INTERVENTIONS FOR ADOLESCENT IDENTITY DEVELOPMENT

OTHER RECENT VOLUMES IN THE
SAGE FOCUS EDITIONS

INTERVENTIONS FOR ADOLESCENT IDENTITY DEVELOPMENT

Sally L. Archer
editor

SAGE PUBLICATIONS
International Educational and Professional Publisher
Thousand Oaks   London   New Delhi

For information address:

SAGE Publications, Inc.
2455 Teller Road
Thousand Oaks, California 91320

SAGE Publications Ltd.
6 Bonhill Street
London EC2A 4PU
United Kingdom

SAGE Publications India Pvt. Ltd.
M-32 Market
Greater Kailash I
New Delhi 110048 India

Printed in the United States of America

Library of Congress Cataloging-in-Publication Data

Main entry under title:

Interventions for adolescent identity development / edited by Sally L.
   Archer.
      p. cm.—(Sage focus editions; vol. 169)
   Includes bibliographical references and index.
   ISBN 0-8039-4188-9 (cloth). —ISBN 0-8039-4189-7 (pbk.)
   1. Identity (Psychology) in adolescence. 2. Teenagers—Counseling
of. 3. Identity (Psychology) in adolescence—Social aspects.
4. Group identity. 5. Adolescent psychotherapy. I. Archer, Sally
L.
   BF724.3.I3I57   1994   93-38497
   155'.5—dc20   CIP

94 95 96 97 10 9 8 7 6 5 4 3 2 1

Sage Production Editor: Yvonne Könneker

For my family's children:
Aaron and Jeremy,
Vikki, Jenni, Penni,
Jacob, Rae, Dusty Lynn,
Leigh, and Robbie,
and those of our children
yet to be.

May each of you revel
in discovering and being
your own unique you.

Love, S.

Contents

Foreword

Identity is a central concept for those concerned with adolescence. The study of identity was dominated first by Erik Erikson and more recently by James Marcia. Both have had a profound influence on the field, shaping the framework within which adolescent identity has come to be viewed. This volume represents a courageous move to bring together the concerns of both these major figures and to move forward in establishing a new perspective. Such an endeavor will be widely welcomed.

There is another reason why the publication of this book is significant. In today's world we are faced with continually increasing levels of problem behaviors among young people. Although politicians and commentators wring their hands, counselors, social workers, psychiatrists, and others are daily faced with the daunting task of finding appropriate interventions for troubled adolescents. In fact—and it is something not always fully acknowledged—we do not have a particularly impressive range of options open to us. Although conventional psychotherapy is frequently either inappropriate or unavailable, and behavioral approaches have limited application, there are multitudes for whom straightforward counseling only goes so far. This volume is exciting and important precisely because it offers new possibilities and new approaches in an area in which they are urgently needed. I am confident that this book will come to be seen as a landmark in the development of new interventions for young people.

As editors of the *Journal of Adolescence,* Gerald Adams and I were pleased indeed that Sally Archer agreed to act as guest editor for a special edition of the journal, which was published in December 1989 as "Adolescent Identity: An Appraisal of Health and Intervention." This special issue signified an important step forward in the thinking of a small group of clinical and developmental psychologists. The issue was well received, and I like to think that it was this publication that encouraged Dr. Archer to develop further her ideas and to persuade her colleagues across the United States to collaborate on an even more ambitious project. The project has now come to fruition—in the shape of this volume—and I wish it every success.

—JOHN C. COLEMAN

Acknowledgments

First I would like to thank the authors of this book for responding to my vision, for extending their expertise, sometimes into uncharted waters, and for thoughtfully providing constructive feedback to one another. Together we wish to express our appreciation to our external reviewers for their excellent recommendations, among them Michael Berzonsky (State University College of New York at Cortland), Chet Bowers (University of Oregon), Richard Dunham (Florida State University), Stuart Hauser (Harvard Medical School), John Ogbu (University of California at Berkeley), Pamela Reid (City University of New York), Ritch Savin-Williams (Cornell University), and Fred Vondracek (Pennsylvania State University).

Throughout this complicated process, the editors and staff of Sage Publications have been very supportive. In particular my thanks are extended to C. Deborah Laughton, Nancy S. Hale, and Yvonne Könneker.

On the home front, thanks go to my colleagues and our secretaries in the Psychology Department at Trenton State College, who provided me with emotional and practical support. In addition, my appreciation to our student secretary, Heather DiSciascio, who compiled the Author Index. My gratitude to the college for its support through a Faculty Research Grant (FIRSL). Most of all, my heartfelt thanks to my colleague and spouse, Alan, who helped me maintain a sense of humor when my strong need for organization could not always be met.

—SALLY L. ARCHER

PART I

The Framework

1

An Overview

SALLY L. ARCHER

The Status of Identity for Interventions

The theoretical and empirical history of the construct of identity has been a long and rich one. This volume is written for those of us who are interested in exploring the application of this construct to the lives of adolescents and their development.

Historically, the construct of identity has been examined in several spheres. In the theoretical and clinical spheres we are aware of its multiple definitions and forms of expression (Erikson, 1958, 1968, 1969; Waterman, 1988). Indeed, the construct is so complex that practitioners and scholars have concluded that it would be wrong to develop a single operationalization of this overarching entity (Archer, 1992; Waterman & Archer, 1990).

In the empirical sphere, although multiple measures of the identity construct have been encouraged (e.g., Bourne, 1978), the most influential framework has been that developed and elaborated by James Marcia (1966; also Marcia, Waterman, Matteson, Archer, & Orlofsky, 1993), who investigated the processes of exploration and commitment as applied to values, beliefs, and goals in numerous life domains. Over the past 25 years, this single operationalization of identity as process, focused on four status derivations of the interrelationship of exploration and commitment, has resulted in several hundred studies that have documented the validity of the construct with personality, cognitive, and behavioral correlates and developmental, gender, and ethnic patterns of self-definitional formation (e.g., Marcia et al., 1993).

Replication of findings has resulted in some central "facts" about the identity process. These lead to intervention questions. For example, the majority of adolescents and youth do not explore alternatives but rather unquestioningly make commitments to the first major value, belief, or goal to which they are exposed, if they make a commitment. Is this a developmental norm? Does this lead to weak life commitments? Are there critical periods for identity activity? How does this information translate into interventions?

With increase in age, there is an increased likelihood of the exploration of alternatives. College and divorce are two additional factors that at least correlate with increased sophisticated identity activity. Regarding interventions, what are the catalysts for such changes in identity activity? And how much sophisticated identity activity is needed and in which life domains—career, family, ideology—to qualify as "healthy" development for whom?

Males and females use the processes of exploration and commitment comparably. The timing of their identity activity is comparable. They address the identity task similarly in numerous domains of life to include career, religion, gender role, marriage, and parenting. In some areas, females have been found to have engaged in more sophisticated identity activity to include the areas of sexuality, friendship, and marriage and career prioritizing, whereas males have been more likely to become committed to political ideology than have females. Should we have similar expectations for interventions for males and females?

Ethnic identity is an important component of self-definition that must be appreciated in as many aspects as the ethnicities investigated. Should we have similar expectations for interventions for different ethnicities?

Individuals who explore alternatives and subsequently arrive at self-definitional commitments are more likely to express personality characteristics, cognitive and interpersonal stages, and other behaviors that are deemed healthy and sophisticated relative to individuals who do not make commitments or do so without considering alternatives. These findings have been among the most powerful influences on the call for intervention. However, the complexities of individual pathways to identity addressed in the next paragraph demonstrate the need for a sophisticated assessment of the meaning of these correlates for intervention, because people typically do not fall neatly into the global status of explorer of alternatives or one who is demonstrating commitment across life domains. Perhaps most important, these "facts" must be assessed and, in time, reassessed in the context of their historical and social environments. (For reviews, see Archer, 1989; Archer & Waterman, 1994; Marcia et al., 1993.)

In a special issue of the *Journal of Adolescence* (Archer, 1989), an attempt was made to bring together many of these findings in a manner that might be meaningful for intervention. It is hoped that readers found many useful ideas and some proposals for interventions. Also provided were caveats about the status of our understanding of the enormous complexity of the identity task. For example, although developmental by nature, should we not honor individual timetables of identity formation? For different individuals different domains of life are significant and perhaps at different points in time. While some 16-year-olds are working through tentative career plans, others are focusing on religious beliefs or sexuality. A 35-year-old may be giving serious consideration to career plans for the first time. And the same individual may use different processes of identity at the same point in time, each in a different domain. A given 15-year-old may be exploring alternatives about gender roles, uninterested in identity activity pertaining to religion and demonstrating an unquestioned commitment to a single career plan at the same point in time. How does one account for complexities such as these when designing interventions in part guided by findings such as the previously mentioned personality, behavioral, and such correlates? Which are appropriate and healthy behaviors? Which are not? By whose standards? The special issue was an exciting beginning.

The Task

The task set for the authors of this book was not a simple one. Scholars and practitioners who are well versed about identity were asked to address their specialty and then to take a further step. Regarding some themes there is a substantial research literature from which to generate proposals, such as Dennis Papini's chapter on family and Randall Jones's chapter on behavioral deviance. For others, there is a substantial theoretical or clinical literature but little empirical grounding, such as John McConnell's chapter on lesbian and gay therapy and Pat Raskin and Al Waterman's chapter on counseling for identity and intimacy. Several areas are being addressed, perhaps for the first time, such as Phil Dreyer's curriculum chapter. In each instance, authors were asked to step out from a strong branch to a less certain limb. It is my hope that the readers of this volume will appreciate our efforts in that spirit. Let me introduce you more specifically to the five parts of this book.

An Overview

The second chapter in this first part of the volume is provided as an introduction to the theory of identity development and the question of intervention. Ruthellen Josselson provides an insightful framing of identity as an intersection of the individual and society. She elaborates on both process and content issues for both. She further describes the efforts that have been made to study identity psychologically. In particular, she focuses on Marcia's conceptual framework and the operationalization of four categories of identity resolution, namely, the identity statuses. She next explores the relationship between the identity statuses and psychological health. She concludes with the identification of essential issues of intervention and leaves us with provocative questions to address.

Part II of this volume comprises five chapters that focus on issues of intervention for specific populations. In Chapter 3, Jim Marcia addresses identity and psychotherapy. He continues to break new ground by exploring the nature of psychosocial developmental theory, the relationship between theory and therapy, the dialectics of development, and psychotherapy within a psychosocial developmental framework. Drawing on his many years of experiences in private practice and the teaching of psychodynamically based therapy, Marcia raises difficult and essential issues. The final section of his chapter focuses on possible therapeutic directions one might take with persons in different identity statuses, whether late adolescents or adults, and some potential difficulties arising in psychotherapy focused on psychosocial development.

Family interventions is the theme of Chapter 4, where Dennis Papini provides a comprehensive description of recent models of adolescent psychosocial development in the context of the family. Having provided this framework, Papini offers a selective summary of research that demonstrates linkages between family processes and adolescent identity development. Attention is especially concentrated on family affect, structure, adaptability, and communication. Intervention proposals are provided in the context of significant questions pertaining to family processes, as well as the level, form, and timing of those interventions.

Ethnic identity interventions are addressed in Chapters 5 and 6. In Chapter 5, Mary Jane Rotheram-Borus and Karen Fraser Wyche examine the relationship between identity and ethnicity for adolescents. Important factors that contribute to the definition of a healthy identity are discussed and include the contexts of diversity of ethnicity, race, and socioeconomic status. Additional ethnic complexities are addressed using gender roles and self-esteem as exemplars. Rotheram-Borus and Wyche subsequently examine the role of ethnic identity in identity development. They then examine major environmental and family factors that contribute to shaping ethnic identifications, concluding with implications for interventions.

In Chapter 6, Carol Markstrom-Adams and Margaret Beale Spencer introduce a model for identity intervention with minority adolescents. After addressing a series of critical factors that limit opportunities in perspective taking and exploring alternatives for minority adolescents, they examine the appropriateness of three models of identity formation for these adolescents. The focus of the rest of their chapter is on interventions per se. Here they examine the application of the models for intervention, the role of the domains of identity, and the structure of the intervention, each in the context of perspective taking and exploration.

Lesbian and gay male identity formation is the focus of John Hazen McConnell in Chapter 7. After providing a historical perspective of Eriksonian and Freudian theories on unconventional erotic life, McConnell introduces contemporary models of lesbian and gay identity, with primary focus on Troiden's model. Here parallels are made between the Troiden model and the Eriksonian and Marcia frameworks. Next is a focus on data that address prevalence and demographics of sexual orientation, the phenomenon of an extended moratorium, the defining of social sex roles, and contrasts of experiences between lesbians and gay men. McConnell then discusses a paradigm shift for erotic identity and its implications for clinical work and research. He concludes his chapter with important caveats and a call for specialization to provide appropriate interventions with lesbians and gay men.

Part III of this volume comprises four chapters that explore curricula interventions. In Chapter 8, Philip Dreyer outlines ways in which educational environments and curricula can be structured to promote identity achievement in adolescents. He begins the chapter by advocating identity theory as a theoretical basis for curriculum design. He breaks new ground by examining the relationships among identity theory, cognitive development, and educational reform movements. Dreyer subsequently addresses the characteristics of identity-enhancing curricula and provides examples from a variety of disciplines. In this chapter, a major step has been taken to draw together the psychosocial development of students and the traditional instructional sequence.

A working curriculum for gender-role identity formation is the focus of Karen Greenlaw Bieri and Mindy Bingham in Chapter 9. Examining gender concerns for males and females, the authors address the need for conscious choice and reflective compromises that might dispel stereotypical demands that bode ill health for both sexes. A central thrust of the chapter is to describe a series of programs and their textbooks that explore self-awareness and life planning and which have been implemented with more than half a million students. Evaluations of the programs and texts provide interesting data and anecdotes that document the importance of this form of curricula intervention with adolescents.

Career counseling is the focus of Chapter 10. Patricia Raskin elaborates on the development of the adolescent's vocational identity and addresses the vocational tasks of exploration and tentative choice, cautioning the reader to consider the impact of gender, ethnicity, and class. The chapter continues with a concentration on vocational interventions. Specifically, the identity-status model is applied to career counseling. Raskin takes the reader through the preadolescent, junior high or middle high, senior high and college groups, carefully distinguishing their needs and capacities for exploration and commitment. She offers recommendations for group and individual interventions and concludes with some thoughts about the roles of community organizations.

In Chapter 11, the last of Part III, Randall Jones provides a valuable critique of existing forms of curricula interventions pertaining to various forms of behavioral deviance. After addressing the role of home, religion, and education, he examines more specifically cognitive-skill-based approaches to intervention. Having laid this groundwork, Jones continues the chapter by examining the research findings relating identity development to substance use as well as to cognitive style. In a further step, he makes an interesting connection between the literature on resilient children, the pressures involved with substance use and associated at-risk behaviors and psychosocially advanced children. Jones concludes the chapter with a section focused on proposals for prevention at the elementary and secondary school levels that target underlying developmental issues.

The interface of identity and intimacy for intervention is explored in the two chapters that constitute Part IV. Controversy has surrounded the relationship between the fifth psychosocial stage of development, namely, identity-identity confusion, and the sixth stage, intimacy-isolation.

In Chapter 12, Gerald Adams and I explore the thesis that identity is a precursor to intimacy. The operationalization of the constructs of identity and intimacy is examined, followed by a selective summary of some of the evidence testing the association between identity and intimacy. Three comparative models of the identity-intimacy association and their gender-specific implications are detailed and evaluated. The chapter concludes with a discussion of implications for socialization.

In Chapter 13, Patricia Raskin and Alan Waterman explore the bidirectional impact of counseling on identity and intimacy developments. They first propose counseling techniques for individuals in each of the four identity statuses. Then they consider counseling with clients in various intimacy statuses. In the final section of the chapter, Raskin and Waterman provide two examples of intimacy-identity counseling, demonstrating potential dynamics of the interrelationship between these two psychosocial constructs.

The final section of the book comprises two chapters that are designed as commentary on the intent of this volume. In Chapter 14, Alan Waterman explores ethical considerations in interventions for promoting identity development. Working from a benefit-cost analyses framework, he evaluates how attending to the identity-related implications of interventions with adolescents and youth in both the clinical or counseling and educational settings makes salient several ethical issues. For example, he particularly attends to the complexities of informed consent and the therapeutic contract in clinical settings. For both clinical or counseling and educational interventions, Waterman provides guidelines for minimizing the risks of intervention and closes with a statement of the need to openly analyze each new intervention to minimize risk.

In the final chapter, John McKinney draws from his own clinical experiences in his assessment of the themes and proposals for interventions for identity development. He examines each arena proposed for intervention, making insightful connections across populations and environmental contexts and generating thoughtful questions that require future consideration. McKinney also shares his own perspective on how adolescents respond to the prospect of change, noting potential relationships between his styles and the processes of exploration and commitment. After addressing the linkage between identity and intimacy—and including relationships between client and caregiver—and noting the fertile network of linkages with other constructs, McKinney concludes that identity may well be a powerful guiding concept in our interventions with youth.

An overview of this text must be summarized as follows: The time has come to realize that we have been exploring the use of the identity construct for the lives of adolescents. We have been stretching this construct in a myriad of directions in terms of its definitions, contexts, behavioral expressions, relationships with other components of living, and meaning for diverse populations. In part, this book is intended to advance the task of testing the appropriateness of these activities.

These chapters are not meant as an exhaustive examination of identity and interventions, but they should reveal areas of theoretical and empirical strength as well as weakness, questions asked, questions yet to be asked, interlocking themes, and disconnection. In essence, applying identity theory and research to intervention is work in progress.

In conclusion, I hope that this book will spur the continued development of interventions that could enrich our youths' opportunities to more effectively embrace the process of identity decision making as it pertains to the various themes of their self-definitions. May the dialogue among theorist, empiricist, and practitioner expand and bring to fruition models of productive pathways for our adolescents and youth to traverse toward a healthier, personally expressive sense of self.

References

Archer, S. L. (Ed.). (1989). Adolescent identity: An appraisal of health and intervention [Special issue]. *Journal of Adolescence, 12*(4).
Archer, S. L. (1992). A feminist's approach to identity research. In G. R. Adams, R. Montemayor, & T. P. Gullota (Eds.), *Advances in adolescent development* (Vol. 4, pp. 25-49). Newbury Park, CA: Sage.
Archer, S. L., & Waterman, A. S. (1994). Adolescent identity development: Contextual perspectives. In C. B. Fisher & R. M. Lerner (Eds.), *Applied developmental psychology* (pp. 76-100). New York: McGraw-Hill.
Bourne, E. (1978). The state of research on ego identity: A review and appraisal. Part 2. *Journal of Youth and Adolescence, 7,* 371-392.
Erikson, E. H. (1958). *Young man Luther.* New York: Norton.
Erikson, E. H. (1968). *Identity: Youth and crisis.* New York: Norton.

Erikson, E. H. (1969). *Gandhi's truth*. New York: Norton.

Marcia, J. E. (1966). Development and validation of ego identity status. *Journal of Personality and Social Psychology, 3,* 551-558.

Marcia, J. E., Waterman, A. S., Matteson, D. R., Archer, S. L., & Orlofsky, J. L. (1993). *Ego identity: A handbook for psychosocial research*. New York: Springer Verlag.

Waterman, A. S. (1988). Identity status theory and Erikson's theory: Commonalities and differences. *Developmental Review, 8,* 185-208.

Waterman, A. S., & Archer, S. L. (1990). A life-span perspective on identity formation: Developments in form, function, and process. In P. B. Baltes, D. L. Featherman, & R. M. Lerner (Eds.), *Life-span development and behavior* (Vol. 10, pp. 29-57). Hillsdale, NJ: Lawrence Erlbaum.

2

The Theory of Identity Development and the Question of Intervention

An Introduction

RUTHELLEN JOSSELSON

Identity represents the intersection of the individual and society. In framing identity, the individual simultaneously joins the self to society and the society to the self. As a result, identity comes to serve not only as a guardian of the integration and continuity of self-experience, but also as a mechanism for shared meaning-making that embeds the individual with those with whom life will be lived. Erikson's (1950, 1968) rich exposition of this process made it possible not only to better understand the adolescent transition but also to break ground for the study of adult development.

In adolescence, young people first confront the challenge of finding a place for themselves in the larger social world. As children move toward and into adulthood, society begins to take them more seriously as members. Identity is the process of claiming membership in the social world, standing for something, being known for who one is. Once constructed, identity then forms the framework for adulthood.

Identity is both process and product. It is an unfolding bridge linking individual and society, childhood and adulthood. To understand identity then, we must be able to think about its basis in the individual and its expression in social existence, its roots in early development and its realization in adult purpose. Because identity forms the foundation of adult life, as a society we have a large stake in seeing that this takes place as optimally as possible. Questions of intervention must focus on when it might be necessary to help this unfolding process along and, if necessary, how.

Identity From the Side of the Individual

To form an identity, the individual must have a reasonable understanding of the raw materials—that is, knowledge of the self. Erikson says that identity requires the synthesis of "constitutional givens, . . . favored capacities, selective identifications, effective defenses, successful sublimations and consistent roles" (1968, p. 163). What individuals come to understand about themselves may both delimit and govern identity choices. Some highly talented people, for example, experience a "calling" as though from inside. Musical talent or early intense spirituality might direct the life path in a determined search for expression of inner truth. For others, wishes for achievement may be beyond talents or capabilities. The questions "What is in me?" and "How do my parts fit together?" become significant building blocks of identity. In learning about the self subjectively in terms of felt experience ("I tried that and didn't like it, and it's not for me") and learning about the self objectively in terms of how one is viewed by others ("Everyone always comes to me with their problems, so people must think I'm a good listener"), the individual gathers information about what the self might be capable of doing or being, what beliefs or life goals are most consonant with what feels most essential in the self.

The process of identity formation requires sufficient personality structuralization and management of internal conflict for the individual to be able to attempt joining the self to a larger purpose. Young people burdened by unresolved residues of previous stages of development find it hard to finish being children. What they most deeply want is what they needed much earlier on, and the prospect of growth appears terrifying rather than inviting. Thus when we conceptualize the process of identity formation, we are postulating a reasonably integrated and self-aware young person, a person with sufficient internalization to have an inner world, a sense of self, and adequate defenses against overwhelming anxiety. For such people, Erikson postulates that, with development, there will be an inner "push" toward identity formation. The task of identity formation forms the fifth stage of Erikson's eight-stage epigenetic model of development (see Table 2.1). In each stage, a developmentally necessary psychosocial crisis becomes central to the individual and is resolved with some balance of its positive and negative polarity as the individual moves on to the next developmental challenge. By the time the young person reaches the identity stage, he or she will have achieved some balance between trust and mistrust, autonomy and shame or doubt, initiative and guilt, industry and inferiority. In addition, the identity stage has precursors in each previous stage. All of these earlier resolutions will find structure in the young person's personality and will color and shape the course of the identity-formation phase.

Identity From the Side of Society

More traditional nonindustrial and ritualized societies provide "place" for the individual at prescribed times. The more restrictive the society, the more the individual has to adapt to what is socially dictated. The individual is absorbed into preassigned roles, a transition marked by more or less elaborate rites of passage. The individual has little or no choice: He or she is usually born to a place that then may or may not have to be earned through proving oneself.

The expanse of identity possibility that necessitates a whole developmental phase devoted to the quest for identity is a product of modern technological society. Where these societies make individual freedom an important value and offer the individual a panoply of choice, identity formation also becomes a process of learning about what might be available as potential ways of living. The larger the smorgasbord of choice the society offers, the greater freedom the individual has to express what is inner. In very open societies, the society might go so far as to invite the individual to reshape the society to make a unique place for the self, forcing, in Erikson's phrase, the society to adapt to him or her.

Complex societies that offer wide choice make (more or less) available to young people a moratorium in which it is understood that choices are tentative, playful perhaps, and not for keeps. In this period, the young person is (more or less) free to explore ways of thinking, being, doing, and valuing that might fit. One thing the young person may learn in this phase is how the society responds to different choices: What is valued by others? What is tolerated by others? In our society, college offers such a moratorium. The young person is free of the necessity to be taken too seriously and allowed to make mistakes and to

Identity issue at Integrity Stage →

CHRONOLOGICAL AGE

CHRONOLOGICAL AGE	1 T—M	2 A—S,D	3 I—G	4 Ind—Inf	5 Id—ID	6 Int—Is	7 Gen—S	8 Integrity and Despair
VIII OLD AGE	T—M Intg.	A—S,D Intg.	I—G Intg.	Ind—Inf Intg.	Id—ID Intg.	Int—Is Intg.	Gen—S Intg.	Intg—D
VII ADULTHOOD	T—M Gen.	A—S,D Gen.	I—G Gen.	Ind—Inf Gen.	Id—ID Gen.	Int—Is Gen.	Generativity and Stagnation Self-absorption	Intg—D Gen.
VI YOUNG ADULTHOOD	T—M Int.	A—S,D Int.	I—G Int.	Ind—Inf Int.	Id—ID Int.	Intimacy and Isolation	Gen—S Int.	Intg—D Int.
V ADOLESCENCE Genital Mature intrusion-inclusion	T—M Id.	A—S,D Id.	I—G Id.	Ind—Inf Id.	Identity and Identity Diffusion	Int—Is Id.	Gen—S Id.	Intg—D Id.
IV SCHOOL AGE Latent	T—M Ind.	A—S,D Ind.	I—G Ind.	Industry and Inferiority	Id—ID Ind.	Int—Is Ind.	Gen—S Ind.	Intg—D Ind.
III PLAY AGE Phallic (oedipal) Intrusion-inclusion Individuation	T—M I	A—S,D I	Initiative and Guilt	Ind—Inf I	Id—ID I	Int—Is I	Gen—S I	Intg—D I
II EARLY CHILDHOOD Anal Eliminative-retentive Practising	T—M A	Autonomy and Shame, Doubt	I—G A	Ind—Inf A	Id—ID A	Int—Is A	Gen—S A	Intg—D A
I INFANCY Oral 1. Passive-active Incorporative 2. Attachment 3.	Basic Trust and Basic Mistrust	A—S,D T	I—G T	Ind—Inf T	Id—ID T	Int—Is T	Gen—S T	Intg—D T
	1	2	3	4	5	6	7	8

↑ Precursor to Autonomy at Trust Stage

1. Psychosexual zone
2. Related behavioral modality
3. Object relational phase

Key:

T—M = Trust—Mistrust
A—S, D = Autonomy—Shame, Doubt
I—G = Initiative—Guilt
Ind—Inf = Industry—Inferiority
Id—ID = Identity—Identity Diffusion
Int—Is = Intimacy—Isolation
Gen—S = Generativity—Stagnation
Intg—D = Integrity—Despair

Table 2.1 Psychosocial Stages

SOURCE: From Marcia, Waterman, Matteson, Archer, & Orlofsky (1993). Reprinted with permission from Springer Verlag.

15

investigate belief systems, relationships, and occupational choices while society (in the forms of parents, teachers, and friends) regards the proceedings with bated breath. North American society schedules this moratorium at late adolescence, and the young person is expected to settle these matters sometime between ages 21 and 25, although the period often extends to age 30. The society then, through its expectations, its willingness to suspend judgment, and its subsequent haste to form them, grants this time and milieu to the individual and then withdraws it by declaring the period at an end. Thus the moratorium is not of the individual's creation but a product of the coming together of individual growth needs and societal timetables. For the individual out of phase with the society, who wishes to explore identity either too early or too late, or who is unable to bring the time for exploration to closure in the form of commitments, grave difficulties may ensue.

Erikson discusses the fact that because the society moves on inexorably, even those young people who are developmentally unready to tackle identity formation tasks are nevertheless swept into the tides of this stage. At a certain point the society simply expects young people to declare themselves. Where the young person abrogates choice or flirts with deviance, the society may supply a (usually negative) label such as schizophrenic, delinquent, or dropout, taking seriously what may have only been intended to be a temporary "negative identity."

Changes in society will drastically alter the identity-formation process by changing possibility and expectations. Women, for example, now have many more options for public achievement than they did a generation ago; at the same time, values of care and devotion to others are often treated contemptuously. Homosexuals now have much more latitude for self-expression; for nonwhites in North American society, possibility and social response are always complex and always changing.

To understand identity, then, we must keep in focus both individual dynamics and social organization. To intervene in the process of identity formation, we might try to make changes in either the individual or in the social climate within which identity formation takes place.

The Effort to Study Identity Psychologically

Erikson's legacy of the concept of identity was heuristic and connotative rather than operational and concrete. Trying to define identity as emergent, he discussed its core (the interface of individual and society) and some of its edges. But because identity is an integrative concept that describes both process and product of the marriage between individual and society, it cannot be precisely demarcated. How then could psychologists study it?

The earliest efforts to operationalize identity tended to follow the traditions of personality research and locate identity as an intraindividual trait. The first steps thus tried to think about people as having more or less identity or tried to view identity as comprising separate intrapsychic components.

When James Marcia invented an operational way of thinking about identity that preserved the holistic and integrative nature of Erikson's concept, researchers abandoned other approaches. Rather than trying to splinter identity into components or locate it solely in the individual, Marcia treated identity as the process by which the individual comes to take a place in the social world. His style of assessing it tried to pinpoint the individual's position along the path toward that end.

In Marcia's (1980) conceptualization, the essence of Erikson's idea about identity formation is that the individual ideally makes a commitment to a way of being after a period of exploring possibilities. Commitment is the endpoint of the process of exploration. At any given moment, however, the adolescent may be found at any point along the path. The individual may not yet have reached the identity "bridge." He or she may still be experiencing the ascribed identity of childhood, embedded in the subgroup and values into which he or she was born or without any sense of place at all, seeing those choices as belonging solely to a distant future or imagining that decision may be delayed indefinitely. Possibility and choice may not yet seem real or imminent. Or the individual could be on the bridge in the process of trying things out, thinking about things, taking advantage of the psychosocial moratorium the society makes available. Or the individual may have reached the opposite shore, may have made a commitment to a way of being, and thus be said to have formulated an identity.

Marcia, thinking along these lines, was able to define four categories of individuals making identity resolutions that he called *statuses*:

1. the *identity achievement* group—those who made identity commitments after a period of exploration
2. the *foreclosure* group—those who made identity commitments without a period of exploration, foreclosing possibility by bringing along unquestioned childhood ascriptions

3. the *moratorium* group—those *in* a period of crisis or exploration in an effort to discover values or goals that fit them

4. the *identity diffusion* group—those without identity commitments who were making no effort to explore or create them

Unlike most psychological constructs that emerge, generate interest, and then fade away, this paradigm for identity development has lasted 25 years and spawned hundreds of research investigations around the world. In every postindustrial culture, one can find the four statuses. Furthermore, they are consistent groups, although they differ on a wide range of variables and behave differently under different circumstances. We now have an increasingly clear and complex understanding of the four groups and know something about how and why people are in one place or the other.

This research also has allowed us to think more incisively about identity development and how it proceeds. One question, for example, reemerges to vex all identity researchers: Are these four statuses really developmental stages or are they personality types? The emerging answer seems to be that they may encompass both. Some individuals, for example, because of their prior experience, are so rigidly organized that they have neither the capacity nor the inclination to explore identity possibility. These people follow instead a fairly narrow path laid out for them by their families, their subgroup, or their own childhood expectations. These are foreclosures who, instead of yet being in the exploration phase, are people who intend to avoid it at all costs.

There are also some individuals who, because of lack of personality organization caused by serious psychopathology, do not have the inner resources to experience themselves as entities who can join a society. This is a form of identity diffusion linked to intrapsychic deficits, and it is not a preidentity position.

Similarly, there appear to be some people for whom the moratorium phase becomes a way of life. Rather than a path toward identity, it becomes itself a way of living, and such people are unable to choose or to commit themselves. They just extend their adolescence as far into adulthood as possible.

Studies of the stability of identity statuses show that, as expected, there is an increase in identity achievement over the course of the college years. With time, as a group, young people move out of the uncommitted and prematurely committed statuses and make choices of their own through greater self-understanding and greater knowledge about what possibilities the society offers. Longitudinal studies that follow people after college, however, attest to the relative stability of identity status measured at the end of college. Those who are at the threshold of graduation from college and who are foreclosures or diffusions are likely to remain so into adulthood. Moratoriums and achievements, surprisingly, sometimes regress in adulthood to foreclosed or diffuse positions (Josselson, 1987; Marcia, 1976).

As identity researchers have come to better understand the characteristics of the four groups, it has seemed increasingly necessary to formulate subtypes: One may, for example, then discriminate the characterological foreclosure from the transient one. In addition, one might discriminate the "lost" diffusion from one keeping options open to meet an economically uncertain social climate (see Archer & Waterman, 1990, and Marcia, 1989, for fuller discussion).

Identity Status and Psychological Health

The notion of identity achievement built into the name of one of the identity statuses reflects researchers' idea that formulation of identity is an achievement—that is, something to be valued, encouraged, and viewed as in the service of psychological health. And this seems beyond dissent. To take a place in the social world, a place reached through dialogue between individual capacity and inclination on the one side and social possibility on the other, is certainly to be lauded. Surely this serves growth and can be deemed healthy. No one seriously contests this.

But what of the other statuses? Can it be healthy to foreclose possibility? Are those in the moratorium status just as healthy as the achievements but just not yet finished with the task? And what of the diffusions? Is this just a phase or a style of being to worry about?

Empirical research with the identity statuses has both answered some of these questions and raised others. In Marcia's initial conceptualization, the identity statuses that included crisis or exploration—identity achievement and moratorium—were deemed to be the "high" statuses, while those that bypassed exploration were viewed as the "low" statuses. And, indeed, subjects' performance on other instruments and tasks reflected this division. The high statuses showed more self-confidence, more advanced moral reasoning, internal locus of control, more resistance to pressure to conform, and generally better adjustment (see

Marcia et al., 1993, for a complete review of this research). When the same investigations were conducted with women, however, a different pattern emerged. For women, the high statuses tended to be the committed ones. On the usual measures of personality functioning and successful adaptation, foreclosure women resembled achievements, while moratorium women were more like the diffusions. Other research suggested that while this pattern held true for women on the more superficial measures, the "deeper" measures of personality differentiation and integration would reveal that moratorium women had a core of strength, while foreclosure women were more deeply brittle. The reasoning thus held that while the culture may make life easier for women who have made commitments—whether automatic and unquestioned or thoughtful and individually won—women who had undergone a period of exploration were, like men, more deeply healthy. The contradictory sex-linked results obtained about moratoriums and foreclosures thus made it difficult to make simple statements about the relative health of these statuses. (See Patterson, Sochting, & Marcia, 1992, for the most recent and complete discussion of this issue.)

About diffusions there has been less confusion but no less disagreement. Although most researchers agree that diffusion is an undesirable state, some regard this as a nonpathological way station, while others have argued that identity diffusion is a sign of a possibly serious emotional problem that ought to be responded to as such. Here it may be that identity diffusion also has different meanings at different times in a society's history. During the late 1960s and early 1970s, when a great many studies of identity status were conducted, to be diffuse was to be at a far distance from the ideological whirlpools and the occupational opportunities that swirled around the college campuses. In this age of commitment and activism, to be uncommitted and uninterested in choice was perhaps a reflection of inner blocks to doing so. By the late 1980s, a period of ideological quiescence and economic bleakness, to remain diffuse not only reflected the moral tempo of the times but also made it possible to take hold of whatever occupational opportunity might emerge. The relativity of identity status to social conditions therefore makes it difficult to make absolute judgments about the relative health or pathology of the four statuses.

Marcia tends to see each status as having both positive and negative attributes. Thus the identity-diffuse individual leaves him- or herself open to possibility, buying flexibility at the price of certainty. One might view the diffusions as either creative or alienated, carefree or

confused. Those who remain in the moratorium phase keep alive struggle, awareness, and openness at the cost of much anxiety. They are
philosophical, but they also may suffer. Foreclosures trade freedom and
choice for certitude and escape from doubt and ambivalence. They
conform, but also cooperate. Identity achievements gain choice and the
sense of self-direction but must renounce other possibilities, perhaps
too completely or prematurely. Identity achievement, especially after
adolescence, can become entrenched and rigidified and impervious to
the refinement and reworkings necessitated by truly vital adult life.

It may be that any of these options, given the right personality
configuration and social circumstances, could be adaptive. We do not
yet have enough follow-up data to make final determinations as to
health. Before deciding health and pathology, one must carefully review
the unique situation rather than rush to label one status or another as
healthy or sick. One must also recognize that relative health and pathology of these routes through the identity-formation stage are also reflective of cultural values and constraints that may change over time.

My own longitudinal follow-up study (Josselson, 1987) of women
who had been classified into the identity-status categories as college
seniors failed to show that any of the statuses were universally un-
healthy. Foreclosures were found to be leading well-adjusted productive lives, just as much so as those who had been achievements or
moratoriums in college. The diffusion group contained both those who
had experienced serious problems in college and those who had merely
been drifting or impulsive during that time. Some of these women
continued to experience difficulty and problems in adjustment. Others
found ways of living that, although perhaps not exemplary of ideal
mental health, certainly represented adequate adjustment. Thus women
in all statuses went on to live reasonably happy and fruitful lives. Using a
retrospective method, Mallory (1983) also found no differences among the
identity statuses in long-term happiness or adjustment.

The identity statuses themselves, then, are neither healthy nor un-
healthy; there can, however, be pathological aspects of identity formation within any of them (see also Archer, 1989). (Within identity
achievement, there can be a spectrum of psychopathology, but it may
not directly affect identity.) Within the moratorium status, guilt and
anxiety can become so overwhelming that the clear thinking necessary
to exploration becomes clouded or blocked. Or the young person in a
moratorium phase may become stuck and despair of ever finding a
social choice that feels right. The presence of excessive guilt, anxiety,

or depression within the moratorium group may thus signal pathological processes at work. It is more difficult to assess the health of foreclosure solutions because these become so much a function of the values of the observer. For example, for women who make primary identity commitments to care and tradition and who plan to return or remain in the communities in which they were raised, being bearers of culture is their identity choice. Psychologists, however, tend not to approve of foreclosures. The foreclosure lack of self-reflection, tendency to self-denial and moralism, together with their often smug authoritarian certainty, all clash with values implicit in psychology that stress openness, self-awareness, self-realization, and liberalized values. On the other hand, psychologists, who have a natural affinity for moratoriums, tend to overvalue the moratorium status and perhaps have a harder time recognizing some of the pain and pathology in this form of adolescent passage.

The Question of Intervention

Questions about intervention are directly tied to underlying assumptions about health and pathology of the identity statuses. One intervenes when one believes that one can make things better or smoother for another. We would intervene then if we believed that the process of identity formation is going off track and needs help. Because identity formation is, as we have seen, a product of the individual interface with the society, two points of intervention become possible: the individual and the social.

Individual intervention involves either education or psychotherapy of some kind. Intervention here is aimed, status by status, at helping the individual better traverse the identity bridge and get by whatever obstacles block the way. Here one thinks in terms of assisting foreclosures to consider exploration, to bear guilt and anxiety, or to find a group of similar peers with whom to explore. Or one might want to find a way to take the temperature of the uncommitted statuses, to find out if distress is too high or possibilities too overwhelming in order to help the young person with strategies of decision making.

Issues of individual intervention concern identification of those in trouble and the creation of both individual and group mechanisms to provide assistance. Here questions of education enter as well. The aim is the assessment of what the individual needs in order to know optimally his or her own capacities and predilections, to maximally explore, to make realistic decisions and choices, and to manage the affective distress that accompanies the process.

Social intervention requires thinking about the society end of the bridge. What options does the society make available to the initiate? Is there sufficient structure so that the individual can identify choices and values? Are there social gatekeepers available to greet and orient the new members, or is the society closed, viewing newcomers as rivals or threats and making entry difficult? As a society becomes morally confused and itself diffuse, possibilities for meaningful joining lessen. Identity, to the extent that it is a form of shared meaning-making, requires a society that regards itself as meaningful. Today many young people are diffuse in identity because they are coming of age in families and communities where values are unspecified, religion disowned, and occupation tedious and unstimulating. For such young people, the burning issues are those of consumption: for example, which are the best stereo speakers? Identity then tends to be phrased not in terms of what the individual will stand for, be faithful to, or try to become or to generate in the world, but instead what the individual will purchase.

Further, a society beleaguered by racism, sexism, and homophobia seriously interferes with possibility extended to large segments of its membership. Issues of identity formation among those who feel estranged from or misconstrued by the social world they enter are not issues of individual exploration and choice. Rather, they are issues of the society foreclosing individual possibility, disallowing the expression of potential and choice.

Social intervention necessitates an analysis of the role of the external world in supporting or hindering the process of identity formation. The adolescent does not do it alone: The process, in its essence, requires dialogue. Thus there must be people there for the adolescent to explore with and against. Someone must be making limits so the adolescent can find boundaries. Someone must provide support so the adolescent can go on when the way becomes frightening. Someone must be there to exemplify and take an interest so that the adolescent can measure himself or herself while feeling invited to join. Mentors, for example, are critically important in this regard, a role that we in psychology are just beginning to conceptualize and learn about.

Intervention thus must take account of both sides of this process. To intervene on the individual side, we try to make changes in the internal world of the adolescent so that he or she is more able to undertake and complete the journey. To intervene on the social side, we attempt to reform our social institutions so that they promote optimal development. Thus we may choose to make more counselors available at the counseling center, thereby encouraging individual change, *or* we can reduce the size of classes and faculty teaching loads in order to encourage personal interaction between faculty and students in the conviction that education for identity is beyond what one learns in books and can be evaluated on exams. Providing conditions where students can get to know new (and perhaps admired) others in unpressured circumstances and learn about possibilities for being and doing in a way that can make some personal sense to them is an example of intervention at an institutional level. Intervening on the individual level, we may choose to include value-clarification exercises in classes to help young people see more clearly what their values are. Intervening on a social level, we might try to reduce the racism and sexism that make people despair of having a meaningful role in society regardless of their values.

For 25 years we have reaped the benefits of Erikson's provocative work. We have thought about identity in its many functions and manifestations, and we have found a way to investigate it that is theoretically sound, reliable, and replicable and that yields interesting results. We then came to understand more and more the characteristics of each of the four statuses and to learn something about their eventual fate. This brought us to the need to further differentiate and subdivide, to see that within each of the four statuses are subgroups, some of which do better than others. And all of this understanding brought us to thinking about the young people whom we, as adults in the society, must invite to join us and must welcome as members. Can we help out in this process? Can we make the way easier or surer? (And do we want to?) How can we help those who seem to be stumbling? And how can we make the society a more tolerant and desirable world to join? These are the questions of intervention.

References

Archer, S. (1989). Adolescent identity: An appraisal of health and intervention [Special issue]. *Journal of Adolescence, 12*(4).

Archer, S., & Waterman, A. (1990). Varieties of identity diffusions and foreclosures: An exploration of subcategories of the identity statuses. *Journal of Adolescent Research, 5,* 96-111.

Erikson, E. (1950). *Childhood and society*. New York: Norton.

Erikson, E. (1968). *Identity, youth and crisis.* New York: Norton.

Josselson, R. (1987). *Finding herself: Pathways to identity development in women.* San Francisco: Jossey-Bass.

Mallory, M. (1983). *Longitudinal analysis of ego identity status.* Unpublished doctoral dissertation, University of California, Davis.

Marcia, J. E. (1976). Identity six years after: A follow-up study. *Journal of Youth and Adolescence, 5,* 145-160.

Marcia, J. E. (1980). Identity in adolescence. In J. Adelson (Ed.), *Handbook of adolescent psychology* (pp. 159-187). New York: John Wiley.

Marcia, J. E. (1989). Identity diffusion differentiated. In M. A. Luszcz & T. Nettlebeck (Eds.), *Psychological development: Perspectives across the life-span* (pp. 289-294). New York: Elsevier North-Holland.

Marcia, J. E., Waterman, A. S., Matteson, D. R., Archer, S. L., & Orlofsky, J. L. (1993). *Ego identity: A handbook for psychosocial research.* New York: Springer Verlag.

Patterson, S. J., Sochting, I., & Marcia, J. E. (1992). The inner space and beyond: Women and identity. In G. R. Adams, T. Gulotta, & R. Montemayor (Eds.), *Adolescent identity formation* (Vol. 4, pp. 9-24). Newbury Park, CA: Sage.

PART II

Population Interventions

3

Identity and Psychotherapy

JAMES E. MARCIA

This chapter concerns relationships among psychosocial developmental theory, the identity-status paradigm, and psychotherapy. Included are some of the author's opinions on psychotherapy, based on 25 years of private practice and teaching psychodynamically based therapy. Although psychotherapy is the focus of this chapter, and some of the examples given are of moderately long-term work with adults, the points made are applicable to briefer interventions undertaken by counselors and educators with adolescents (see also Marcia, 1986).

Psychosocial Developmental Theory

Psychosocial developmental theory (Erikson, 1959, 1963) is an extension of ego psychoanalytic theory (A. Freud, 1936; Hartmann, 1964; Rapaport, 1969; White, 1959), which was itself an extension of classical Freudian psychoanalytic theory. This theoretical progression represents a movement from pathology to adaptation, from libidinal determinants to autonomous ego functions, from intraindividual psychodynamics to individual-societal interaction. These different levels of discourse are complementary, not contradictory. Incorporated within psychosocial developmental theory are Freudian psychosexual stages, which are

AUTHOR'S NOTE: The author expresses his appreciation to Dr. Janet Strayer, who read an early draft of this chapter, and Drs. Stuart Hauser and Alan Waterman, who made usefully critical comments on a later draft.

described in terms of focal body zones and related modalities of behavior, as well as those ego mechanisms of primary and secondary autonomy assumed to develop given an "average expectable environment." What Erikson has added to these earlier concepts is a developmental chart of stages of ego growth cast in the form of age-specific "crises." Each crisis in growth has both its individual and societal components. For example, the individual component of the basic trust-mistrust crisis involves the infant's needs for oral gratification and abilities in the form of the sucking reflex and rudimentary motor and perceptual apparatuses. The social component involves the society's particular institution of mothering.

Erikson's most important contributions have been to specify stages of ego development and to direct attention to differing social institutions that provide the milieus within which this growth takes place. If one takes the orthodox psychoanalytic perspective narrowly, society may be seen as a composite of individual compromise formations writ large or as an individually oppressive condition essential for human survival. Within an Eriksonian perspective, it is viewed also as the provider of those necessary contexts that we have developed over time to nourish and expedite human psychological growth. The individual is viewed as a participant in a social contract wherein personal demands can be moderated voluntarily with the reasonable expectation of a societal response good enough to ensure survival and growth.

If Erikson's schedule for stages of human development is valid, then one can begin to assess social institutions in terms of the extent to which they facilitate or hinder that developmental schedule. One motive for the psychosocial developmental research we are currently undertaking is to determine and establish the validity of this developmental scheme (Bradley & Marcia, 1990; Hearn, 1994; Marcia, Waterman, Matteson, Archer, & Orlofsky, 1993; Stephen, Fraser, & Marcia, 1992). Only a scheme that considers the cultural developmental context of the individual, as well as the individual's particular psychosexual or psychosocial stage, can provide the breadth of scope necessary for the most individually relevant interventions. If one is to aid in the commitment aspect of the exploration-commitment process of psychotherapy, one must be aware of the cultural context within which the individual resolved previous developmental issues as well as the extent and limitations of the culture within which he or she is currently trying to effect an adaptation.

Theory and Psychotherapy

Before the question of the relationships among psychotherapy, psychosocial developmental theory, and identity can be addressed, a prior issue must be dealt with: the relationship between theory and psychotherapy. In spite of the way in which most clinical psychology programs prepare their students to be psychotherapists—that is, requiring theory courses before practice—the relationship between theoretical knowledge and psychotherapeutic practice is not clear-cut. Probably the people who are most enthusiastic about the primary role of theory and related techniques in making psychotherapists effective are beginning psychotherapists. One can hardly blame them for this. To be faced with the sometimes overwhelming "otherness" of another person—to try to understand this and to be of help—is an extraordinary burden to place on the novice therapist, who is usually a young adult in his or her late 20s or early 30s. Small wonder that a clearly articulated theory and a set of learnable techniques are so appealing to the novice practitioner. But most experienced therapists know better. It is primarily the relationship that cures, and the major responsibility for that, at least in the beginning of any therapeutic endeavor, lies with the therapist. Hence it is the person of the therapist that is at the heart of psychotherapy. Whether this crucial ingredient is called transference, or relationship, or becoming a certain kind of required self-object,[1] there is no theoretical refuge large enough to conceal that necessary (and sometimes sufficient) condition for effective psychotherapy: the person of the therapist.

If the essential ingredient of psychotherapy is the person of the therapist, of what use then is theory? Radical Rogerians would reply, "None at all." Freudians would disagree. The rest of us would be somewhere in the middle. I would like to try to make that middle a bit more specific. Probably the choice of operating theory of psychotherapy (assuming that one goes to a training institution that permits choice), is a function of a beginning therapist's world view. The novice chooses the theory that meshes best with his or her current values and aesthetic sense (some people prefer complexity and complex theories, others prefer simplicity and theories with only a few major constructs). Hence we are back again to the person of the therapist. But what happens next, or at least what happens to persons who are going to become good therapists, is that by listening to their patients they identify the weaknesses of their theories. Clearly, there are parts of this other person not captured by the theory's constructs. They discover something else. Embedded in the theory are certain values that may not have been apparent to the novice therapist before the theory was tested in the actual therapeutic crucible. And these values must mirror in some way the values of the therapist who chose the theory. The beginning therapist who undergoes the process described above is learning one of the basic lessons of psychotherapy: to allow oneself to be instructed by one's patients.

Faced with a theory disconfirmed by therapeutic events, the novice therapist, if he or she is to become more than a hack, must now either change his or her theory or change theories. Usually, one does the former, until that theory is stretched to its conceptual limits and another must replace or supplement it. (Our patients, if we listen to them, insist on asserting their independence from our theories.) Also, not only do therapists change theories, but also theories change therapists. The process is gradual but inevitable if one operates authentically and in good faith. How could one work daily within a theoretical framework embodying particular values (is there anyone so naive as to think that any psychological theory is value-free?) and not absorb those values into the fabric of one's life? Therefore, one must be somewhat circumspect in the choice of theory, for one will become, to some extent, a creation of that theory.[2]

Developmental Dialectics

One must choose a theory with which one—and one's patients—can live and grow. Is it enough to settle for misery transformed into mere unhappiness—which is one classical psychoanalytic view of therapeutic reality? Can one really achieve total responsibility for oneself—the Gestalt prayer? Is it too much to expect transformation and transcendence—the Jungian dream? Perhaps these ask too little and too much. I would suggest considering the possibility of the heroics of everyday life. From an Eriksonian perspective, there are those qualities attainable within the life cycle of the average human being, living in an average expectable environment, that are the naturally occurring outcomes of a life honestly and fully lived. The virtues are homely ones—hope, justice, fidelity, wisdom, and so on—and the schedule of developmental tasks whose resolutions yield these virtues are assumed to occur in a guaranteed, built-in, epigenetic sequence. One of the beauties of Erikson's theory is that the values by which one might gauge one's life are not superimposed, but are organically embedded within everyone's life cycle; they develop out of the very process of being a human being living among others.

The foregoing picture appears a bit rosy. Growth is built-in and guaranteed. There is an accrual of virtues based on the resolution of developmental tasks occurring in an epigenetically determined sequence. Societies have developed more or less attuned to these individual stages of development and provide institutions within which ego growth may take place. Why, then, even suggest the word *heroics*?

Because there is a dark side to Erikson's theoretical picture, darker perhaps than even he would prefer to paint. Looking only at basic trust, autonomy, initiative, industry, identity, intimacy, generativity, and integrity, one can conceive of a sort of Jacob's ladder of development, from the earth of infancy to the heaven of an integrated and fulfilled old age. But at the end of that ladder is also despair. And at the beginning lies also mistrust. No matter how successfully one has rolled one's particular rock up a particular mountain, one knows that the rock and the mountain will be there long after one has gone, and that the excellence of one's rolling is finally irrelevant. What meaning does integrity have when everything so visibly falls apart with age? At infancy, no matter how devoted one's earliest caretaker, one is still subject to the storms and rages of one's impulses and the absolutely total cravings that batter at one's whole being from the inside. Does such an apparently indifferent world that permits these daily cataclysms merit trust?

As Erikson himself has said, his psychosocial stages are not an achievement scale; in his later writings, he has acknowledged their dialectical character. If one takes dialectics out of the realm of philosophical speculation and locates it directly in the life of individuals, it can be cruel and brutal stuff. Read in what I think is its fullest, most accurate way, Erikson is saying that there is no identity without diffusion, no intimacy without isolation, no autonomy without shame and doubt, and so on. That means that to achieve these "homely" virtues, one must immerse oneself in the dark antithesis as well as the bright thesis to achieve some balanced synthesis. Without the negative poles, Erikson's theory would become a kind of bank statement reflecting the accumulated interest of successfully resolved stages. However, having cast the life cycle into a dialectic of development, Erikson has achieved a sometimes anguishing existential accuracy.

Every psychotherapist knows that, no matter how much protest there is to the contrary, no one really wants to change. One just wants to feel better, to be happy. The bitter pill of knowledge in psychotherapy is that happiness, as a lasting state, is not possible, and that change is both necessary and painful. Does it now seem so "optimistic" to say that growth is continuous throughout the life cycle? Is this really to be experienced as a gift bestowed on humankind by a nurturant nature? Not if one considers the hard truth that all growth involves change, that all change involves loss, and that loss is painful. It is clear why we do not really want to change, and that clarity is spelled out in the form and content of Erikson's theory. To change, to grow is to permit oneself to experience fully both the negative and positive aspects of any developmental period. Considering this, one can more easily have compassion for those in the foreclosure identity status, who, rather than permit themselves to enter that trough of anxious uncertainty—moratorium—would prefer to bear those ills with which they are familiar than fly to unknown others, even though by doing so they stunt themselves.

This, then, recommends Erikson's psychosocial developmental theory to psychotherapists: It incorporates almost all of the human experience from the essential physicality of toilet training to the numinosity of an integral vision of the articulation of one's life cycle with those of others' past and present. To the extent that theories do have a structuring effect on those who hold them, a full understanding, a lived understanding, of Erikson's theory will aid in the creation of a therapist to whom no human experience is foreign. I think that patients will appreciate this.

Psychosocial Theory and Psychotherapy

The long view taken in the above section may be most appealing to experienced psychotherapists. New practitioners could use something somewhat more practical. I think that psychosocial developmental theory offers this. For one thing, it provides a sequential description of age-specific personality developmental issues that can inform a therapist of the life-cycle context of any particular presenting problem. For example, if an adolescent comes in with a problem in relationships, that problem is going to be set within the context of identity development. If a middle-aged adult presents with a similar issue, it will be occurring within the context of generativity. Clearly, relationships have different meanings according to whether one is resolving identity issues or generativity concerns. In addition, there are therapeutic implications of the theoretical assumption that most people most of the time possess the personal and social resources to resolve satisfactorily the stage-specific crises. This means that problems that require psychotherapy probably have their origins in the unsatisfactory resolution of some psychosocial stage prior to the current one. What is required at the outset of therapy then is a kind of diagnostic excursion back to the point of earliest failed resolution. When this point has been identified, one can then address that prior stage-specific concern in therapy within the context of the current psychosocial stage. As is clear from Table 2.1, because every stage issue recurs at every other stage, there is the chance for remediation of past stages within a contemporary chronological context.

Even though a young adult's primary difficulty may lie, say, at the autonomy level, this does not mean that one has to make either a diagonal or vertical reversion in the level of therapeutic techniques back to toilet training. Although finger painting may be cathartic and "release creativity," coloring outside the lines is probably best treated metaphorically and translated into attempting alternative resolutions of issues arising in everyday contexts. In addition to being unnecessary, there is a problem involved with employing regressive therapeutic techniques (such as rebirthing) to deal with inadequately resolved early psychosocial stages. Such techniques often involve that kind of magical thinking on which the ego defense mechanism of undoing is based. According to this logic, an arm severed by a locomotive could be healed by means of running the locomotive backward over it. In addition to the questionable metaphysics involved, a danger lies in such magical thinking. There is frequently a profound disappointment that ensues when the magic fails and the patient comes to understand that real-life change can be accomplished only through hard work in the everyday world. At this point, many otherwise amenable patients leave therapy altogether.

The way in which one might proceed with the psychosocial developmental approach in psychotherapy is illustrated in the following case history. Although the client was chronologically beyond the age of adolescence, he was psychologically very much in an "adolescing" period, and the developmental principles described are appropriate also to chronological late adolescents. My client was a 35-year-old computer programmer who was floundering in his job. He was extremely vulnerable in his self-esteem to others' opinions. And he was remarkably unempathic, especially with women. Although on the basis of his age he might be expected to have been on the threshold of generativity, he had not had a truly intimate relationship. His occupation remained just a job for him, unintegrated into an identity. He was unable to work industriously; he just put in his time. His sense of initiative, by contrast, seemed intact. Hence, we faced the re-resolution of three psychosocial stages: industry, identity, and intimacy. We began work at an industry level with an emphasis on industry in the context of his current life. This consisted primarily of my mirroring positively his sometimes numbingly boring descriptions of the intricacies of programming. As he began to be able to use me more as a self-object and to treat himself more as I was treating him, he came to experience his work more as a part of himself and to take more pride in it. His performance subsequently improved, and this bolstered his self-esteem so that he became better able to treat the comments of others with equanimity. In fact, those comments began to become increasingly positive and directed not only toward his work, but also toward himself as a person and friend. As his self-esteem increased and his relationships improved, he became less vulnerable to and more empathic with women. We terminated therapy when he made a decision to move to a new city, to finally separate from his parents, to begin a new job that was a career advancement, and to attempt to reestablish a previously failed relationship. Whether that relationship would provide the context for generativity, we both felt that he was now in a position where the next one might.

An important point in this description is that the earliest level of "stuck" development was addressed and dealt with in a contemporaneous context—that is, industry in the context of the current job. Psychotherapists familiar with personality theory will also note that one therapeutic technique—*mirroring*—derives not from Erikson but from Kohut's self-psychology (see Note 1). Although psychosocial developmental theory was formulated by a psychoanalyst, a variety of therapeutic techniques may be used when cases are construed within its context. These techniques may be chosen on the following bases: the therapist's values, ethics, abilities, and aesthetic preferences and the patient's needs and abilities. Although the theory does not prescribe techniques, it does provide a descriptive developmental context wherein one can determine what prior issues might be unresolved, what the relevant constituents of the current situation are, and what future directions the person's life is likely to take. Hence there is technical flexibility within a defined developmental framework.

Thus far we have discussed the nature of psychosocial developmental theory, the relationship between theory and therapy, the dialectics of development, and psychotherapy within a psychosocial developmental framework. However, this is a book on identity, and there are some indications for therapeutic procedure with the identity statuses that have emerged from our research. These will be discussed in the next section.

Exploration and Commitment: Psychotherapy and Identity

To be a psychotherapist is to participate with another person in the process of exploration—of current difficulties and the history of their development, of the solutions tried and now about to be reluctantly abandoned, and of new alternatives. An equally difficult task for the client is to make real-life commitments to untried directions. The related task for the therapist is to establish those protective and nurturant conditions in the therapy situation that will enable the other person to begin to make these commitments. This could be called the *encouraging* aspect of psychotherapy. To explore requires patience, a moderate level of anxiety, and some cognitive flexibility. To make commitments requires courage.

These therapeutic components of exploration and commitment are also the defining criteria for identity formation, as discussed in Chapter 2. That both therapy and identity formation have these processes in common bears on an aspect of the identity statuses that has been puzzling: their continuing existence. Constructs in psychology have their half-lives, and the identity-status constructs as useful ideas might be expected to have begun to disintegrate some 5 to 10 years ago. I think that the reason they have not is certainly not because of their felicitous titles, but because the process variables of exploration and commitment underlying them represent essential elements of human change and growth—whether that occurs in the realm of cognitive development, moral development, self-development, identity development, or psychotherapy.

Psychotherapy is a means by which a "stuck" developmental process may be freed to move ahead again. Although there are those for whom psychotherapy can become life, for most of us, including Freud, psychotherapy is but a means to the ends of "leben und arbeiten." Psychotherapies successful in getting persons "unstuck," moving out of therapy and on with their lives, are likely to be those that enhance the exploration-commitment process. And because this process is also the basis for identity formation, it is highly probable that any significant change occurring during psychotherapy also involves an identity transformation.

We developed the identity statuses in order to describe the different ways in which late adolescents might be found to be dealing with Erikson's fifth stage. When the identity statuses were initially conceived, they were just vehicular concepts intended to facilitate empirical research. However, probably because the subjects in the early identity studies were very carefully listened to by genuinely interested investigators, these concepts seem to have apprehended something fundamental about the ways in which persons form not just their identities, but also their general approaches to life. For example, a foreclosure is, to be sure, a late adolescent who has seemed reluctant to explore meaningfully occupational and ideological directions different from those with which he or she grew up. But foreclosure has come to mean more than that. It is also a way of being in the world, a mode of relating to others and oneself. Hence it appears that the identity statuses, although formulated initially as labels applied to late adolescents' styles of resolving the identity issue, can also be seen as descriptions of states of essential developmental processes.

As a result of the more than 300 studies that have been conducted on the identity statuses, we have a fairly clear idea of their characteristics, family settings, developmental antecedents and consequences, and interactional styles. This information provides us with possible therapeutic directions to take with persons in the different identity statuses, whether they are late adolescents or adults. These directions and possible difficulties arising in psychotherapy will be discussed below.

Foreclosure

I begin with foreclosure because it is the most common status appearing before moratorium and because it is probably the most frequent status overall. Also, understanding some of the dynamics of the foreclosure in particular yields insight into the identity-formation process itself.

Foreclosures whom we have studied are persons who, even though they live in a society that sanctions and encourages an exploratory period during adolescence (Erikson's "institutionalized moratorium"), have not used this period to consider seriously departures from their childhood beliefs and occupational directions. They usually remain closely tied to their families: internalized, externalized, or both. Our hypothesis (Marcia et al., 1993) has been that a primary reason for this is the guilt and anxiety attendant to questioning parental values. We also have assumed that this reluctance to deviate significantly from the beliefs inculcated by childhood authorities has its origin at least in the oedipal, and perhaps pre-oedipal, period. Hence foreclosures likely come out of late adolescence and enter early adulthood with a fairly unreconstructed superego. This has direct implications for psychotherapy, especially if therapy is seen as a process whereby exploration is encouraged. For the foreclosure, genuine exploration will reactivate all of those fears and anxieties that precluded such exploration in the first place. Thus to invite a foreclosure to explore is to ask him or her to do and be the opposite of what he or she learned under anxiety-arousing conditions to not do and not be.

Foreclosure families are notable for their closeness and warmth. But this closeness and warmth is conditional, contingent on one's adherence to the family rules. Regardless of the content of those rules, the requirement of adherence itself serves to preclude exploration. Hence for the foreclosure, it is not so much what is explored that is threatening, but the very fact of exploration itself. It becomes clear then why foreclosures so seldom appear for psychotherapy and, when they do, why it is usually following some kind of external precipitating crisis such as low grades that jeopardize an occupational direction, a failed love affair, or the death of a close family member.

One of the most memorable foreclosures I have seen in therapy was a 47-year-old lawyer. He had been maintaining a five-year affair with his secretary, who was threatening to leave him if he did not leave his family. What brought him to therapy was not even this conflict but the warning from his physician that his blood pressure was reaching the danger point and something had to be done (in addition to beta blockers) to decrease the effects of stress. We spent two years of therapy exploring the consequences of his no longer being a "good boy." This is absolutely not a trivial question for a foreclosure. Because he or she has not reconstituted the superego by means of the strengthening of the ego ideals at adolescence (Blos, 1974; Josselson, 1980), his or her entire self-esteem rests on living up to the standards of parental introjects. Failure to maintain one's self-esteem is one of the recognized conditions for suicide. It is difficult to live with oneself and others if one does not feel worthwhile, and the foreclosure's conditions for feeling worth-while were inculcated when he or she was a child (and parents were gods and goddesses). By asking a foreclosure to meet one essential condition for psychotherapy—exploration—one is posing a threat to his or her existence. If one truly explores, one questions; if one questions those internalized figures, one risks their rejection and consequent guilt and anxiety. If one overcomes this and successfully departs from parental precepts, one risks having no internalized standard by which to judge one's worth. The resulting feeling of emptiness may be as bad as feelings of guilt and anxiety.

Thus a danger in treating foreclosures lies in being too successful, too quickly. To strip the person of superego values before these can be supplemented by newly formed ego ideals is to risk acute depression. Unless one wishes to undertake a brief crisis-intervention approach (which is not psychotherapy), then the rule with foreclosures must be to proceed gradually. One procedure that I have found effective is to locate some values held by the foreclosure with which the therapist can authentically identify (perhaps honesty or hard work). Proceeding from this "companionable" position, one may then make forays into the more dangerous territory of, say, sexual values and lifestyle orientations. But care must be taken along the way that new ideals, to which the person can refer for self-esteem, are being developed.

During this period of superego reformulation, the therapist can expect a transference fluctuating between extreme dependence and gratitude ("I wish that my father, mother, etc., had been more like you") and extreme resentment ("How dare you suggest that my parents, my church, . . ."). Many foreclosures will leave therapy in outrage during this period. However, leaving outraged is better than leaving depressed. Although not wishing to be melodramatic, it does seem at times in treating foreclosures that one is fighting for them to recover their soul.

Moratorium

Moratoriums have already launched themselves into the exploration phase and are suffering its consequences. Some of the therapist's work has been done for them by pressures internal or external to the individual. If this is the first crisis period the individual has undergone, he or she may be anxious and confused because he or she probably has come from a stable foreclosure position in which direction was quite clear.

Such individuals are not used to being uncertain and may feel as if their worlds are collapsing.

The impetus for the identity-status research was a diagnostic evaluation I had done on a 16-year-old boy whose projective tests yielded responses indicating a severe thought disorder (e.g., edging the Rorschach, dividing Thematic Apperception Test, or TAT, responses into "good" and "bad" based on picture shadings, etc.). When he left the hospital six months later in quite good health, it was apparent to my supervisor and myself that we had been dealing not with a schizophrenic episode, but with a severe identity crisis. The precipitating event for his hospitalization had been his decision not to go into the Coast Guard academy as his career military father had ordered.

What a moratorium needs most is a therapist who does not get in the way. What he or she needs least is a zealous practitioner eager to dispense "insights." It must be recognized that a moratorium is already doing what developmentally he or she ought to be doing; what is required is a patient, caring, and responsive witness to the process. No wonder our moratoriums produce the longest identity-status interview tapes as they use the listening ear of the researcher to work out their concerns. No wonder that client-centered therapy had its origin within that institutionalized moratorium: the university. A mistake that is easy to make with moratoriums because they are so engaging is to fall into the trap of siding with one or the other aspect of their ambivalence—that is, to be led into supporting one alternative over another. This just rescues moratoriums from undergoing their own useful struggles because now they are free to endorse the alternative wholeheartedly and can confront their therapists rather than themselves. Because moratoriums do elicit concern and interest, it is sometimes difficult to remain uninvested. However, the therapist who can do that in a caring way communicates to the moratorium that the process he or she is undergoing, although painful, is necessary and ultimately productive.

Identity Achievement

Identity achievements are more likely to come into therapy for growth than for remediation. Hence they are more receptive to "creative approaches" such as art therapy, psychodrama, and journal writing. Another situation that might bring the identity achievement into therapy is an identity crisis succeeding the initial one at late adolescence. Before the individual learns that change is an integral aspect of being truly alive, he or she may be dismayed to find him- or herself "having to do it all again." The therapeutic procedure indicated for persons undergoing these moratorium-achievement (MAMA) cycles is the same as that for moratoriums: attentive listening and the conveyance of reassurance about the necessity and normality of the process. The expectation that there will be subsequent identity crises after the first one at late adolescence is built into psychosocial developmental theory. Every stage has its accompanying identity issue, so every significant life change means an identity reformulation. I recall wincing at a dinner conversation during which a psychologist (not a clinician) spoke dismissingly of her husband's "midlife crisis" as if it were something that no grown-up should be found to be undergoing. Even the word *adolescent* has come to be something of a pejorative. However, most experienced identity researchers and psychotherapists know that a true adolescence, a period of exploration and commitment, is the primary condition for ego growth, and, although it is often an occasion of discomfort for those who are "adolescing" and those who care for them, it is to be valued and supported, rather than disparaged.

Identity Diffusion

In discussing undertaking psychotherapy with diffusions, it is necessary first to distinguish among different types of diffusions (see Archer & Waterman, 1990; Marcia, 1986, 1989). The diffusion persons most likely to appear for psychotherapy are the borderline personality, the "disturbed" diffusion, and the "carefree" diffusion. Although borderline personalities are diffuse in identity, the origin of their difficulties lies developmentally earlier, and the pathology involved is more in the nature of ego fragmentation than just diffuse identity. There is a considerable literature now on the treatment of borderlines, so that topic will not be covered here (see Adler, 1985).

Carefree diffusions seldom appear in therapist's offices because they are seeking help for themselves. They are more likely to be brought there by others who have become anxious about them. The carefree diffusion seems to avoid assiduously commitment situations, whether occupational, ideological, or interpersonal. They may be charming and socially skilled; they often are also shallow. Authority figures such as parents and teachers describe them as "wasting their time," "not living up to their potential." They do not take themselves especially seriously, this task being relegated to others who seem always to be "on their case." If the therapist becomes too "heavy," the carefree diffusion "splits"; if the therapist is too nonchalant, he or she and the client drift into chatter. It is the rare therapist who can get through to a carefree diffusion. One tactic is to go along with the diffusion's insouciance and then throw in a well-placed "zinger" that surprises the person and induces some anxiety. Although it is impossible to teach or even adequately define "zingers," in this context they would be one-line statements that would cast into immediate and chilling relief the consequences of the vacuousness and meaninglessness of the carefree diffusion's current life course.

Disturbed diffusions seem to be of two varieties: the schizoid loner and the "empty vessel." The schizoid loner shuns social contact, preferring solitary activities such as collecting hockey statistics alone in his or her room or sorting mail in the post office at night. There is a certain kind of social reticence that a therapist who is to be effective with loners must cultivate. A psychotherapist who oozes warmth and is expressively empathic is too interpersonally hot for this kind of client to handle. Rather, what is indicated is a relatively quiet, dependably available, nondemanding person who is not too easily shocked by the bizarre fantasies that the schizoid loner is liable eventually to disclose. During the four-year period in which I had been seeing such a loner, there was a six-month period when he became unable to look at me directly. Finally, he told me that this was because he thought I despised him for some masturbatory fantasies he had described. Actually, I had not found them to be that unusual and I had no idea what expression had crossed my face when he described them, but he had hypersensitively registered it as strongly disapproving. Gentleness, patience, and a low level of reactivity are important in treating these persons. Also, because of their usually emotionally impoverished background, there is a paucity of strongly held introjects, and the therapist, rather than becoming a transference figure, is more likely to become a primary object. Hence, it would be a grave mistake ever to underestimate one's significance for the loner type of diffusion.

The other type of disturbed diffusion is the individual who complains of being "empty inside." Frequently, other people do not perceive them to be like this. That is probably because a fair degree of insight and sensitivity is required to experience oneself in this way, and cases (e.g., narcissistic character disorders) in which there truly is "nobody home" are usually not characterized by such introspection. The task for the therapist in this situation is to help the person construct an identity. In so doing, there are three things these persons bring to therapy that are uniquely their own and from which an identity can be built: (a) their unique personal history, (b) their dreams and fantasies, and (c) their body and feelings arising therefrom. The psychotherapist becomes a temporary receptacle for these facts and also serves as an external guarantor of that experience of continuity of self that Erikson describes as essential for a sense of identity. Gradually, the patient can organize and internalize the personal details that the therapist feeds back to him or her and can experience him- or herself as having continuity in time without constant reminders from the therapist. Working with these people, therapists often find themselves saying things such as "Remember in one of our early sessions when you were describing . . ." and "Last year at this time, I recall you said that . . ." (continuity); and "What you said about . . . kind of goes together with how you seem to feel about . . ." (organization).

Different from working with the other identity statuses, treating identity diffusions involves neither structure disequilibration as with foreclosures nor structure accommodation as with moratoriums, but structure building. Unavoidably, this is a long process and requires more of the person of the therapist as a necessary ingredient than does therapy with the other identity statuses.

Summary

Compared with other theories of personality and associated theories of psychotherapy, psychosocial developmental theory has the advantages of being continuous with classical and ego psychoanalytic theory and of providing a fairly specific developmental schedule for stages of ego growth that takes into account both individual and social factors. This theory, because of the dialectical form given to the stage-specific resolutions, grounds what otherwise might remain theoretical essences in the concrete existence of existential dilemmas. The choice of theory is important to practitioners because it both reflects and creates their own system of values within which they carry on their practices. Psychosocial developmental theory suggests values that derive not from some structure of ethics superimposed on life, but which arise naturally within the expectable course of human development. Research

on one psychosocial developmental stage—identity-identity confusion—
has provided four categories of identity-resolution styles. Each identity
status has its own empirically based characteristics that suggest different psychotherapeutic approaches to be taken with persons in the different identity statuses: cautious disequilibration of structure with
foreclosures; nonintrusive attention with moratoriums and identity
achievements who are reentering an identity crisis; and structure building, using fairly extensively the person of the therapist, with identity
diffusions. Research into the other psychosocial developmental stages
continues with the hope that additional specific suggestions for intervention across the life cycle will be forthcoming.

Notes

1. Kohut (Kohut & Wolf, 1986) describes the developmental need for three kinds of
persons necessary to the growth of the self in infancy and early childhood: (a) a mirroring
person who reflects back to the child his or her essential importance (adorableness,
grandiosity); (b) an idealizable person, or someone whom the child can live up to; and (c)
a "twin"—that is, a treasured companion. All of these figures are experienced in a
somewhat undifferentiated fashion, more as a necessary and valued part of oneself than
as separate and independent others. The need for such self-objects is assumed to continue
in a diminished fashion throughout life. And psychotherapy is assumed to be effective,
especially with narcissistically organized persons, according to the extent to which the
therapist becomes for the client the appropriate self-object.

2. As one editorial reviewer, Professor Waterman, noted, the therapist is also in an
ongoing process of identity formation and may model this process for the client.

References

Adler, G. (1985). *Borderline psychopathology and its treatment*. New York: Jason Aron-
son.
Archer, S. L., & Waterman, A. S. (1990). Varieties of identity diffusions and foreclosures:
An exploration of subcategories of the identity statuses. *Journal of Adolescent Re-
search, 5*(1), 96-111.
Blos, P. (1974). The genealogy of the ego ideal. *Psychoanalytic Study of the Child, 29*,
43-89.
Bradley, C., & Marcia, J. E. (1990). *Towards construct validity of generativity-stagnation:
A status approach*. Unpublished manuscript, Simon Fraser University, Burnaby, British
Columbia, Canada.
Erikson, E. H. (1959). Identity and the life cycle. In *Psychological Issues* (Issue 1,
Monograph No. 1). New York: International Universities Press.
Erikson, E. H. (1963). *Childhood and society*. New York: Norton.

Freud, A. (1936). *The ego and mechanisms of defense*. New York: International Universities Press.

Hartmann, H. (1964). *Essays on ego psychology*. New York: International Universities Press.

Hearn, S. (1994). *Development and construct validation of a measure of Eriksonian integrity*. Unpublished manuscript, Simon Fraser University, Burnaby, B.C., Canada.

Josselson, R. (1980). Ego development in adolescence. In J. Adelson (Ed.), *Handbook of adolescent psychology* (pp. 188-210). New York: John Wiley.

Kohut, H., & Wolf, E. (1986). The disorders of the self and their treatment: An outline. In A. Morrison (Ed.), *Essential papers on narcissism* (pp. 175-196). New York: New York University Press.

Marcia, J. E. (1986). Clinical implications of the identity status approach within psychosocial developmental theory. *Cadernos de Consulta Psicologica, 2,* 23-35.

Marcia, J. E. (1989). Identity diffusion differentiated. In M. A. Luszcz & T. Nettlebeck (Eds.), *Psychological development: Perspectives across the life-span* (pp. 289-294). New York: Elsevier North-Holland.

Marcia, J. E., Waterman, A. S., Matteson, D. R., Archer, S. A., & Orlofsky, J. L. (1993). *Ego identity: A handbook for psychosocial research*. New York: Springer Verlag.

Rapaport, D. (1969). The structure of psychoanalytic theory. In S. Koch (Ed.), *Psychology: A study of a science* (Vol. 3, pp. 55-183). New York: McGraw-Hill.

Stephen, J. E., Fraser, E., & Marcia, J. E. (1992). Lifespan identity development: Variables related to Moratorium-Achievement (MAMA) cycles. *Journal of Adolescence, 15,* 283-300.

White, R. W. (1959). Motivation reconsidered: The concept of competence. *Psychological Review, 66,* 297-323.

4

Family Interventions

DENNIS R. PAPINI

Marcia (1989) has speculated that interventions involving adolescent identity development are most likely to succeed if (a) the focus of the intervention is placed clearly on the processes underlying the identity statuses and (b) the intervention is implemented during a time of natural intrapsychic destructuring. Following Marcia's first suggestion, this chapter will examine how the identity processes of exploration and commitment are affected by family processes. Not only has the transition into adolescence been found to involve significant intrapsychic restructuring, but also many researchers have argued that the family environment undergoes restructuring as family relations are redefined, renegotiated, and realigned (Collins, 1990; Steinberg, 1990). Thus this chapter will (a) review the theoretical models designed to explain adolescent psychosocial development in the family context, (b) summarize research that demonstrates an empirical link between family processes and adolescent identity development, and (c) suggest a model of family intervention that may be useful in promoting healthy and adaptive ego identity development during adolescence.

AUTHOR'S NOTE: Address correspondence and requests for reprints to Dennis R. Papini, Department of Psychology, Western Illinois University, Macomb, IL 61455.

Models of Adolescent Psychosocial
Development in the Family

As a developmental passage, adolescence is by definition a time of intrapsychic and extrapsychic restructuring (Adams, Gullotta, & Montemayor, 1992; Erikson, 1968; Feldman & Elliott, 1990). Marcia (1983, 1988) has suggested that the biopsychosocial changes associated with the child's transition into adolescence are characterized by questioning, revision, and eventual rejection of childhood identifications with parents. Thus early adolescence may involve the child's deidealization of identifications with parents and a search for autonomy (Steinberg & Silverberg, 1986). This deidealization of parental identifications generates self-disequilibration and is associated with a period of ego exploration in which the middle adolescent actively searches for roles and values that reflect his or her own unique skills, abilities, and personal preferences. Late adolescents begin to make commitments that integrate these new elements of the self into a coherent identity structure, thereby replacing the self-regulatory function of childhood identifications with parents (Sabatelli & Mazor, 1985).

The adolescent's ability to successfully negotiate this intrapsychic process depends in large part on the presence or absence of certain qualities in the family environment. The ability to construct an identity capable of *self*-regulation holds forward the promise of efficient and effective adaptation to the demands of the adult world. The failure to replace childhood identifications with parents through the processes of exploration and commitment may result in short-term pseudoadaptation but long-term maladjustment (see Archer, 1989a, for a review of the psychological correlates and consequences of the identity statuses). There is a definite need to establish intervention strategies that facilitate adolescents' ability to co-construct with parents an identity that is adaptive for the long-term. I contend that such interventions should be family-based, preventative, and implemented during late childhood.

Perhaps the most comprehensive statement on the role of the family in the identity-formation process has been advanced by Grotevant and Cooper (1985, 1986; Cooper, Grotevant, & Condon, 1983), who contend that the family plays a significant role in adolescent identity formation by allowing the adolescent to express differences of opinion from parents (individuality) while maintaining a sense of emotional connectedness with them. In general, findings reported by Grotevant and Cooper indicate that adolescents engaged in significant identity exploration were embedded in families whose interactions were characterized by statements reflecting separateness (e.g., how one's point of view differs from others) and moderate levels of permeability (e.g., openness toward others' points of view). Adolescents who engaged in little identity exploration were found to be engaged in family relationships characterized by an active avoidance of interpersonal disagreements and high levels of permeability. This process of establishing individuality and connectedness has important implications for the adolescent's ability to explore and make commitments to various life alternatives.

Research by Hauser and colleagues (Hauser, Powers, Noam, & Jacobson, 1984) has also revealed that the interactional style of families is associated with adolescent ego development. These researchers distinguish between two interactional styles in families—enabling and constraining—both of which have cognitive and affective components. Enabling interactions encourage family members to express their own thoughts and perceptions. Cognitive enabling involves focusing on problem solving, engaging in the curious exploration of family issues, and explaining individual points of view to other family members. Affective enabling involves the expression of empathy and acceptance of other family members. Ego development appears to be facilitated through the use of enabling interactions during family problem solving. Constraining interactions interfere with the individual's movement toward autonomy and differentiation. Cognitive constraining involves distracting family members away from the problems they face, withholding information from the interaction, and expressing indifference toward family members and family issues. Affective constraining includes excessive judging (both devaluation and gratification) of other family members and their points of view. Ego development appears to be inhibited by the use of constraining interactions during family problem solving. Although this model is built on the study of ego development, it is not difficult to recognize the implications of these interactional styles for identity development. Parents may, through the use of enabling and constraining interactions, shape and direct adolescent identity exploration and commitment.

Adams (1990) and Dyk (1990) have attempted to integrate these two models and have been studying patterns of family interaction that enable or constrain both individuality and connectedness. Dyk (1990) has recently reported data that indicate that middle-adolescent identity development is facilitated by interactions with fathers that reflect enabling individuation and connectedness. In addition, identity development was inhibited by patterns of family interaction in which there was low enabling individuation and high enabling connectedness. This particular pattern of interaction was associated with adolescent identity foreclosure. Future research conducted from this integrated model may further our understanding of familial contributions to adolescent identity development.

The circumplex model of family systems has been receiving increased attention from researchers interested in the study of adolescent development in the family context (Olson, Russell, & Sprenkle, 1980). These theorists view the dynamics of the family system along three dimensions: cohesion, adaptability, and communication. Olson and his colleagues hold that *cohesion* refers to the quality of the emotional bonding that family members feel for one another, ranging from disengaged to connected to enmeshed. *Adaptability* refers to the family's ability to change control structures, relationships, and rules in response to situational or developmental stress; it ranges in value from rigid to flexible to chaotic. The quality of *communication* between and among family members is viewed as a mediator of cohesion and adaptability, and it is evaluated on the basis of the openness of communication patterns within the family. Although this model has not been directly employed in the study of identity development, the three dimensions may generate some interesting theoretical expectations that can be tested.

Adolescent identity exploration and commitment should be facilitated by family contexts that are emotionally connected, flexibly adaptive, and characterized by open patterns of interpersonal communication. Emotionally detached and enmeshed families may be unable to provide the emotional security adolescents need to explore and commit to life alternatives, resulting in identity diffusion and foreclosure, respectively. Similarly, rigid and chaotic families may be unable to adapt to the developmental needs of their maturing children, resulting in very little adolescent exploration of life alternatives. The rigid family would be more likely to produce identity foreclosure, as the adolescent is presented with a parentally prescribed identity. The chaotic family would be more likely to produce identity diffusion, as the adolescent would lack a sense of direction and guidance from parents during the process of exploration and commitment. The openness of family communication patterns may serve to mediate the effects of these extreme forms of cohesion and adaptability.

Although each theoretical model discussed has a slightly different conceptualization of adolescent development in the family context, all of these models share common features. Each model views the affective quality of the family context as an influential aspect of the child's ability to engage in the construction of an adaptive identity. Similarly, each model emphasizes the family's need to adapt to the changing biopsychosocial needs of individual family members. The co-construction of a sense of identity by adolescents and parents depends heavily on the ability of each family member to be sensitive to, supportive of, and flexible in their reactions to the adolescent's identity exploration and commitment activities (Youniss, 1983). The review of research that follows lends empirical credence to these theoretical speculations.

Family and Identity Processes: Research Linkages

This review incorporates what is currently known about the relationship between identity development and family affect, as well as family structure, adaptability, and communication. These family processes have been found to be systematically related to the exploration or commitment activities of early, middle, and late adolescence. Before proceeding with this review, I would like to clarify my position on identity processes during early adolescence. Archer (1982) studied early and middle adolescent identity development on the grounds that the biopsychosocial changes associated with these epochs might be a catalyst for identity-construction activities. This research revealed that the vast majority of early and middle adolescents were identity-foreclosed or identity-diffused. Archer and Waterman (1983) found that even though some 6th graders did exhibit evidence of identity construction, the greatest amount of change in identity occurred from 10th to 12th grade and involved moving from the nonexploration statuses (foreclosure and diffusion) into the active exploration statuses (moratorium and achievement). I am not suggesting that early adolescents are identity achieved, only that they may be actively engaged in self-exploration (for example, deidealization of parental identifications) and that the family may facilitate or inhibit this active search and discovery of self.

Family Affect

Family affect has been broadly dimensionalized in studies of adolescent identity development; included in this array are attachment (Campbell,

Adams, & Dobson, 1984; Marcia, 1988; Papini & Roggman, 1992; Schiedel & Marcia, 1985), parent-adolescent conflict (Collins, 1990; Papini, Sebby, & Clark, 1989), and perceptions of parental acceptance or rejection (Adams, 1985; Adams & Jones, 1981, 1983; LaVoie, 1976). A brief consideration of the research in each dimension may prove insightful.

Attachment

Several researchers investigating adolescent psychosocial development have argued that the quality of parent-adolescent attachment may affect adolescent identity exploration and commitment (Adams et al., 1992; Marcia, 1988; Schiedel & Marcia, 1985). Adolescents who enjoy a secure sense of attachment to parents have a safe foundation from which to explore and sample life alternatives and make self-chosen commitments to life directions. Conversely, adolescents who do not possess a secure sense of attachment to parents are less likely to face the risks that inevitably go hand-in-hand with exploration and commitment. In general, healthy identity development has been observed in family contexts characterized by a moderately high degree of parent-adolescent affection (Campbell et al., 1984). Families in which there are secure parent-adolescent attachment relations provide the emotional support necessary for meaningful identity exploration and commitment. Thus the quality of attachment relations to parents may buffer the adolescent from feelings of role confusion.

Family theorists have conceptualized attachment as a continuum ranging from detachment to enmeshment (Hess & Handel, 1968; Olson et al., 1980). Both detachment and enmeshment are thought to interfere with the establishment of self-other boundaries during adolescent psychosocial development. In families characterized by detachment, the adolescent's ability or willingness to explore and make commitments is undermined by a lack of feedback from parents. The adolescent lacks the confidence that parents will respond in a supportive fashion as he or she experiments with new roles and relationships. In families characterized by enmeshment, the adolescent's ability to construct an adaptive identity is inhibited because the adolescent is unable or unwilling to venture away from the safety and security provided by the family. To venture away from the family is to risk the loss of safety by charges of disloyalty to parental imperatives. Several researchers have shown that adolescents who are identity-foreclosed tend to have the most loving and affectionate perceptions of their families (Archer, 1989a; Papini, Micka, & Barnett, 1989). Thus in thinking about the relationship between parent-child attachment and identity development, there can be too much as well as too little of a good thing.

Conflict

Another dimension of family affect that has been empirically related to adolescent identity development is parent-adolescent conflict. Identity exploration involves questioning childhood identifications, values, and beliefs, and it appears to involve greater conflict with parents. A variety of researchers have suggested that low to moderate levels of parent-adolescent conflict may function to promote psychosocial development during adolescence (Cooper, 1988; Papini, Sebby, & Clark, 1989; Steinberg, 1990). Research reported by Papini, Sebby, and Clark (1989) has revealed that identity exploration was highest when there was a moderate degree of conflict between parents and teens. The results of these studies clearly indicate that more research is needed to better understand the relationship between family conflict and identity exploration during adolescence. The child's transition into early adolescence may well involve affective changes in the quality of family relationships that have important implications for subsequent adolescent identity development.

Parental Acceptance or Rejection

A final dimension of family affect that has been found to be related to identity development is adolescent perceptions of parental acceptance or rejection (Adams, 1985; Adams & Jones, 1983; Enright, Lapsley, Drivas, & Fehr, 1980; LaVoie, 1976). In general, research on the relationship between parental acceptance or rejection and identity development reveals that (a) identity-achieved adolescents perceive their parents as exhibiting minimal control coupled with a high degree of praise; (b) adolescents experiencing psychosocial moratorium perceive their parents as encouraging; (c) identity-foreclosed adolescents perceive their parents as being warm and supportive, with little open expression of emotion; and (d) identity-diffuse adolescents perceive their fathers as being highly negative and rejecting and feel that their family relations are detached (Campbell et al., 1984; Papini, Micka, & Barnett, 1989).

Thus the affective quality of family life appears to play an important role in the child's ability to negotiate successfully the psychosocial crises of adolescence. The affective quality of the family context influences the adolescent's sense of trust and security, thereby influencing his or her willingness to explore and make commitments to various life alternatives.

Family Structure, Adaptability, and Communication

The intent of a family systems perspective has been to describe how transactional relationships within the family facilitate or inhibit adolescent identity development (Ackerman, 1980; Hess & Handel, 1968). Several authors (e.g., Bell & Bell, 1983; Berzonsky, 1988; Grotevant, 1983) have suggested that the functioning of family systems can be characterized by the degree of openness and flexibility in processing information. Family systems that encourage open patterns of communication and flexible adaptability to change may facilitate the development of these characteristics among family members. Adolescents who are participants in social contexts that facilitate openness and flexibility should be better equipped to actively explore and make commitments to life alternatives than adolescents from family systems characterized by closedness and rigidity.

Steirlin (1981) has discussed adolescent psychosocial growth in the family context in terms of the ways in which psychological distance and adaptations are made within the family. Taking cues from the developmental changes of family members, the differentiating family is able to adjust to changes in the individual's need for emotional closeness and distance. Adolescents in differentiating families are able to explore and make commitments in a family system that is sensitive to and supportive of their identity-construction activities. The nondifferentiating family is unresponsive to the developmental needs of family members, and adolescents who attempt to engage in identity exploration may be kept in their existing individual and family role through the use of guilt-induction strategies (Anderson & Fleming, 1986). Again, the family's ability to adapt to the changing needs of family members may affect adolescent identity development. Thus the adolescent's construction of an adaptive ego identity requires him or her to destructure childhood identifications and restructure the self in the context of a structurally balanced family that is flexible and adaptive to the developmental changes of family members.

Intervention

The call to explore identity intervention during the process of adolescent identity development has come from several different scholars (Adams & Gullotta, 1983; Archer, 1989b). Unfortunately, these calls have been followed by little basic or applied research. To date, I have found only one published identity-intervention study that incorporates family concepts. Working with late adolescents, Ganiere and Enright (1989) developed an intervention strategy aimed at helping adolescents better understand others' perceptions of self, early childhood identifications with parents, and values. Although this is a positive first step, I believe we have a firm enough understanding of adolescent identity development in the family context to pursue more comprehensive intervention strategies.

Three basic questions will be addressed in the remainder of this chapter. First, what family processes could or should be altered to promote the construction of a healthy and adaptive identity during adolescence? Second, at what level of the system and in what form should interventions into adolescent identity development be implemented? Third, when should interventions be implemented? The answers to these questions are highly dependent on the specific developmental characteristics of individuals and families.

What Family Process Should Be Targeted?

Both theory and research converge on the central importance of family affect, family adaptability, and family communication on the adolescent's ability to co-construct with parents a healthy and adaptive identity. Accordingly, interventions should be developed that are aimed at helping families establish cohesion, flexible adaptability, and open patterns of communication. Although these family processes are important, the role of affect in the family seems to be crucial to the adolescent's exploration and commitment activities. If families are unable to provide an appropriate level of emotional support, many adolescents find the anxiety and guilt associated with self-exploration to be psychologically overwhelming. The tendency for adolescents in enmeshed families is to retreat to the safety and security of parent-child relationships, while the tendency for adolescents from detached and rejecting families is to continue their aimless psychological wanderings. The establishment of emotionally secure relationships with parents seems to be a prerequisite for adolescent identity exploration and commitment. More extensive and intensive clinical interventions may be required for families that exhibit dysfunctional levels of enmeshment or detachment.

The family's ability to adapt to the developmental changes of family members also appears to play a critical role in adolescent identity development. Rigid and chaotic families stifle exploration and provide little or no guidance for adolescents as they make commitments and try to integrate and consolidate elements of their emerging identity. Many rigid and chaotic families will also exhibit dysfunctional structural properties such as fusion and triangulation that may require clinical family intervention (Anderson & Fleming, 1986). Family members' ability to adjust to the adolescent's exploration of new roles, relationships, values, and beliefs allows them to play a constructive role in guiding the adolescent toward an identity that is healthy and adaptive for both the adolescent and the family.

Adolescent identity exploration also appears to be facilitated by families in which there are open patterns of communication. Such patterns allow families to overcome problems of cohesion and adaptability by discussing their problems and differences. One reason that moderate amounts of family conflict are positively related to adolescent identity exploration is that these families are able to discuss and resolve their differences of opinion (Robin & Foster, 1989). Open communication not only allows the adolescent an opportunity to express newly acquired perspectives and beliefs, but also allows parents to monitor and validate or invalidate these expressions. By intervening in family communication patterns, it may be possible to ameliorate deficiencies in family cohesion and adaptability that adversely affect identity exploration and commitment.

What Level and What Form Should Interventions Take?

The level of the system at which interventions should be directed is largely a matter of personal preference and professional training. Because identity development is usually conceptualized as an intrapsychic process, there may be a tendency to intervene at the level of the individual adolescent. Clinical work with severe identity-diffused adolescents reveals that successful intervention requires the creation of a warm and supportive relationship between therapist and client (Marcia, 1989). However, adolescent identity development almost always occurs in the family context. What happens to the adolescent when he or she returns to the family environment and deals with inappropriate levels of family cohesion, adaptability, and communication? By intervening at the level of the family, it may be possible to help families change these maladaptive patterns of behavior and develop the family strength that is necessary for optimal adolescent psychosocial growth and development (Hess & Handel, 1968; McCubbin & Patterson, 1981; Stinnett, 1981). Thus the key to optimizing adolescent identity development may lie in directing strength-promoting interventions toward the family as a whole.

Many different intervention formats may be potentially useful, ranging from self-help groups to clinical family therapy. The clinically based interventions are designed primarily for use with adolescents and families experiencing severe psychosocial disturbances. The promotion of optimal identity exploration and commitment among normal functioning adolescents and families may be facilitated by the implementation of self-help and planned parent or family education programs. Peer self-help groups may also be helpful if adolescents are able to express their family and identity concerns in a nonthreatening setting. Adult-headed self-help groups generally provide more structure and feedback to the adolescent about how to communicate these concerns to family members. Thus self-help groups may facilitate identity development by allowing adolescents to question and revise childhood identifications with parents while exploring self-chosen roles, values, and beliefs.

Existing parent and family education programs are typically designed to help parents deal with conflicts arising from adolescent autonomy and independence-seeking behaviors with little awareness of the potential psychosocial value of these conflicts. Thus there is a need to develop educational programs that will help families develop a greater sensitivity to how the developmental changes associated with the child's transition into adolescence are related to subsequent psychosocial development. This program should include research-based information about developmental changes in family cohesion, adaptability, and communication (Steinberg, 1990), as well as exercises that develop family sensitivity, tolerance, and strength in coping with these biopsychosocial changes.

When Should Interventions Be Implemented?

A growing body of evidence suggests that the family's adaptation to the biopsychosocial changes associated with the child's transition into early adolescence serves a psychosocial function (Steinberg, 1990). This transition requires families to alter existing patterns of family affect, adaptability, and communication in such a way that adolescents are able to explore their individuality while maintaining feelings of emotional connectedness with other family members. The first step in exploring individuality is taken when the early adolescent begins to question and revise childhood identifications with parents. Although the deidealization process may not immediately result in the construction of an identity, it probably does signal the beginning of the psychosocial crisis of identity versus role confusion. Given the pervasive restructuring of the intrapsychic and extrapsychic worlds of the early adolescent, identity interventions should probably be implemented during late childhood. Families with 10-year-olds would benefit from programs that educate them about (a) the biopsychosocial changes that will be taking place in their adolescents; (b) the affective, adaptational, and communication challenges that families may encounter during this transition; (c) constructive strategies that families can employ to cope with these changes; and (d) the need to facilitate adolescent identity development by allowing them to express their own individuality in a family context that is characterized by emotional connectedness.

An ideal family-intervention model would begin with an acknowledgment that the intrapsychic destructuring that accompanies the child's transition into adolescence is associated with changes in family affect, adaptability, and patterns of communication. Many parents (and teens) fail to recognize the psychosocial importance of these normative changes; in so doing, they may fail to provide the emotional support and encouragement that adolescents need during the exploration of and commitment to various life alternatives. Intervention programs need to be implemented during late childhood and must be designed to inform parents and teens about the psychosocial implications of the changes that the family is about to experience. Such a strategy would undoubtedly alleviate some of the parental confusion that accompanies the child's growth toward young adulthood.

The most effective means of disseminating this information would be to design and integrate into the junior high or middle school curriculum (for example, through health or family life class) a series of vignettes that present descriptions of the normative changes that take place during early adolescence. More important, this work would be assigned as family "homework." Family members would have to sit down together, become familiar with the normative changes that will take place in the family in the near future (self-exploration, separation and individuation, quest for autonomy, pubertal maturation), and develop strategies about how to deal with these changes. Through the vignettes and feedback from the teacher, parents and children will be exposed to familial qualities (family affect and adaptability) that facilitate optimal identity development. Families that express qualities associated with less optimal identity development could be referred to a school-counselor-sponsored family-education workshop. This more intensive workshop would be designed to promote appropriate patterns of family affect and interaction.

Given the relatively consistent linkages between some ego-identity statuses and adolescent problem behaviors (Jones, 1992), the inclusion of such an education-based intervention in the school curriculum is justifiable. This intervention model would also facilitate parent-school partnerships. The workshop for families might require additional training for school counselors. However, the relatively recent explosion of research and theory on adolescent behavior and development has created the need for updating professional staff anyway. Regardless of the approach we adopt for facilitating adolescent identity development, the psychological health and well-being of adolescents in our complex world requires us to begin developing active intervention strategies.

References

Ackerman, N. J. (1980). The family with adolescents. In E. A. Carter & M. McGoldrick (Eds.), *The family life-cycle: A framework for family therapy* (pp. 147-173). New York: Gardner.

Adams, G. R. (1985). Family correlates of female adolescents' ego-identity development. *Journal of Adolescence, 8,* 69-82.

Adams, G. R. (1990). *Identity development.* Logan: Utah State University, Laboratory for Research on Adolescence.

Adams, G. R., & Gullotta, T. (1983). *Adolescent life experiences.* Belmont, CA: Brooks/Cole.

Adams, G. R., Gullotta, T. P., & Montemayor, R. (1992). *Advances in adolescent development: Adolescent identity formation.* New York: Russell Sage.

Adams, G. R., & Jones, R. M. (1981). Female adolescents' ego development: Age comparisons and childrearing perceptions. *Journal of Early Adolescence, 1,* 423-426.

Adams, G. R., & Jones, R. M. (1983). Female adolescents' identity development: Age comparisons and childrearing perceptions. *Developmental Psychology, 19,* 249-256.

Anderson, S. A., & Fleming, W. M. (1986). Late adolescents' identity formation: Individuation from the family of origin. *Adolescence, 21*(84), 785-796.

Archer, S. L. (1982). The lower age boundaries of identity development. *Child Development, 53,* 1551-1556.

Archer, S. L. (1989a). Adolescent identity: An appraisal of health and intervention. *Journal of Adolescence, 12,* 341-343.

Archer, S. L. (1989b). The status of identity: Reflections on the need for intervention. *Journal of Adolescence, 12,* 345-359.

Archer, S. L., & Waterman, A. S. (1983). Identity in early adolescence: A developmental perspective. *Journal of Early Adolescence, 3,* 203-214.

Bell, D. C., & Bell, L. G. (1983). Parental validation and support in the development of adolescent daughters. In H. D. Grotevant & C. R. Cooper (Eds.), *Adolescent development in the family: New directions for child development* (pp. 27-42). San Francisco: Jossey-Bass.

Berzonsky, M. D. (1988). Self-theorists, identity status, and social cognition. In D. K. Lapsley & F. C. Power (Eds.), *Self, ego and identity: Integrative approaches* (pp. 243-262). New York: Springer Verlag.

Campbell, E., Adams, G. R., & Dobson, W. R. (1984). Familial correlates of identity formation in late adolescence: A study of the predictive utility of connectedness and individuality in family relations. *Journal of Youth and Adolescence, 13,* 509-524.

Collins, W. A. (1990). Parent-child relationships in the transition to adolescence: Continuity and change in interaction, affect, and cognition. In R. Montemayor, G. R. Adams, & T. P. Gullotta (Eds.), *Advances in adolescent development: From childhood to adolescence* (pp. 85-106). Newbury Park, CA: Sage.

Cooper, C. R. (1988). Commentary: The role of conflict in adolescent-parent relationships. In M. R. Gunnar & W. A. Collins (Eds.), *Development during the transition to adolescence: The Minnesota Symposia on Child Psychology* (Vol. 21, pp. 181-188). Hillsdale, NJ: Lawrence Erlbaum.

Cooper, C. R., Grotevant, H. D., & Condon, S. L. (1983). Individuality and connectedness in the family as a context for adolescent identity formation and role-taking skill. In H. D. Grotevant & C. R. Cooper (Eds.), *Adolescent development in the family: New directions for child development* (No. 22, pp. 43-60). San Francisco: Jossey-Bass.

Dyk, P. A. H. (1990, April). *The impact of family relations on adolescent identity development.* Paper presented to biennial meetings of Society for Research on Adolescence, Atlanta, GA.

Enright, R. D., Lapsley, D. K., Drivas, A. E., & Fehr, L. A. (1980). Parental influences on the development of adolescent autonomy and identity. *Journal of Youth and Adolescence, 9,* 529-545.

Erikson, E. H. (1968). *Identity: Youth and crisis.* New York: Norton.

Feldman, S. S., & Elliott, G. R. (1990). *At the threshold: The developing adolescent.* Cambridge, MA: Harvard University Press.

Ganiere, D. M., & Enright, R. D. (1989). Exploring three approaches to identity development. *Journal of Youth and Adolescence, 18,* 283-295.

Grotevant, H. D. (1983). The contribution of the family to the facilitation of identity formation in early adolescence. *Journal of Early Adolescence, 3,* 225-237.

Grotevant, H. D., & Cooper, C. R. (1985). Patterns of interaction in family relationships and the development of identity exploration in adolescence. *Child Development, 56,* 415-428.

Grotevant, H. D., & Cooper, C. R. (1986). Individuation in family relationships: A perspective on individual differences in the development of identity and role-taking skill in adolescence. *Human Development, 29,* 82-100.

Hauser, S. T., Powers, S. I., Noam, G. G., & Jacobson, A. M. (1984). Familial contexts of adolescent ego development. *Child Development, 55,* 195-213.

Hess, R. D., & Handel, G. (1968). The family as a psychosocial organization. In G. Handel (Ed.), *The psychosocial interior of the family* (pp. 10-24). Hawthorne, NY: Aldine.

Jones, R. M. (1992). Ego identity and adolescent problem behaviors. In G. R. Adams, T. P. Gullotta, & R. Montemayor (Eds.), *Advances in adolescent development: Adolescent identity formation* (pp. 216-233). New York: Russell Sage.

LaVoie, J. C. (1976). Ego identity formation in middle adolescence. *Journal of Youth and Adolescence, 5,* 371-386.

Marcia, J. E. (1983). Some directions for the investigation of ego identity development in early adolescence. *Journal of Early Adolescence, 3,* 215-223.

Marcia, J. E. (1988). Common processes underlying ego identity, cognitive/moral development, and individuation. In D. K. Lapsley & F. C. Power (Eds.), *Self, ego, and identity: Integrative approaches* (pp. 211-225). New York: Springer Verlag.

Marcia, J. E. (1989). Identity and intervention. *Journal of Adolescence, 12,* 401-410.

McCubbin, H., & Patterson, J. (1981). Broadening the scope of family strengths: An emphasis on family coping and social support. In N. Stinnett, J. DeFrain, K. King, P. Knaub, & G. Rowe (Eds.), *Family strengths: Vol. 3. Roots of well-being* (pp. 154-172). Lincoln: University of Nebraska Press.

Olson, D.H., Russell, C. S., & Sprenkle, D. H. (1980). Circumplex model of marital and family systems II: Empirical studies and clinical intervention. In J. Vincent (Ed.), *Advances in family intervention, assessment, and theory* (pp. 129-176). Greenwich, CT: JAI.

Papini, D. R., Micka, J. C., & Barnett, J. K. (1989). Perceptions of intrapsychic and extrapsychic functioning as bases for adolescent ego identity statuses. *Journal of Adolescent Research, 4,* 460-480.

Papini, D. R., & Roggman, L. A. (1992). Adolescent perceived attachment to parents in relation to competence, depression, and anxiety: A longitudinal study. *Journal of Early Adolescence, 12,* 420-440.

Papini, D. R., Sebby, R. A., & Clark, S. M. (1989). Affective quality of family relations and adolescent identity exploration. *Adolescence, 24,* 457-466.

Robin, A. L., & Foster, S. L. (1989). *Negotiating parent-adolescent conflict: A behavioral-family systems approach.* New York: Guilford.

Sabatelli, R. M., & Mazor, A. (1985). Differentiation, individuation, and identity formation: The integration of family systems and individual developmental perspectives. *Adolescence, 20,* 619-633.

Schiedel, D. G., & Marcia, J. E. (1985). Ego identity, intimacy, sex role orientation, and gender. *Developmental Psychology, 18,* 149-160.

Steinberg, L. D. (1990). Autonomy, conflict, and harmony in the family relationship. In S. S. Feldman & G. R. Elliott (Eds.), *At the threshold: The developing adolescent* (pp. 255-276). Cambridge, MA: Harvard University Press.

Steinberg, L. D., & Silverberg, S. (1986). The vicissitudes of autonomy in early adolescence. *Child Development, 57,* 841-851.

Steirlin, H. (1981). *Separating parents and adolescents.* New York: Jason Aronson.

Stinnett, N. (1981). In search of strong families. In N. Stinnett, B. Chesser, & J. DeFrain (Eds.), *Building family strengths: Blueprints for action.* Lincoln: University of Nebraska Press.

Youniss, J. (1983). Social construction of adolescence by adolescents and parents. In H. D. Grotevant & C. R. Cooper (Eds.), *Adolescent development in the family: New directions for child development* (pp. 93-109). San Francisco: Jossey-Bass.

5

Ethnic Differences in Identity Development in the United States

MARY JANE ROTHERAM-BORUS
KAREN FRASER WYCHE

A 16-year-old tells his friend, "I need to figure out who I am." He is getting poor grades but is popular with his peers. He wears torn jeans, shirts with holes, and a leather jacket, and he listens to hard rock. He knows the steward at the carpenter's union, with whom he has discussed working on a construction project after high school graduation. He has a girlfriend who hopes to marry him someday; they have sexual intercourse about once per month. He is Catholic, and his parents are registered Republicans. Lately, however, this young man has been questioning his job plans, has been wanting to date other girls, has stopped attending church, and is fighting with his parents and friends.

This young man appears to be initiating an identity search. Research data are accumulating in support of the hypothesis that the process of identity formation for this adolescent will differ significantly depending on whether he is Chinese-, Mexican-, African-, or Irish-American. This chapter examines the role of ethnicity in shaping an adolescent's search for identity and the factors influencing the extent to which ethnicity becomes a focus of that search. Also discussed are the implications of these issues for the development of intervention programs targeting identity formation for adolescents of different ethnic backgrounds.

Ethnicity and Adolescence

The concept of ethnicity refers to the identification of an individual with a larger social group on the basis of common ancestry, race, religion, language, or national origin (Shibutani & Kwan, 1965). Ethnicity not only shapes an individual's values, attitudes, patterns of behavior, and feelings, but also influences how others respond to the individual. By puberty, one's self-concept and social persona are integrally related to one's ethnicity. During adolescence, as the primary developmental task becomes the establishment of a personal identity, ethnicity continues to play a critical role in two major ways.

First, ethnicity shapes the adolescent's exploration and commitments to occupational, religious, political, and gender roles (Erikson, 1968). The ethnically linked patterns of attitudes and behaviors acquired during childhood affect how, when, where, and in what manner the adolescent initiates the search. The adolescent's ethnicity also continues to be a central feature that determines the extent to which society facilitates or limits the adolescent's search for adult roles. Within certain ethnic groups, fundamental differences in life views even bring the value and desirability of an adolescent initiating an identity search into question. For example, the search for an individual identity may be minimized among Chinese-American adolescents, whose culture emphasizes a group orientation, which is in contrast to adolescents who emigrate from England, whose culture promotes an individual orientation. Moreover, ethnicity has different implications for the pursuit of personal identity, depending on whether the adolescent is male or female, rich or poor, or newly immigrated; this leads to differences in achievement of personal identity within ethnic groups.

Second, in considering who they are and who they want to be, adolescents also adopt a stance toward their own ethnicity and ethnic group. An adolescent's ethnicity becomes a focus of the identity search, similar to the search initiated for one's gender role, occupation, political affiliation, and religious beliefs (Phinney, 1990; Rotheram-Borus, 1989). Adolescents must recognize their feelings toward their ethnic heritage, choose the intensity of ethnic identification, and acknowledge the salience of ethnicity in structuring their lives. These are complex decisions affected by factors such as the status of the ethnic group within the broader culture, as well as each adolescent's own community. For example, it is quite different to identify oneself as a Dominican in

New York City, which has a large Dominican population, than as one living in Las Vegas, where this population is very small.

In light of these considerations, in this chapter we will (a) review the empirical evidence concerning ethnic differences in the definition and achievement of a healthy identity, (b) examine how the process of identity formation differs for males and females within various ethnic groups, (c) discuss the concept of ethnic identity, and (d) identify environmental factors that contribute to identity formation by minority adolescents. Highlighted in this discussion will be cultural norms of specific ethnic groups, emphasizing the limited applicability of existing research models of personal identity to these groups. The final portion of the chapter is devoted to discussion of the implications of these issues for designing and implementing interventions regarding the process of identity formation.

In the discussion that follows, keep in mind the relationship between socioeconomic status and ethnicity in the United States. African-Americans, Hispanic-Americans, and American Indians are over-represented in groups of lower socioeconomic and educational status and underrepresented in those of higher status; Japanese-Americans, however, do not follow this pattern. Before 1980, most research on adolescents compared minority group members from lower socioeconomic backgrounds to middle-class European-Americans and African-Americans. Therefore, in much of the early research in this area, ethnicity was not distinguished from socioeconomic status. Furthermore, the ethnic composition of the communities in which information was gathered was rarely specified. Recently, there has been the recognition that prejudicial treatment and attitudes toward African-American, Latino, or American Indian adolescents may be in response to these youths being a minority in terms of their numbers in the population; this fact, rather than simple group minority status, dramatically influences the interpretation of data concerning these adolescents.

In addition, ethnicity must be distinguished from race, which involves social and political categorizations as well as physical characteristics, such as skin color, that cannot be changed. Race is also a characteristic of an ethnic group insofar as it comes to be associated with various values, patterns of behavior, and attitudes within a given ethnic group. In the search for identity, adolescents can choose to retain or abandon race-associated aspects of their ethnicity but cannot substantially magnify or alter the permanent physical markers of their race.

The Ethnic Specificity of Healthy Identity

In his examination of variations in child-rearing practices between the Sioux and Yurok tribes, Erikson (1963) acknowledged the influence of culture in the process of searching for and establishing identity. However, Erikson went beyond stating simply that cultures differed with regard to their influence on this process; he suggested that the search for and achievement of personal identity is superior in Western civilized societies. This judgment presumably developed from his own identification with the norms of mainstream Western culture. Western culture emphasizes individuation as "healthy" over an orientation toward the group or enmeshment with the family, task accomplishment and the assertive pursuit of one's goals over passive acceptance of the natural unfolding of events, and evaluation of competence according to the current status hierarchy over evaluation independent of status (Ogbu, 1988). Although these norms of development may be usefully applied to white, European-American, middle-class males (Ogbu, 1988), these norms ignore ethnic diversity, as well as gender diversity (Cote & Levine, 1987).

Ethnic groups appear to vary along four dimensions (Rotheram-Borus, 1993; Rotheram & Phinney, 1987a): (a) the degree of orientation to a group, (b) activity versus passivity, (c) acceptance of authority, and (d) emotional expressiveness. These dimensions are relevant to the discussion of identity formation because the apparent differences among ethnic groups along these dimensions challenge the universality of Erikson's (1968) model of healthy adolescent development. For example, cultures that endorse a strong group and family orientation do not place great value on individuation, which is a cornerstone of Erikson's model (Thompson, 1990). Relative to mainstream European-Americans, Hispanic-, African-, Asian-Americans, and American Indians are all typically more oriented to a group or the family. Variations from the European-American mainstream also occur along the remaining three dimensions. Hispanic-Americans tend to be relatively less assertive in pursuing individual goals, accepting of hierarchical relationships, and emotionally expressive. African-Americans tend to be relatively active and emotionally expressive, but less accepting of hierarchical relationships than European-Americans. In addition to being extremely group-oriented, Asian-Americans are relatively emotionally restrained and accepting of hierarchical relationships, yet they tend to play an active role in shaping their own experiences. American Indian culture places value on the passive acceptance of the unfolding natural order, emotional restraint, and the honoring of hierarchical status. Thus the notion of healthy development for an American Indian youth, for example, may involve a somewhat greater emphasis on social conformity and acceptance of a tribal social role, rather than the active search for independent identity prescribed by Erikson (1968). Such normative differences among ethnic groups undoubtedly have a dramatic effect on adolescents' examination and development of personal identities.

Reconsideration and revision of the concept of healthy identity development also appears warranted regarding the extent to which ethnicity, race, and lower socioeconomic status are assumed to limit the search for and achievement of identity. Erikson assumed that the stigma associated with membership in minority ethnic, racial, or socioeconomic group would make the successful (i.e., healthy) completion of the identity search difficult. This assumption regarding the difficulty of identity achievement among minorities is partially justified. Members of the dominant social group do, in fact, typically command greater economic resources and have broader or more plentiful vocational and educational opportunities, both of which can facilitate the search for identity. Those who are not members of the dominant social group typically do not have these resources and opportunities, and this may influence choices adolescents make as they establish their personal identities. For example, young African-American males living in impoverished inner cities encounter few positive role models in their neighborhoods, with the available models of success being restricted largely to nonmainstream occupations. These youths are bombarded by information about the skyrocketing rate of unemployment within their ethnic group, the relatively large percentage of their peers who are in jail or on probation, and the high school dropout rate among their peers. To the extent that the lack of positive role models of successful employment is likely to have a dramatic influence on the vocational choices made by these youths as part of their identity search (Spencer & Markstrom-Adams, 1990), Erikson's assumption regarding difficulty in actually achieving identity owing to the complex yet restricted range of alternatives facing minority youth is warranted. However, the assumption that one ethnic group's normative resolution of the identity search can be considered more successful (i.e., healthier) than ethnic-specific alternatives remains untenable.

Actual empirical support for Erikson's lowered expectations for identity achievement among minority group members has been mixed. Membership in the dominant cultural group has been found to be associated with more successful identity achievement among youths in Canada (Marcia, 1980), New Zealand (Chapman & Nicholls, 1976), and Israel (Tzuriel & Klein, 1977), as well as within a single sample in the United States (Hauser, 1972). Contrary to what would be predicted from Erikson's model, however, Rosenthal, Moore, and Taylor (1983) found no greater identity achievement by European-Australians than by Greek- and Italian-Australians. In the United States, Rotheram-Borus (1989) found similar levels of identity achievement among European-, African-, Hispanic-, and Asian-Americans when groups were similar in socioeconomic status. Clearly, the impact of ethnicity on identity achievement is complicated by other factors such as socioeconomic status.

Erikson's model also has been criticized for conceptualizing identity development as a linear progression—for instance, from enmeshment to individuation. Cognitive styles of ethnic groups have been described as varying along a linear-cyclical dimension. European-American thought styles and developmental cycles are perceived as more linear, while those of Hispanic culture and women better described as complex spiral (Cote & Levine, 1987). Thus, for example, the identity search for girls is likely to be shaped by more diverse sources of information and life experiences with a pattern of stopping and starting sporadically over time.

Finally, feminist theorists (Cote & Levine, 1987) argue that Erikson's definition of healthy development is based on male models of traditional sex roles that appear very limited in the context of today's changing family structures and work roles, and that this to some extent reduces the possibility of women successfully achieving identity within the model. In addition, the developmental norms within a given ethnic group may differ significantly for males and females. Thus what it means to have achieved a healthy identity needs to be examined not only by ethnicity, but also by gender and socioeconomic status.

Ethnic Differences in Normative Gender Roles

Gender Role Differences Among Minority Groups

Differences in the definition of appropriate social roles for males and females among ethnic groups lead to further modifications to the concept and definition of a healthy identity, dependent on both ethnicity

and gender. Anthropologists have provided rich accounts of the quali-
tative differences between men's and women's roles in various cultures
and ethnic groups, and some evidence exists that gender and ethnicity
interactively influence personality development (Armstrong, 1984; Reid
& Comas-Diaz, 1990). It also appears that minority adolescents are
socialized into gender roles that differ from those of European-American
males and females (Armstrong, 1984), and that gender stereotyping is
less salient within some ethnic groups than within the European-American
group (Albert & Porter, 1988; Allen & Majidi-Abi, 1984). However,
little research has been done to clarify the processes underlying these
differences; most of the data examining cultural influences on gender-
role development come from clinical accounts rather than epidemiolog-
ical data (Gibbs & Huang, 1989). Because the gender roles of a youth's
ethnic group and socioeconomic status will define the context of his or
her search to a significant extent, research in this area is greatly needed
in the future.

  One example of this type of research comes from adolescents with
Chinese-American backgrounds. In a Chinese family, the eldest son is
responsible for providing emotional support to the mother and uphold-
ing the family honor; the youngest daughter is responsible for the care
of aged parents. Because the rules regarding these social roles are
explicit and detailed, eldest sons and youngest daughters who reject
their assigned roles are likely to experience culturally linked stress and
be subject to negative sanctions from parents and members of their ethnic
community. It seems reasonable to hypothesize that these individuals'
exploration of their own identities and the commitments they choose to
make during the course of establishing their ethnic identity will be
strongly influenced by these sanctions. Considering how dramatically
the definitions of these gender-specific social roles differ from the roles
mainstream European-American culture presents to the Chinese-American youth, it should come as no surprise that Chinese-Americans
occupying these two family positions have the highest rates of psychopathology relative to their siblings (Huang & Ying, 1989).

  The answer to the question of whether it appears to be healthier to
arrive at an identity consistent with the gender- and ethnic-specific
norms of one's own reference group is problematic. This is an area in
which a great deal more theoretical and empirical work remains to be
done. For example, traditional Asian women are highly deferential to
men. However, life satisfaction and self-esteem appear to be significantly higher among those Asian women who have not conformed to

these norms and who have adopted a more androgynous identity (Chow, 1987). The question remains, is this healthy identity achievement or not?

The influence of gender on shaping ethnic styles will vary based on the adolescent's level of acculturation, as well as the acculturation of his or her parents. For example, among Mexican-American families, this process is reflected in generational patterns of acculturation (Buriel, 1987). First-generation immigrants are likely to attempt assimilation into mainstream culture, adopting European-American gender roles and gender-laden values. This is a slow process, in which language often is a primary barrier. The second generation tends to continue this process, but third-generation members of immigrant families are likely to return to more traditional gender roles and customs. Because new immigrants are continually arriving, a Mexican-American adolescent initiating his or her identity search typically has role models available at every stage of acculturation. No wonder, then, that Mexican-American adolescents adopt a variety of orientations toward their ethnic identity, with no one orientation characterizing them as a group. These varying orientations affect the adolescent's identity search in significant and diverse ways. For example, recognition of such diversity recently has led researchers to challenge the concept of rigidly delineated gender roles in Mexican-American families (Ethier & Deaux, 1990; Vasquez-Nuttall, Romero-Garcia, & DeLeon, 1987). In assessing the impact of ethnicity on gender roles and the identity search, researchers clearly must specify the degree of acculturation with the family and local community.

Ethnically Linked Methods of Encouraging Self-Esteem

Self-esteem and an individual's style of processing information are factors that vary by ethnic group and also affect personal identity development (Grotevant, 1987). For example, self-esteem among minority adolescents is as high as and often higher than nonminority youths (Cross, 1987; Scheinfield, 1983). In particular, African-American urban girls consistently report higher self-esteem than their European-American female peers (Housley et al., 1987). Gilligan (Daley, 1991) has argued that African-American culture encourages emotional expressiveness among adolescent girls, helping them to maintain self-esteem in contrast to their European-American peers.

Because ethnic groups encourage self-esteem in different ways, self-esteem serves to facilitate the minority adolescent's identity search in different ways from European-American peers. For example, European-Americans endorse an "open" style of enhancing self-esteem (Grotevant, 1987). Identifying this style as optimal is ethnocentric and inconsistent with both Asian- and Hispanic-Americans cultures' emphasis on interpersonal relationships. Relationships and social rewards are more important and adolescents are encouraged to please others, a style defined as "closed" and less functional in the identity search (Grotevant, 1987). Therefore, one may hypothesize that adolescents who adopt the orientation of their culture may be less effective in pursuing their identity search by Grotevant's (1987) description. Similarly, Grotevant (1987) identified an undesirable "avoidant" decision-making style that is inconsistent with some American Indian tribes' definitions of harmony with the universe. Inaction is the desirable response for some American Indians when faced with ambiguous decisions. Therefore, when interpreting research data describing the influence of ethnicity on identity development of minority youths, awareness of differences in the ethnic norms is again critical.

The Role of Ethnic Identity in Identity Development

Typically, an individual is a member of an ethnic group at birth, and his or her ethnicity affects how others respond to him or her and dramatically shapes the acquisition of values, attitudes, and patterns of behavior from childhood through adulthood (Tajfel, 1978). However, the norms of the dominant culture also shape and influence minority youths through daily contact with that culture. For example, even in ethnically homogenous communities, all adolescents in the United States watch television and are shaped by that exposure. Therefore, minority youths must establish their stance toward their own ethnicity within the context of the dominant culture, which is an integral component of their identity development. This process results in the formation of *ethnic identity,* which is one component of personal identity and refers to one's sense of belonging to an ethnic group, as well as to the part of one's thinking, feelings, perceptions, and behavior that is due to ethnic group membership (Rotheram & Phinney, 1987a). Making a commitment to an ethnic identity is a complex process, similar to that involved in making the commitments in other areas of one's life—

vocational, religious, political, and gender-related roles—that are part of establishing one's identity (Rotheram-Borus, 1989).

Four similar models have been proposed to describe ethnic identity formation (Phinney, 1990). The framework proposed by Marcia (1980), for example, allows the description of an adolescent's ethnic identity as *diffuse, foreclosed, in moratorium,* or *achieved* (Rotheram-Borus, 1989). *Diffuse ethnic identity* refers to a lack of exploration and commitment to an ethnic role. Adolescents with diffuse ethnic identification are unlikely to see their ethnicity as a central characteristic influencing their relationships, believe prejudice to be uncommon, and not believe their lives to be substantially different from their crossethnic peers (Phinney & Tarver, 1988). *Foreclosed ethnic identity* refers to the outright adoption by an adolescent of his or her parents' values, attitudes, and behaviors. Youths who are actively exploring their identity but have not yet resolved their feelings, attitudes, and commitments to their ethnic roles are considered *in moratorium* with respect to their ethnic identity. Finally, the concept of *achieved ethnic identity* refers to the choice of an ethnic label (e.g., Hispanic, Mexican-American, Mexican, Chicana, or Latina), identification and selection of desired role models (i.e., mainstream, strongly ethnic, or bicultural), adoption of a set of attitudes toward one's own and other ethnic groups, and demonstration of patterns of behavior consistent with these choices (e.g., language usage).

The process of developing an ethnic identity is more complex for minority youths than for mainstream European-Americans. For members of the dominant cultural group, in general, the issues related to exploring and defining one's own ethnic identity appear to have little salience compared to the tremendous salience of these issues for minority youths (Phinney & Tarver, 1988). In part, this is because socializing agents for children outside the family, such as media and schools, typically present European-American models as ideal. Therefore, there is consistency between media portrayals of the ideal model and the norms, values, and behavioral routines of adolescents for European-American youths. In contrast, non-European-American youths must choose from among the norms, values, and behaviors of their own group as well as from those of the majority European-American group. Specifically, minority youths are faced with the choice of identifying themselves as (a) multiculturally synthesized (i.e., personally identified and competent to interact effectively with one or more groups), (b) multiculturally competent but oriented to the mainstream, (c) multiculturally competent but oriented to their own ethnic group, (d) strongly ethnically identified with their own ethnic group or monocultural, or (e) closely affiliated and adoptive of mainstream European-American values, attitudes, feelings, and behaviors (Ramirez, 1983).

These basic patterns of ethnic identity have received validation from a variety of sources. In an integrated school, Rotheram-Borus (1990) found 45% of the African-, Puerto Rican-, and Filipino-American students identified themselves as bicultural; one third reported that they were strongly identified with their ethnic group; and the remaining 20% to 25% identified themselves as mainstream. Predictably, white European-American students were far more likely to identify themselves as mainstream. Ogbu's (1988) rich anthropological description of roles adopted by African-American teenage boys includes roles that could be considered mainstream ("squares" and "Ivy Leaguers"), multicultural ("regulars"), and strongly ethnically identified ("gowster," "antagonist," "street men"). Sociolinguist Heller (1987) has described how children signal their choice of ethnic identity by their use of language on the playground. Children attending French schools in Canada are fluent in both French and English; however, at recess some children choose to speak only French, others use only English, and some switch their language depending on their peers' language use. Finally, minority persons who have experienced a series of stages in their own identity development have written autobiographies that provide critical insights into the psychology of identity development (Delgado, 1990; Thompson, 1990).

It also appears that consistency among various aspects of ethnic identity—attitudes, values, social expectations, and patterns of behavior—increases with age (Katz, 1976). For example, African- and Hispanic-American adolescents who are strongly identified with their ethnic group report significantly greater ethnic pride in their own groups, are separatist and hold less positive attitudes toward the mainstream, are less sensitive to differences in social expectations of crossethnic peers in everyday social encounters, demonstrate more traditional behaviors in the frequency of use of their heritage language, and report less frequent crossethnic contacts (Rotheram-Borus, 1990). These patterns associated with ethnic identification are quite different among their minority peers identifying themselves as close to mainstream European-Americans. Adolescents who are bicultural report less ethnic pride, more positive attitudes toward the mainstream, less traditional values, and more crossethnic contact than those who are strongly ethnically identified. Among younger children, inconsistent patterns are reported. Those who are strongly ethnically identified are also high on cross-ethnic contacts; there is less consistency between a child's choice of ethnic reference group, same-ethnic and cross-ethnic attitudes, and behavior.

Ethnicity may affect the personal identity and adjustment of minority youth in several ways. Stonequist (1935) assumed that every person from a minority group would experience stress when interacting with European-Americans because of the group's marginal status relative to the mainstream. This stress would be associated with feelings of insecurity, anxiety, increased emotionality, distrust, hostility, and defensiveness (see review by Rotheram & Phinney, 1987b). More recently, it has been proposed that having the flexibility of choosing their role in reference to the mainstream gives minority adolescents an advantage compared to European-American adolescents because of the availability of alternative models and definitions of success (Padilla, 1980; Ramirez & Castaneda, 1974). It is further proposed that the benefits of bicognitive flexibility, understanding various cultural norms and values, increased options, enhanced creativity, and greater adaptability may accrue with minority ethnic status (Ramirez, 1983). However, data regarding these hypotheses have been inconclusive. Johnston (1972), Kourakis (1983), and Taft (1974) found no relationship between biculturalism and adjustment. Rotheram-Borus (1990) also found no relationship between biculturalism and identity development in ideal integrated school settings. However, Wiseman (1971), Giggs (1977), and Greco, Vasta, and Smith (1977) found negative associations between biculturalism and adjustment. Such inconsistencies emphasize the importance of research regarding the contextual and environmental factors affecting identity development for minority youths.

Environmental and Family Factors Shaping Ethnic Identification

Three factors are particularly influential in shaping the identity search of the minority adolescent, particularly into ethnic identity: (a) the political and social climate experienced by the adolescent's cohort, (b) the ethnic balance and crossethnic tension in the adolescent's school and community, and (c) the ethnic identities of the adolescent's family and peers.

Social Climate

Political and social movements lead to rises and falls in ethnic pride and identification. For example, during the late 1960s and 1970s, ethnic pride was high; phrases such as "Black is beautiful" and "I am proud to be Latino" were familiar to most minority and nonminority Americans. Banks's (1976) review of data assessing self-esteem among minority youths revealed that self-esteem tended to be lower among youths raised before a period of ethnic pride and higher among successive cohorts of minority youths. Hamburg (1986) has asserted that there has been increasing acceptance of the behavioral routines of African-American culture among European-Americans, altering the social climate toward acceptance of African-American ethnic identity and easing the process of identity formation among African-American adolescents. These shifts in acceptance of ethnic diversity among the broader culture dramatically affect the adjustment of individual youths, and this acceptance varies by cohort.

School and Community Climate

Weinreich (1983) has argued that the saliency of ethnicity will increase in threatening environments and decrease in integrated, nonconflictual contexts. Consistent with this assertion, Rotheram-Borus (1993) found substantial variation in ethnic identification and the adolescent's search and commitment to a personal identity at different schools within the same community. At a successfully integrated school, some 40% of minority youths identified themselves as bicultural, and no ethnic differences were found in identity achievement or adjustment. In contrast, minority youths attending an integrated school that was not ethnically balanced and was characterized by high crossethnic tension demonstrated different identity patterns. African-American youths at this school were far more likely to be strongly identified with their own ethnic group and to have strongly negative attitudes toward European-American and Hispanic peers than were African-American youths at the well-integrated school. In addition, significant ethnic differences were found in the sample from the tense school environment in the process of identity formation, such that African-American adolescents were more likely to be diffuse or foreclosed in their identity search. These results were similar to Hauser (1972), but only at the unbalanced school. These findings emphasize the importance of creating supportive school environments in which ethnic conflict is reduced.

Ethnic Identification of Family and Peers

Minority families vary dramatically in their acceptance of their adolescent children's contact with and adoption of mainstream values and behaviors. An adolescent's identity search may threaten to under-mine the cultural traditions of the parent's culture, leading to substantial family conflict. For example, it appears that New York City mothers who immigrate from the Dominican Republic typically do not want their daughters to engage in any identity search regarding their gender role, vocation, religion, or political beliefs (Rodriguez & Zayas, 1990); conflict between these mothers and daughters thus is likely. Similar-ly, conflict can be anticipated for adolescents who take identity paths different from their peers. It is reasonable to suppose that, as youths initiate explorations of alternative life paths, the degree of support or punishment they experience within their social networks becomes a critical determinant of their perseverance in pursuing these various options and opportunities.

A study of transracial and intraracial adoption (McRoy, Zurcher, Lauderdale, & Anderson, 1982) has provided additional information regarding the significant influence of parents' ethnic identity on their child's ethnic identity formation. European-American parents who have adopted racially mixed children tend to be reluctant to socially and legally define their children as African-American; the children them-selves deemphasize the salience of their ethnic heritage. In contrast, African-American parents who have adopted biracial children tend to emphasize African-American heritage. Biracial children raised by African-American parents report greater comfort in discussing their racial iden-tity and more positive attitudes toward their racial group membership. The parents' ethnic heritage clearly shapes the adolescent's identity choices.

Substantial differences in parenting styles among ethnic groups are also likely to influence the course of an adolescent's search for personal and ethnic identity. Differences exist both within and among ethnic groups regarding the patterns of autonomy and social competence sanc-tioned by parents. For example, compared to European- and African-Amer-ican parents, Hispanic-American parents place less emphasis on individual responsibility for behavior, are more protective, foster greater dependency in their children (Escovar & Lazarus, 1982), and expect greater obedience and respect from their children (Ramos-McKay, Comas-Diaz, & Rivera, 1988). Asian-American parents are more likely to encourage obedience and conformity to their ethnic group's norms compared to European-Americans (Huang & Ying, 1989; Nagata, 1989). American Indian parents encourage their children to be independent and autonomous, but also committed to their tribe (LaFromboise & Low, 1989). African-American parents use a humanitarian but restrictive parenting style to encourage early independence, flexibility in gender roles and interpersonal competencies, and acceptance of family responsibilities (Gibbs & Huang, 1989). These ethnic variations in parenting style, as well as variations in endorsement of ethnic identification within the adolescent's family and peer group and within the larger culture, shape an adolescent's search for identity. The ethnic style necessarily emphasizes the need for the search to focus on certain issues more than others, define certain choices as better than others, and highlight areas of potential conflict depending on ethnicity.

Implications for Intervention

Altogether, the information presented here indicates that ethnic identity and gender are important dimensions of adolescents' personal identity—dimensions that must be considered in developing intervention programs to facilitate the identity search among minority youths. Interventions must be designed to develop sensitivity to ethnic differences while enhancing personal identity development (see Chapter 6).

As the review of the existing research has indicated, interventions designed to develop sensitivity to ethnic differences may have several foci. First, explicit identification of one's own cultural norms would be a useful process for both minority and nonminority youths. Second, teaching adolescents to respect ethnic diversity in identity development is important (Berry, 1993). As already discussed, ethnic groups have quite different norms and social expectations, and these normative differences can engender crossethnic conflict. For example, when African-American adolescents comfortably express angry feelings through behaviors endorsed by and accepted within their own ethnic group, their European-American peers may be extremely uncomfortable (Kochman, 1981; Schofield, 1982). European-Americans typically interpret this expressiveness as offensive and intrusive rather than as reflecting ethnically related differences. The development of sensitivity to the ethnic context of behavioral differences is an important factor in reducing crossethnic conflict—which can, in turn, influence the course of an adolescent's search for identity.

In addition to reducing cross-ethnic conflict, the recognition by adolescents of their own ethnically linked norms can increase self-understanding and encourage the exploration of options regarding ethnic and personal identity. Self-awareness can facilitate and guide occupational, political, religious, and gender-role choices. Being able to evaluate which social settings and norms are most consistent with one's upbringing can help adolescents to identify those situations and contexts that are likely to elicit the greatest sense of ease, satisfaction, and belonging. This knowledge also can help them to anticipate those settings that will present novel or challenging social routines and norms.

Finally, the goals of desegregation and reduction of cross-ethnic tension have remained unrealized in the United States, despite their articulation more than 20 years ago (Brewer & Miller, 1984). The research reviewed here suggests that these goals may be better met by attending to the interpersonal and environmental influences on the identity development of minority adolescents than by expending time, energy, and funding on political solutions (e.g., busing). Moreover, without attention to interpersonal and environmental influences, forced political solutions invite failure and may even escalate cross-ethnic tension. Thus school curricula can be outlined to enhance identity development and decrease cross-ethnic tension. Implementation of the curricula by nonprejudiced teachers who encourage positive cross-ethnic interaction is critical. The process of implementation, rather than the content of the program, will determine if a curriculum decreases prejudice.

School-Based Interventions

Effective preventive interventions for adolescents are most likely to be school-based (W. T. Grant Consortium, 1992). First, issues of ethnic identity must become integrated into the school district's curriculum guideline. In many high schools, efforts to enhance cross-ethnic understanding and increase ethnic pride typically focus on changing textbooks and expanding the range of classes available to students (e.g., offering a class in African-American history). In addition, discussion of issues of ethnic pride, the impact of discrimination and prejudice on members of both the majority and minority ethnic groups, and choice of ethnic role models can be introduced by teachers, particularly in history and literature classes. A drawback to this approach is that most teachers have not received special training regarding issues of ethnic identity. However, when there is a mandated curriculum requirement, training of teachers and the allocation of resources and time specifically to address ethnic issues become priorities.

Consideration of the process of identity formation in designing the school curriculum not only can have benefits for minority youths, but also influence attitudes of European-American youths toward their crossethnic peers. For instance, prevention programs emphasizing the role of ethnicity in the process of identity formation have the potential to effectively reverse prejudicial attitudes held by Eurocentric American students—to whom the salience of ethnicity is typically lower than it is for minority students (Rotheram-Borus, 1989). European-American students must be made more aware of why the process of ethnic identity formation is important to their minority peers and come to understand the dimensions of that process.

Training in problem solving would be a specific curriculum-based context in which identity-focused interventions could be framed to advantage. Most states (e.g., New York, New Jersey, California) have adopted curricula that include training adolescents in interpersonal problem solving and social competence in the school setting; these methods are used to address problems of substance abuse, suicide, HIV transmission and AIDS, and teenage pregnancy. It is interesting to note, however, that these prevention programs typically focus on eliminating negative or so-called problem behaviors, rather than on enhancing coping strategies and personal development. Mandating programs focused on encouraging identity processes would reverse this trend. Rather than focusing on what not to do, prevention programs would focus on the development of positive behaviors and skills to encourage a healthy identity search (see Chapter 11 in this volume). In addition, Erikson (1968) and other identity researchers (Grotevant, 1987; Marcia, 1980) have noted that the identity search is more likely to be initiated in environments that pose challenges to the adolescent. For example, asking adolescents about their career aspirations, forcing them to consider choices of colleges, stimulates an identity search. Therefore, by using identity as a focus of the problem-solving training programs already in place in many school settings, a challenge would be presented that would stimulate the identity search process.

Another way of facilitating identity-focused interventions is through multicultural education. For a school system, adopting a policy of multiculturalism results in an institutional shift from the transmission of Eurocentric American values to values of pluralism and diversity, going beyond mere identification of cultural diversity to emphasize value and respect for diversity, the importance of interpersonal relationships, and a commitment to positive change in the world (Modgil,

Verma, Mallick, & Modgil, 1986; Ramsey, 1987). This systemwide commitment to a new perspective in all phases of the educational process, not limited to curriculum guidelines, results in the exposure of youth to new ways in which to interpret and participate in social relationships (Ramsey, 1987).

Interventions Based on Role Models

Positive role models within the minority community are critical participants in any intervention program that targets identity processes among minority youths. A goal of any such intervention program should be to represent the spectrum of choices regarding an individual's ethnic identity.

Presentation of diverse role models as part of an intervention program is critical for several reasons. First, given that minority youths' exposure to alternative models is often limited (e.g., by family, by geographical location), formalized exposure to alternative models is likely to stimulate and expand their search process. For example, many American Indian youths living in New York City may have no contact with tribal members who have chosen traditional lifestyles; the youths thus perceive a limited range of potential paths regarding their ethnic identity. Second, exposure provides specific information about the benefits and costs of a given alternative, particularly about how certain benefits may be difficult to obtain. Third, the consideration of alternative paths is a central prerequisite to effective problem solving; therefore, exposure to alternative models encourages the evaluation of alternatives before a choice is made.

In the adolescent's own family and community, the degree of acculturation will differ among individuals and vary according to the environment in which the adolescent lives (e.g., in the city versus on a reservation). The extended family, in particular, plays an important role in helping the adolescent to clarify potential roles for him- or herself in the context of the larger community (La Fromboise & Low, 1989). For example, an American Indian youth familiar with tribal members who have renounced mainstream European-American culture and norms and instead identified with traditional culture and rituals also may gain an understanding of the extent to which this choice is primarily associated with benefits within the American Indian community at the cost of some rewards available from the mainstream European-American culture. However, this American Indian youth also needs exposure to tribal members who have succeeded in mainstream European-American culture to fairly compare their experience of a different distribution of costs and benefits. Finally, some American Indian adults have kept a foot in both worlds, facing complex choices resulting in new cost-benefit ratios. The American Indian adolescent can also benefit from exposure to this model for incorporating ethnicity into personal identity as he or she begins to make choices regarding his or her own life.

In summary, the challenge of forging ethnic identity will vary substantially with the adolescent's ethnic group. The norms, values, and behavioral routines of each ethnic group vary, shaping the challenge for males and females. The concept of a highly individuated identity based on exploration and commitment to roles and beliefs is European-American centered. The definition of a healthy identity and the route leading to identity formation will reflect the adolescent's ethnicity and acculturation. Interventions can be initiated to encourage the search for identity. However, these intervention programs must again be tailored to the cultural norms of the ethnic group being served.

References

Albert, A., & Porter, J. (1988). Children's gender role stereotypes: A sociological investigation of psychological models. *Sociological Forum, 3,* 184-210.

Allen, L., & Majidi-Abi, S. (1984). Black American children. In J. Gibbs & L. Huang (Eds.), *Children of color: Psychological interventions with minority youth* (pp. 148-178). San Francisco: Jossey-Bass.

Armstrong, M. J. (1984). Ethnicity and sex-role socializations. A comparative example using life history data from Hawaii. *Sex Roles, 10,* 157-181.

Banks, W. C. (1976). White preference in blacks: A paradigm in search of a phenomenon. *Psychological Bulletin, 83,* 1179-1186.

Berry, J. (1993). Identity in a pluralistic society. In M. Bernal & G. Knight (Eds.), *Formation and transmission of ethnic identity in children* (pp. 272-296). Tucson: University of Arizona Press.

Brewer, M., & Miller, N. (1984). Beyond the hypothesis: Theoretical perspectives on desegregation. In N. Miller & M. Brewer (Eds.), *Groups in contact: The psychology of desegregation* (pp. 281-300). New York: Academy Press.

Buriel, R. (1987). Ethnic labeling and identity among Mexican-Americans. In J. S. Phinney & M. J. Rotheram (Eds.), *Children's ethnic socialization: Pluralism and development* (pp. 134-153). Newbury Park, CA: Sage.

Chapman, J. W., & Nicholls, J. G. (1976). Occupational identity status, occupational preference, and field dependence in Maori and Pakeah boys. *Journal of Cross-Cultural Psychology, 7,* 61-72.

Chow, E. C. (1987). The influence of sex-role identity and occupational attainment on the psychological well-being of Asian American women. *Psychology of Women Quarterly, 11*, 69-82.

Cote, J. E., & Levine, C. (1987). A formulation of Erikson's theory of ego identity formation. *Developmental Review, 7*, 273-325.

Cross, W. (1987). A two factor theory of black identity: Implications for the study of identity development in minority children. In J. S. Phinney & M. J. Rotheram (Eds.), *Children's ethnic socialization: Pluralism and development* (pp. 117-133). Newbury Park, CA: Sage.

Daley, S. (1991, January 9). Little girls lose their self-esteem on way to adolescence, study finds. *New York Times*, p. 6.

Delgado, M. (1990). Hispanic adolescents and substance abuse: Implications for research, treatment, and prevention. In A. R. Stiffman & L. E. Davis (Eds.), *Ethnic issues in adolescent mental health* (pp. 303-323). Newbury Park, CA: Sage.

Erikson, E. (1963). *Childhood and society*. New York: Norton.

Erikson, E. (1968). *Identity: Youth and crisis*. New York: Norton.

Escovar, P. L., & Lazarus, P. (1982). Cross-cultural child rearing practices. Implications for school psychology. *School Psychology International, 3*, 143-148.

Ethier, K., & Deaux, K. (1990). Hispanics in ivy: Assessing identity and perceived threat. *Sex Roles, 22*, 427-440.

Gibbs, J. T., & Huang, L. N. (Eds.). (1989). *Children of color: Psychological interventions with minority youth*. San Francisco: Jossey-Bass.

Giggs, J. A. (1977). The mental health of immigrants in Australia. In M. Bowen (Ed.), *Australia 2000: The ethnic impact* (pp. 174-187). Armidale, New South Wales: University of New England Publishing Unit.

Greco, T., Vasta, E., & Smith, R. (1977). "I get these freaky feelings like I'm splitting into a million pieces": Cultural differences in Brisbane, Australia. *Ethnic Studies, 1*, 17-29.

Grotevant, H. (1987). Toward a process model of identity formation. *Journal of Adolescent Research, 2*, 203-222.

Hamburg, B. (1986, July 12-14). *Ethnicity and social competence*. Paper presented at W. T. Grant faculty scholars annual meeting, New York.

Hauser, S. T. (1972). Black and white identity development: Aspects and perspectives. *Journal of Youth and Adolescence, 1*, 113-130.

Heller, M. (1987). The role of language in the formation of ethnic identity. In J. S. Phinney & M. J. Rotheram (Eds.), *Children's ethnic socialization: Pluralism and development* (pp. 180-201). Newbury Park, CA: Sage.

Housley, K., Martin, S., McCoy, H., Greenhouse, P., Stiggen, F., & Choping, L. C. (1987). Self-esteem of adolescent females as related to race, economic status and area of residence. *Perceptual and Motor Skills, 64*, 559-566.

Huang, L., & Ying, Y. (1989). Chinese-American children. In J. T. Gibbs & H. N. Huang (Eds.), *Children of color: Psychological interventions with minority youth* (pp. 30-66). San Francisco: Jossey-Bass.

Johnston, R. (1972). *Future Australians: Immigrant children in Perth, Western Australia*. Canberra: Australian National University Press.

Katz, P. A. (1976). The acquisition of racial attitudes in children. In P. A. Katz (Ed.), *Towards the elimination of racism* (pp. 95-127). New York: Academic Press.

Kochman, T. (1981). *Black and white styles in conflict.* Chicago: University of Chicago Press.

Kourakis, M. (1983). *Biculturalism: The effect upon personal and social adjustment.* Unpublished master's thesis, University of Adelaide, South Australia.

La Fromboise, T. D., & Low, K. C. (1989). American-Indian children and adolescents. In J. T. Gibbs & H. N. Huang (Eds.), *Children of color: Psychological interventions with minority youth* (pp. 114-147). San Francisco, CA: Jossey-Bass.

Marcia, J. E. (1980). Identity in adolescence. In J. Adelson (Ed.), *Handbook of adolescent psychology* (pp. 159-187). New York: John Wiley.

McRoy, R. G., Zurcher, L., Lauderdale, M., & Anderson, R. (1982). Self-esteem and racial identity in transsocial and uniracial adoptees. *Social Work, 27,* 322-526.

Modgil, S., Verna, G. K., Mallick, K., & Modgil, S. (Eds.). (1986). *Multicultural education: The interminable debate.* Philadelphia: Palmer.

Nagata, D. L. (1989). Japanese American children and adolescents. In J. T. Gibbs & L. N. Huang (Eds.), *Children of color: Psychological interventions with minority youth* (pp. 67-113). San Francisco: Jossey-Bass.

Ogbu, J. L. (1988). Cultural diversity and human development. In D. Slaughter (Ed.), *Black children and poverty: A developmental perspective. New directions for child development* (pp. 11-28). San Francisco: Jossey-Bass.

Padilla, A. (Ed.). (1980). *Acculturation: Theory, models, and some new findings.* Boulder, CO: Westview.

Phinney, J. (1990). Ethnic identity in adolescents and adults: A review of the literature. *Psychological Bulletin, 108,* 499-514.

Phinney, J., & Tarver, S. (1988). Ethnic identity search and commitment in black and white eighth graders. *Journal of Early Adolescence, 8,* 265-277.

Ramirez, M. (1983). *Psychology of the Americas: Mestizo perspectives on mental health.* Elmsford, NY: Pergamon.

Ramirez, M., III, & Castaneda, A. (1974). *Cultural democracy, bicognitive development, and education.* New York: Academic Press.

Ramos-McKay, J., Comas-Diaz, L., & Rivera, L. (1988). Puerto Ricans. In L. Comas-McCay & E. Griffith (Eds.), *Clinical guidelines in cross-cultural mental health* (pp. 204-232). New York: John Wiley.

Ramsey, P. G. (1987). *Teaching and learning in a diverse world: Multicultural education for young children.* New York: Teachers College.

Reid, P. T., & Comas-Diaz, L. (1990). Gender and ethnicity: Perspectives on dual status. *Sex Roles, 22,* 397-407.

Rodriguez, O., & Zayas, L. (1990). Hispanic adolescents and antisocial behavior: Sociocultural factors and treatment implications. In A. Stiffman & L. Davis (Eds.), *Ethnic issues in adolescent mental health* (pp. 147-174). Newbury Park, CA: Sage.

Rosenthal, D. A., Moore, S. M., & Taylor, M. J. (1983). Ethnicity and adjustment: A study of the self-image of Anglo-, Greek-, and Italian-Australian adolescents. *Journal of Youth and Adolescence, 12,* 117-135.

Rotheram, M. J., & Phinney, J. (1987a). Introduction: Definitions and perspectives in the study of children's ethnic socialization. In J. S. Phinney & M. J. Rotheram (Eds.), *Children's ethnic socialization: Pluralism and development* (pp. 10-31). Newbury Park, CA: Sage.

Rotheram, M. J., & Phinney, J. S. (1987b). Ethnic behavior problems as an aspect of identity. In J. S. Phinney & M. J. Rotheram (Eds.), *Children's ethnic socialization: Pluralism and development* (pp. 201-219). Newbury Park, CA: Sage.

Rotheram-Borus, M. (1989). Ethnic differences in adolescents' identity status and associated behavior problems. *Journal of Adolescence, 12,* 361-374.

Rotheram-Borus, M. (1990). Adolescents' reference group choices, self-esteem, and adjustment. *Journal of Personality and Social Psychology, 59,* 1075-1081.

Rotheram-Borus, M. (1993). Biculturalism among adolescents. In M. Bernal & G. Knight (Eds.), *Formation and transmission of ethnic identity in children* (pp. 81-104). Tucson: University of Arizona Press.

Scheinfield, D. K. (1983). Family relationships and school achievement among boys of lower income urban Black families. *American Journal of Orthopsychiatry, 153,* 127-143.

Schofield, J. W. (1982). *Black and white in school: Trust, tension or tolerance?* New York: Praeger.

Shibutani, T., & Kwan, K. (1965). *Ethnic stratification.* New York: Macmillan.

Spencer, M. B., & Markstrom-Adams, C. (1990). Identity processes among racial and ethnic minority children in America. *Child Development, 61,* 290-310.

Stonequist, E. V. (1935). The problem of a marginal man. *American Journal of Sociology, 41,* 1-12.

Taft, R. (1974). Ethnically marginal youth and culture conflict: A problem in cross-cultural sciences. In J. L. M. Dawson & W. J. Lonner (Eds.), *Readings in cross-cultural psychology* (pp. 57-68). Hong Kong: Hong Kong University Press.

Tajfel, H. (1978). *Differentiation between social groups: Studies in the social psychology of intergroup relations.* New York: Academic Press.

Thompson, C. L. (1990). In the pursuit of affirmation: The antisocial inner-city adolescent. In A. Stiffman & L. Davis (Eds.), *Ethnic issues in adolescent mental health* (pp. 131-146). Newbury Park, CA: Sage.

Tzuriel, D., & Klein, M. M. (1977). Ego identity: Effects of ethnocentrism, ethnic identification, and cognitive complexity in Israeli, Oriental, and Western ethnic groups. *Psychological Reports, 40,* 1099-1110.

Vasquez-Nuttall, E., Romero-Garcia, I., & DeLeon, B. (1987). Sex roles and perspectives of femininity and masculinity of Hispanic Americans. *Psychology of Women Quarterly, 11,* 409-425.

Weinreich, P. (1983). Emerging from threatened identities. In G. Breakwell (Ed.), *Threatened identities.* New York: John Wiley.

Weissberg, R. P. (1990). Support for school-based social competence. *American Psychologist, 45,* 986-988.

Wiseman, R. (1971). Integration and attainment of immigrant secondary school students in Adelaide. *Australian Journal of Education, 15,* 253-268.

W. T. Grant Consortium (1992). Drug and alcohol prevention curricula. In J. D. Hawkins, R. F. Catalano, Jr., & Associates (Eds.), *Communities that care.* San Francisco: Jossey-Bass.

6

A Model for Identity Intervention
With Minority Adolescents

CAROL MARKSTROM-ADAMS
MARGARET BEALE SPENCER

The establishment of an identity is a major developmental task for adolescents. The adolescent years are typically filled with the trying on of a variety of roles and lifestyles in an effort to determine the best fit. Erikson (1959) has described the maturation process as a series of conflicts that must be resolved if healthy identity development is to occur. This search, which is common to every adolescent, is particularly complex when the adolescent in question happens to be a member of a minority group—that is, the individual's social unit is physically or culturally identifiable (e.g., American Indians and African-Americans).

Minority adolescents have much in common with all adolescents; for example, they share the same biological imperatives and similar cognitive acquisitions, which include a frequently uncomfortable growing awareness of the social pressures around them. They share the same social needs for fidelity, intimacy, and a sense of a trustworthy world. Commonalities diminish, however, when social context is taken into account. Minority youths find themselves in a social context that, because of their minority status, often does not value and support them. Thus the healthy need to feel competent and the healthy developing cognitive awareness of these youths lead them to turn off the environment in which they find themselves.

The adolescent search for identity includes a particular self-consciousness and aching desire to fit in. This desire to belong, a typical need for all adolescents, may be made extremely complex by obvious differences in skin color and speech patterns and by unchallenged stereotypes (for example, the assumed frightening quality associated with African-American males). Further, the growing—in fact, unavoidable—cognitive skills of adolescents make them sensitive to subtle expectations and biases. For example, in a nonminority setting, young African-American and Hispanic males who had been greeted warmly by majority group members when they were young children may discover that majority group adults appear guarded and distrustful of them as teenagers.

For minority group adolescents, the question "Who am I?" expands to "What does my minority-group membership *mean*?" A belief in a shared origin, common beliefs and values, and a shared sense of survival or a "common cause" are extremely powerful in uniting humans into self-defining in-groups (DeVos, 1982). The importance of the issue of group membership in identity formation cannot be overstated. The results have implications for the rest of the life course: Adolescents who conclude that they are failures (and that their group is not as good as the majority) may fulfill their own prophecies. On the other hand, those who demonstrate a cultural identity that is accepting of their own group appear more stress-resistant and have higher achievement outcomes (Spencer, 1983, 1988).

To design interventions that are relevant to minority youth, it is essential to look at their development *as adolescents* by considering their needs as manifestations of the needs that are shared cross-culturally by their peers. It is equally important to look at general development in terms of these adolescents' specific cultural contexts—both the traditions within their group and the stresses that arise from living in the larger dominant culture (see Chapter 5 for discussion of these topics). It is this interaction between a developmental framework and specific cultural understanding that informs the intervention model described in this chapter.

The identity intervention model that we propose is grounded in the crucial role played by perspective taking in adolescent development. Perspective taking—variously described as social cognition, role taking, person perceptivity, and decentration—is the process by which individuals develop the ability to see the world imaginatively from the perspective of someone other than themselves. This process enhances social interaction and minimizes egocentrism, thereby making available occasions for exploration in identity formation. Social perspective-taking training specifically creates situations in which youths engage in comparison of the self with members of other groups in terms of both similarities and differences.

Davis and Stiffman (1990) assert that minority adolescents are likely to experience difficulties in identity formation. Indeed, a variety of factors affect minority adolescents' opportunities for perspective taking and exploration, which are two critical components of identity formation. For example, many minority adolescents face hostile environments that present obstacles to the successful accomplishment of developmental tasks (Gustavsson & Balgopal, 1990). The more pressing factors highlighted in this chapter are poverty, threats posed by inner-city living, inequities in schooling, limited employment and apprenticeship opportunities, pressures to assimilate, and immigration-related issues. In the subsequent section of this chapter we will examine the effects of these issues on various ethnic minority groups. We will then describe three models that are useful for understanding minority identity formation. The models will then be explored in relation to a specific identity intervention strategy for minority adolescents.

Factors Limiting Opportunities in Perspective Taking and Exploration

Poverty, Inner-City Living, Inequities in Schooling, and Limited Employment and Apprenticeship Opportunities

Two-fifths of minority youths in the United States have the double disadvantage of minority status and poverty (Hamilton, 1990). For example, Hamilton (1990) states that 750,000 African-Americans and 375,000 Hispanics between ages 16 and 19 are disconnected because of poverty, discrimination, or alienation. These circumstances place poor and minority youths at severe disadvantage in their attempts to resist self-destructive behaviors such as teen pregnancy, delinquency, and drug abuse.

Poverty, in conjunction with crowded and stressful conditions of inner-city living,[1] offers special challenges to adolescents who face the task of identity establishment. Certain Hispanic groups (e.g., Puerto Ricans) and African-Americans are especially at risk for living in deteriorating central-city neighborhoods that are accompanied by a myriad of problems (e.g., substandard housing with poor sanitation, depressed local economies, and inadequate access to quality health and mental health facilities (Gibbs, 1989; Inclan & Herron, 1989; Rodriguez & Zayas, 1990). An adolescent whose first priority is survival has diminished energy to direct to identity exploration and perspective-taking tasks.

Inequities in schooling and employment opportunities likewise take a toll on the development of minority adolescents. U.S. schools are thought to be champions of democracy and achievement for all students. In reality, they do little to reduce race, class, and gender inequities (Hamilton, 1990). In addition to educational constraints, a growing awareness of a "job ceiling" is a further limitation: Minority youths have difficulty envisioning work opportunities that are beyond the level of their adult role models. In particular, there appears to be a lack of intermediate role models in the work force for many minority youths (Hamilton, 1990). Further, lack of apprenticeship opportunities makes it difficult for many youths to envision work opportunities beyond the level of their immediate role models. Thus, perspective taking in respect to potential future occupational roles is diminished.

The hostile environments constituted by poverty, hazardous living conditions, and inequities in schooling and apprenticeship opportunities present obstacles to the successful accomplishment of developmental tasks (Gustavsson & Balgopal, 1990). Further, the naturally developing cognitive processes of minority youths in combination with hostile environments create a potential interaction. For example, discriminatory practices limit opportunities for *productive* perspective-taking experiences; nonetheless, adolescents' meaning-making processes continue to develop. It is precisely those *normal, developmentally appropriate* processes that make youths painfully aware of the discrepancies in opportunity that the environment holds for them. Thus their own normal and healthy development puts them further at risk as their correspondingly normal and healthy impulse to shield themselves from hostility and devaluation leads them to increasingly tune out the larger society to secure self-perceptions as persons of value.

Assimilation

Assimilation processes become most salient during the teen years as functions of normal developmental tasks and identity-formation process. The cultural assimilation process includes the incorporation of the cultural patterns of the majority, dominant, or core group in a society by a minority, subordinate, or peripheral group. This incorporation may include language, religious beliefs and observances, dress and food preferences, choice of first names for children and modification of surnames, entertainment patterns, and informal cliques.

The time of the strongest pull toward assimilation confronts minority adolescents at a time in the life span when they are engaged in search processes and have strong needs to fit in. The risk is that these youths may opt to disengage from their ethnic or racial groups to attempt assimilation with mainstream culture. The intervention model proposed in this chapter seeks to support minority individuals in their ethnic or racial affiliations while encouraging them to understand the perceptions of other groups in society.

Immigrants

The sense of belonging is a significant issue for "newcomers" (who quickly become "outsiders"). Isaacs (1976) suggests that "uncertainty of belongingness" challenges self-esteem and personhood "in dealing with members of other groups be they more powerful or less" (Arredondo, 1984, p. 984). For immigrants, moving from a position of majority status to minority or outsider status undermines ego functioning as illustrated in the following quotation: "It's like being born again. You have to find out who you are while getting messages from two sides, saying this is how you were raised, and this is how you should be" (Arredondo, 1984, p. 984).

The multiple dilemma for immigrants is consistent with other minority youths. As indicated by Gay (1978), they are caught in the transition from childhood to adolescence that is common to all humans, and they are in the process of becoming adults in the context of particular ethnic-group membership. Part of the adolescent crisis requires that youths make conscious commitments to their ethnicity by conforming to ethnic-group norms and expectations while simultaneously becoming active, productive members of the common culture and adhering to rules and regulations (Gay, 1978). These processes are confounded for immigrant adolescents because it is difficult to decide when and how to differentiate behaviors and values (e.g., style shifting). The difficulty is also confounded by the fact that the support that their families may need from the larger society is often circumvented by the importance of "face" and privacy for some cultural groups. It is to this kind of complexity that successful intervention must be addressed.

Summary

In the first portion of this chapter we have attempted to highlight issues that are pertinent to identity formation for minority youths. It is imperative that inequities be addressed for minority adolescents to fully experience natural occurrences of perspective taking and exploration in relation to identity issues. Until this occurs, however, identity interventions may be necessary for some minority youths to furnish them with perspective taking and exploration opportunities. In the second half of this chapter we present a conceptualization of a model for identity intervention as it applies to identity issues of minority youths. Before that, however, we present three models of identity development that are pertinent to identity intervention.

Three Models of Identity Formation

Three general theoretical frameworks of identity development have particular applicability to minorities. A psychosocial foundation of identity development based on the works of Erik Erikson (1968) and James Marcia (1966) is one such theoretical base. The second framework is found in the work of Atkinson, Morten, and Sue's (1983) minority identity development model. The third is a phenomenological variant of ecological systems theory (Spencer, in press). We will discuss the characteristics of each of these theoretical frameworks as well as a proposed synthesis of the frameworks.

Eriksonian Conceptions of Identity

Erik Erikson's (1968) psychosocial stage theory is particularly conducive to an understanding of identity formation and identity intervention with minority cultures. Erikson has written of identity as entailing a culmination of experiences from the individual's developmental history and the history of the individual's society (e.g., the histories of African-Americans and various American Indian tribes). Thus identity is a process that occurs in the core of the individual and in the core of his or her communal culture; the process actually establishes "the identity of these two identities" (Erikson, 1968, p. 22). From Erikson's discussions, it is evident that identity is conceived as an intertwining of individual, societal, cultural, and historical experiences.

James Marcia (1966) has been credited with operationalizing Erikson's notions of identity into four identity statuses that develop around the interaction between *crisis*—that is, "the adolescent's period of engagement in choosing among meaningful alternatives"—and *commitment*—or "the degree of personal investment the individual exhibits" (p. 551). Based on adolescents' exploration of and commitment to identities, they may hold statuses of achievement, moratorium, foreclosure, or diffusion (definitions of these statuses are found elsewhere in this volume).

Minority Identity Development Model

The second theoretical framework of identity is specific to minority individuals. Recognizing the works of Cross (1971) and Jackson (1975) on African-American identity development, Atkinson et al. (1983) developed a five-stage minority identity development (MID) model that allows generalization between minority groups. At each stage of identity development, a minority individual displays four sets of attitudes: (a) those directed toward the self, (b) those directed toward others of the same minority group, (c) those directed toward others of different minority groups, and (d) those directed toward the dominant group.[2] (See Table 6.1.)

Stage 1 is called the *conformity stage* and is characterized by disdain for one's own group and other minority groups, as well as a clear preference toward and valuing of the dominant group. At Stage 2, or the *dissonance stage*, previously held notions are called into question. The individual feels dissonance and experiences conflict in relation to attitudes held toward one's own group, other minority groups, and the dominant group. Stage 3, *resistance and immersion,* is characterized by appreciating attitudes toward the self and the individual's own group. The values of the dominant culture are rejected, and ambivalence is felt toward members of other minority groups. At Stage 4, the *introspection stage,* the individual feels discomfort about previous depreciating attitudes held toward the dominant group and becomes concerned with ethnocentrism held toward other minority groups. At Stage 5, *synergetic articulation and awareness,* the individual continues to hold high regard for the self and his or her group *and* appreciates other minority groups and is open to the positive elements displayed by the majority group.

Table 6.1 Summary of Minority Identity Development Model

Stages of Minority Development Model	Attitude Toward Self	Attitude Toward Others of Same Minority	Attitude Toward Others of Different Minority	Attitude Toward Dominant Group
Stage 1: Conformity	Self-depreciating	Group-depreciating	Discriminatory	Group-appreciating
Stage 2: Dissonance	Conflict between self-depreciating and appreciating	Conflict between group-depreciating and group-appreciating	Conflict between dominant held views of minority hierarchy and feelings of shared experience	Conflict between group-appreciating and group-depreciating
Stage 3: Resistance and Immersion	Self-appreciating	Group-appreciating	Conflict between feelings of empathy for other minority experiences and culturocentrism	Group-depreciating
Stage 4: Introspection	Concern with basis of self-appreciation	Concern with nature of unequivocal appreciation	Concern with ethnocentric basis for judging others	Concern with the basis of group depreciation
Stage 5: Synergetic Articulation and Awareness	Self-appreciating	Group-appreciating	Group-appreciating	Selective appreciation

SOURCE: From David R. Atkinson, George Morten, and Derald Wing Sue, *Counseling American Minorities: A Cross-Cultural Perspective*, 4th edition. Copyright © 1993 Wm. C. Brown Communications, Inc., Dubuque, Iowa. All Rights Reserved. Reprinted by permission.

Phenomenological Variant of Ecological Systems Theory

Like the Eriksonian and MID models, the Spencer model (in press) emphasizes the meaning-making experiences of developing youth. In keeping with Bronfenbrenner's (1979) ecological systems theory, this model places those meaning-making processes in a larger ecological context. The five stages of the model are pictured in Figure 6.1.

Unlike much research that portrays a simple and direct relationship between given attributes (such as race and gender) and life-stage outcomes, each step in this model takes into account minority youths' active meaning-making processes: (a) self-appraisal processes with respect to stereotypes and biases (Step 1), (b) perceptions of environmental stress (Step 2), (c) strategic use of coping methods (Step 3), (d) creative development of emergent identities (Step 4), and (e) self-appraisal processes with regard to life-stage outcomes (from Step 5 back to Step 1). It is this active engagement in meaning making on the part of the individual that is central to the intervention model that we are proposing.

Parallels Between the Models

Atkinson et al.'s (1983) MID model and Marcia's (1966) identity-status model have several features in common. Both recognize that a degree of exploration and a consideration of alternatives must occur to achieve the highest level of identity development. Phinney's (1989, 1990) articulation of correspondences between these two models and additional parallels are shown in Table 6.2.

There appears to be no counterpart of the identity status of diffusion in the MID model, as pointed out by Phinney (1989). Such an omission does not mean that this state does not exist in matters of ethnic identity. Diffusion would be characterized by a lack of commitment to any form of identity, whether it be an identity based in one's minority group or in the dominant group. Such a condition is incompatible with Stages 1, 3, and 5 of the MID model, all of which are characterized by some form of commitment. Further, the minority individual in diffusion is not engaged in ethnic-identity conflict or search. Thus the individual could not be characterized as being in Stages 2 or 4 of the MID model, two stages characterized by identity conflicts. It is therefore logical to assert that an ethnically diffused individual is not classified according to the MID stages.

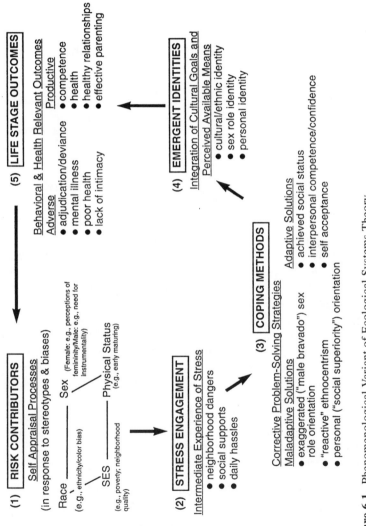

Figure 6.1. Phenomenological Variant of Ecological Systems Theory

Table 6.2 Correspondence Between Marcia's Identity Statuses and Minority Identity Development (MID) Stages

Identity Status	MID Stages	Parallels Between Models
Diffusion	No corresponding stage	
Foreclosure	Stage 1: Conformity Stage 3: Resistance and Immersion	Clear preference for own group Other options in identity not considered Perceptions of others not considered
Moratorium	Stage 2: Dissonance Stage 4: Introspection	Exploration occurs Logic of earlier fore- closed commitments questioned
Achievement	Stage 5: Synergetic Articulation and Awareness	Mature commitments Appreciation of one's own and other groups

Conceptions of the developing identity, represented in both the identity status and the MID models, is incorporated in Stage 4 (emergent identities) of the Spencer model, which places identity processes in the larger context of risk contributors, stress engagement, coping methods, and life-stage outcomes. The model traces the theme of youths' meaning-making processes throughout the five components.

The three models of identity formation are useful for conceptualizing various complexities associated with minority identity development. In the following discussion, a proposed model of identity intervention is articulated and discussed vis-à-vis the models of identity development among minorities.

Identity Intervention Based in Perspective-Taking Training

Enright and Deist (1979) state that two precursors or preconditions critical to identity formation that arise from engagement in social perspective taking are (a) an understanding of what one has in common with others and (b) how the self is unique or different from others. Comparisons of similarities and differences between the self and others is at the core of social perspective-taking training. Some evidence for linkages between social perspective taking and identity formation have been shown in experimental studies (Enright, Ganiere, Buss, Lapsley, & Olson, 1983; Enright, Olson, Ganiere, Lapsley, & Buss, 1984; Markstrom-Adams, Ascione, Bragger, & Adams, 1993). Although the specific needs of minority individuals were not targeted in any of these studies, the mechanisms of change that underlie the interventions may be applicable to minority-intervention programs.

Enright et al.'s (1983, 1984) intervention program is based on Selman's (1980) social perspective-taking levels. Markstrom-Adams et al. (1993) replicated and extended Enright's social perspective-taking training and developed a form of individuation perspective-taking training. The findings of Markstrom-Adams et al. (1993) were mixed, but Enright et al. (1983, 1984) reported more promising results. Perspective-taking training has shown promise in other studies through contributing to higher levels of moral reasoning (Walker, 1980), enhancing interpersonal problem solving (Marsh, Serafica, & Barenboim, 1980), and diminishing delinquent behavior (Chandler, 1973).

Theoretically, perspective-taking skills have been argued to make significant contributions to the diminishment of adolescent egocentrism (Looft, 1971, 1972). As an indirect link between identity and perspective taking, Adams, Abraham, and Markstrom (1987) reported that more mature identity statuses were related to lower levels of self-consciousness and self-focusing behaviors. The converse was found for less mature identity statuses.

We can summarize from this discussion that conceptual and empirical evidence supports a relation between perspective taking and identity and between egocentrism and identity. Further, evidence provided by Markstrom and Mullis (1986) suggests that at least one minority group (American Indians) may be at greater risk for adolescent egocentrism because of the emergence of heightened self-consciousness in minority social contexts. If minority individuals are at greater risk for heightened self-consciousness (or adolescent egocentrism), a further hindrance to identity formation is posed. Thus we propose that an intervention embedded in perspective taking and exploration skills would enhance identity development and diminish adolescent egocentrism.

Identity Intervention With Minority Adolescents

Using perspective taking as a basis, there are additional features to consider in the conceptualization of an identity intervention strategy specifically designed for minority adolescents. It is useful to consider perspective-taking skills as a component of Stage 3 (coping methods) in the Spencer model (see Figure 6.1). Perspective-taking skills are regarded as one component (among many others) that contribute to identity formation. It also is important to consider what forms of Stage 4 (emergent identities, which include Marcia's identity statuses and the stages of the MID model; see Figure 6.1) are best suited for intervention. It also is necessary to consider how ethnic issues might be conceptualized in respect to the domains of identity. A discussion on the structure of an identity intervention model for minority adolescents also follows.

Implication of the Models for Intervention

Individuals holding an achieved identity status or exhibiting synergetic articulation and awareness in the MID model do not need intervention. But what about those individuals in the other identity statuses (i.e., diffusion, foreclosure, and moratorium) and in the other four stages of the MID model (i.e., conformity, dissonance, resistance and immersion, and introspection)?

As noted, there are many features in common between foreclosure and the MID stages of conformity and resistance and immersion. As Atkinson et al. (1983) note, however, clients who are in conformity or resistance and immersion are unlikely to seek intervention or treatment in relation to their cultural identity. Such individuals are characterized by an absence of crisis and conflict and may not be highly motivated to change. Further, there are ethical issues to consider in attempting to force crises for individuals if they feel they are not in need of such treatment, are satisfied with their ethnic identity, or are not in conflict with themselves or others in their immediate environment.

Thus identity intervention might be more potent and appropriate for individuals who are in identity statuses of diffusion and moratorium and in stages of dissonance and introspection in the MID model. Indeed, Atkinson et al. (1983) note that clients in dissonance or introspection are more likely to seek counseling and to be less resistant in intervention. Such individuals, while engaged in exploration and conflict, may benefit from intervention designed to provide structure and organization to their cognitions concerning ethnic identity. Diffused minority adolescents, while not specifically requesting intervention, may come to the attention of professionals because of behavioral problems. Interventions in identity may then be used as a therapeutic tool in working with these adolescents.

Domains of Identity

Every culture must deal with issues related to defining both interpersonal and ideological roles and commitments. In perspective-taking training conducted among minority groups, ethnicity might best be addressed as embedded in the domains of identity (e.g., occupation, politics, sex roles, etc.). Ethnic identity also is conceptualized as a distinct domain of identity, and has been suggested by Phinney, Lochner, and Murphy (1990) to be a critical component of the young person's self-concept as well as having important implications for adjustment. Thus perspective-taking interventions should take into account the specific content that is reflected in varying domains of identity, including ethnic identity.

Structure of Identity Intervention

Earlier in this chapter, several factors were identified that confront many minority adolescents and may inhibit naturally occurring perspective-taking and exploration opportunities. These factors might be addressed in an identity intervention strategy that is organized around the four attitudes of Atkinson et al.'s (1983) MID model. The attitudes provide a structure around which perspective-taking training for minority individuals can occur; that is, attitudes toward the self, toward others of the same minority group, toward others of different minority groups, and toward the dominant group might be explored in relation to the domains of identity. Each domain of identity that is targeted in training is scrutinized according to the four attitudes. The use of perspective-taking and exploration skills is encouraged in this process.

First, in exploring attitudes toward the self, the focus is on understanding feelings of ethnic self-esteem and self-acceptance as well as other aspects of ethnic self-perception. Such attitudes are particularly important given the rejecting messages that some minorities receive through experiences of prejudice and discrimination. Although many minority adolescents do not internalize such negative valuing of their groups, it is important to counteract potential adverse effects.

Second, in targeting attitudes toward others of the same minority group, issues of group pride and feelings of group affiliation and belongingness are addressed. Diversity in views among members of one's group is also explored. This stage in the process is applicable to minority adolescents' exposure to the range of identity outcomes available to them. For example, in considering occupational identity outcomes, minority adolescents might be exposed to adult role models from their group who are engaged in a variety of career options. Given the reality of the "job ceiling" effect, minority adolescents can discover that there are opportunities available beyond those that are readily apparent. Likewise, various educational opportunities also can be explored with minority adolescents.

Third, in exploring attitudes toward members of other minority groups, individuals are encouraged in perspective taking in their experiences. Familiarizing themselves with the values, beliefs, and cultural practices of other groups is important, just as is understanding the effects of prejudice and discrimination on other groups. Exploring the similarities and differences in experiences between other minority group members and the individual's own group should be encouraged. To illustrate this attitude, it would be useful for minority adolescents to examine how other minority groups have been affected by prejudice and discrimination. It also would be useful to heighten awareness of various other minority groups' experiences with poverty, living in the inner city, constraints in respect to education and employment, and pressures to assimilate.

Fourth, in exploring attitudes toward members of the dominant group, the individual is again encouraged in perspective taking on the values, beliefs, and cultural practices of the dominant group. Identifying useful or helpful features of the dominant group is encouraged. Again, exploring the similarities and differences between one's own minority group and the dominant group is promoted.

Additional Considerations

Those who conduct perspective-taking training among minorities should be members of the same minority group as the participants. Adults who are solidly established in their own identities can serve as role models for the youths they are helping. In ethnically diverse communities, identity intervention training could be enhanced by organizing ethnically heterogeneous groups of adolescent participants. Again, the ethnicity of adult leaders should reflect that of the participants.

Although the proposed identity intervention model has been discussed in a general sense, it is critical to design the intervention according to the needs of the target minority group. For example, many minority groups, including Mexican-Americans and American Indians, do not value the individualistic and competitive nature of the broader society. Instead, communal values and extended kinship networks are extremely important to Mexican-Americans, even for families three or more generations removed from Mexico (Ramirez, 1989). Both the Hispanic value of *personalism* or "goodness" and the quality of personal relationships are considered more important than the exhibition of abilities. Thus identity interventions that are counter to the enhancement of kin relations, affiliation, and cooperation will lack effectiveness (Ramirez, 1989). Similarly, given the interdependence that has characterized Asian culture more generally, interventions must focus on the family as a whole and deal sensitively with the tendency of Asian-Americans to prefer handling family matters inside the family (Huang & Ying, 1989).

For immigrant groups, a central concern must be cultural-socialization practices and cognitive interventions that focus on the discontinuity between previous socialization and cultural values and attitudes on the one hand, and current dominant cultural values on the other. Identity interventions for these groups must be sensitive to the transition in which these adolescent find themselves. Youths must be assisted in finding ways to maintain their culture of origin while learning the necessary skills for functioning in American society.

It is important not to overlook the sources of natural perspective-taking opportunities that are found in school and the workplace. However, changes are required to reverse the effects of discrimination that have constrained perspective-taking opportunities for minority youths in these contexts. Although school alone cannot reverse the effects of discrimination, some things can be done to enhance the learning experience of minorities. For example, Hamilton (1990) suggests that discrimination is perpetuated by grouping students according to abilities because such determinations are often made on the basis of race and social class. It would be advantageous if schools' curriculums were sensitized to the needs of the cultural milieus of their students' families and communities. Compensation should be given to those who have been victims of inequality. Recognition and utilization of the talents of all students is needed. In ethnically diverse schools, both minority and majority students could acquire greater respect for the cultural tradition of other groups. Such efforts would ultimately maximize the learning experience for minority adolescents and provide them with social and cognitive perspective-taking experiences that are enhancing to identity formation.

Given that conventional schooling does not offer the needed support for minority youth, Hamilton (1990) suggests that carefully planned apprenticeship programs can enhance both educational and future employment opportunities for minority youth. These opportunities can augment opportunities for perspective-taking opportunities that lead to identity resolution. Such intervention entails a systemic intervention aimed at reducing discrimination in the workplace, particularly discrimination directed at adolescents.

Conclusions and Summary

Three frameworks for understanding the complexities of minority identity formation were featured in this chapter. These frameworks were used as a basis in proposing a model of identity intervention. Given that experimental investigations have been conducted using perspective-taking training to enhance identity interventions, it is timely to extend this line of research to ethnic and racial minorities. In this chapter we have proposed a minority identity intervention model based on perspective-taking skills and exploration. We have suggested that naturally occurring perspective taking and exploration experiences are constrained for some minorities because of poverty, living in the inner city, inequities in education, limited opportunities for employment and apprenticeships, pressures to assimilate, and immigration-related concerns. Thus identity intervention should redress some of these limitations. Interventions that do not deal with these cultural issues from the point of view of the particular culture involved can actually serve as barriers to mental health. Thus effective interventions have the dual task of addressing adolescent needs that generally cross ethnic and racial lines (e.g., need for fidelity, apprenticeship opportunities, and a sense of belonging) and needs particular to minority culture. Careful research and inclusion of family and community participants are essential ingredients for successful identity outcomes.

Notes

1. In many American cities, the youth population is mostly minority (Davis & Stiffman, 1990).
2. Although the term *stage* is used in the MID model, it does not necessarily imply that stages are sequential and invariant or that an individual must progress through the stages as given or that regression cannot occur.

References

Adams, G. R., Abraham, K. G., & Markstrom, C. A. (1987). The relationship between identity development, self-focusing during middle and late adolescence. *Developmental Psychology, 23*, 292-297.

Arredondo, P. M. (1984). Identity themes for immigrant young adults. *Adolescence, 19*, 977-993.

Atkinson, D. R., Morten, G., & Sue, D. W. (1983). *Counseling American minorities* (2nd ed.). Dubuque, IA: William C. Brown.

Bronfenbrenner, U. (1979). *The ecology of human development: Experiments by nature and design.* Cambridge, MA: Harvard University Press.

Chandler, M. J. (1973). Egocentrism and antisocial behavior: The assessment and training of social perspective-taking skills. *Developmental Psychology, 9*, 326-332.

Cross, W. E. (1971). The Negro-to-Black conversion experience. *Black World, 20*, 13-27.

Davis, L. E., & Stiffman, A. R. (1990). Introduction. In A. R. Stiffman & L. E. Davis (Eds.), *Ethnic issues in adolescent mental health* (pp. 13-18). Newbury Park, CA: Sage.

DeVos, G. (1982). Ethnic pluralism: Conflict and accommodation. In G. DeVos & L. Romanucci-Ross (Eds.), *Ethnic identity: Cultural continuities and change* (pp. 5-41). Palo Alto, CA: Manfield.

Enright, R. D., & Deist, S. H. (1979). Social perspective-taking as a component of identity formation. *Adolescence, 14*, 517-522.

Enright, R. D., Ganiere, D. M., Buss, R. R., Lapsley, D. K., & Olson, L. M. (1983). Promoting identity development in adolescents. *Journal of Early Adolescence, 3*, 247-255.

Enright, R. D., Olson, L. M., Ganiere, D., Lapsley, D. K., & Buss, R. R. (1984). A clinical model for enhancing adolescent ego identity. *Journal of Adolescence, 7*, 119-130.

Erikson, E. H. (1959). Identity and the life cycle. *Psychological Issues,* Issue 1, Monograph 1.

Erikson, E. H. (1968). *Identity: Youth and crisis.* New York: Norton.

Gay, G. (1978). Ethnic identity in early adolescence: Some implications for instructional reform. *Educational Leadership, 35*, 649-655.

Gibbs, J. T. (1989). Black American adolescents. In J. T. Gibbs & L. N. Huang (Eds.), *Children of color* (pp. 179-223). San Francisco: Jossey-Bass.

Gustavsson, N. S., & Balgopal, P. R. (1990). Violence and minority youth: An ecological perspective. In A. R. Stiffman & L. E. Davis (Eds.), *Ethnic issues in adolescent mental health* (pp. 115-130). Newbury Park, CA: Sage.

Hamilton, S. F. (1990). *Apprenticeship for adulthood: Preparing youth for the future.* New York: Free Press.

Huang, L. M., & Ying, Y. (1989). Chinese American children and adolescents. In J. T. Gibbs & L. N. Huang (Eds.), *Children of color* (pp. 30-66). San Francisco: Jossey-Bass.

Inclan, J. E., & Herron, D. G. (1989). Puerto Rican adolescents. In J. T. Gibbs & L. N. Huang (Eds.), *Children of color* (pp. 251-277). San Francisco: Jossey-Bass.

Isaacs, H. R. (1976). Basic group identity: The idols of the tribe. In N. Glazer & D. P. Moynihan (Eds.), *Ethnicity: Theory and experience* (pp. 29-52). Cambridge, MA: Harvard University Press.

Jackson, B. (1975). Black identity development. *MEFORM: Journal of Educational Diversity & Innovation, 2,* 17-25.

Looft, W. R. (1971). Egocentrism and social interaction in adolescence. *Adolescence, 6,* 485-494.

Looft, W. R. (1972). Egocentrism and social interaction across the life span. *Psychological Bulletin, 78,* 73-92.

Marcia, J. E. (1966). Development and validation of ego-identity status. *Journal of Personality and Social Psychology, 3,* 551-558.

Markstrom, C. A., & Mullis, R. L. (1986). Ethnic differences in the imaginary audience. *Journal of Adolescent Research, 1,* 289-301.

Markstrom-Adams, C., Ascione, F. R., Braegger, D., & Adams, G. (1993). The effects of two forms of perspective-taking training on ego-identity formation in late adolescence. *Journal of Adolescence, 16,* 217-224.

Marsh, D. T., Serafica, F. C., & Barenboim, C. (1980). Effect of perspective-taking training on interpersonal problem solving. *Child Development, 51,* 140-145.

Phinney, J. S. (1989). Stages of ethnic identity development in minority group adolescents. *Journal of Early Adolescence, 9,* 34-49.

Phinney, J. S. (1990). Ethnic identity in adolescents and adults: A review of research. *Psychological Bulletin, 108,* 499-514.

Phinney, J. S., Lochner, B. T., Murphy, R. (1990). Ethnic identity development and psychological adjustment in adolescence. In A. R. Stiffman & L. E. Davis (Eds.), *Ethnic issues in adolescent mental health* (pp. 53-72). Newbury Park, CA: Sage.

Ramirez, O. (1989). Mexican American children and adolescents. In J. T. Gibbs & L. N. Huang (Eds.), *Children of color* (pp. 224-250). San Francisco: Jossey-Bass.

Rodriguez, O., & Zayas, L. H. (1990). Hispanic adolescents and antisocial behavior: Sociocultural factors and treatment implications. In A. R. Stiffman & L. E. Davis (Eds.), *Ethnic issues in adolescent mental health* (pp. 147-171). Newbury Park, CA: Sage.

Selman, R. L. (1980). *The growth of interpersonal understanding: Development and clinical analysis.* New York: Academic Press.

Spencer, M. B. (1983). Children's cultural values and parental childrearing strategies. *Developmental Review, 3,* 351-370.

Spencer, M. B. (1988). Afro-American adolescents: Adaptational processes and socioeconomic diversity in behavioral outcomes. *Journal of Adolescence, 11,* 117-137.

Spencer, M. B. (in press). Old issues and new theorizing about African American youth: A phenomenological variant of ecological systems theory. In R. L. Taylor (Ed.), *Black youth: Perspectives on their status in the United States.*

Walker, L. J. (1980). Cognitive and perspective-taking prerequisites for moral development. *Child Development, 51,* 131-139.

7

Lesbian and Gay Male
Identities as Paradigms

JOHN HAZEN McCONNELL

This chapter addresses how unconventional erotic identifications from childhood are integrated with adult social constructions of unconventional erotic life in the process we call ego identity. The chapter first places Erikson's views on unconventional erotic identities in historical context, which explains why the early models of positive gay male and lesbian identities that were developed in the 1970s seldom cite Erikson. Many of these models are generally consistent with Erikson's constructs of foreclosure, moratorium, diffusion, and identity achievement, although they have eschewed the use of Marcia's fourfold paradigm in favor of stages that are more refined and operational. A synopsis of Troiden's (1989) developmental model is presented, followed by a brief discussion of the relevant research base. Some differences between gay male and lesbian identities are then highlighted. It is proposed that the paradigm shift underlying Troiden's model applies to other stigmatized erotic identities, such as sadomasochism (SM) and cross-dressing. Finally, consideration is given to therapeutic interventions and criteria for specialization.

For Erikson "there is an element of psychobiological dissatisfaction in any sexual situation not favorable in the long run to procreative consummation and care" (Erikson, 1968, pp. 242-243). Erikson's ideal of intimacy is "*the utopia* of genitality [which] should include . . . mutuality of orgasm . . . with a loved partner . . . *of the other sex* [and] procreation . . . so as to secure to the offspring, too, all the stages of

103

satisfactory development" (Erikson, 1950, p. 266, italics added). As these opening quotes demonstrate, the very groundplan of Erikson's theory of the life cycle assumes a variation of psychobiological Darwinism that is utopian, heterosexist, and homophobic.

To use Erikson's language of ego identity to understand alternative erotic identities as normal developmental variants requires that we go beyond him in two directions: back to Freud's moral and therapeutic neutrality toward erotic variation, and forward to examine the social and self constructions of emergent sociosexual communities.

Erotic expressions and identities are social constructions that change cross-culturally and historically within cultures. Foucault's (1978) landmark work on the history of sexuality documents that the attribution of a character type to a person based on his or her sexual behavior is a historically recent construction that has developed slowly over the last two centuries. Nineteenth-century sexologists, most notably Krafft-Ebing in his 1886 work *Psychopathia Sexualis,* classified varieties of sexual expression—such as homosexuality, transvestism, fetishism, sadism, and masochism—under the rubric of psychopathology. They contributed greatly to the reification of sexual behaviors as sexual types and eventually as personality types: Persons who had homosexual fantasies or engaged in homosexual behavior became homosexuals. The term *homosexual* was first used in English in 1892, and it was in contradistinction to such sexual "pathologies" that the term first appeared in 1900 (Halperin, 1990).

It was in this context that Freud proposed that conflictual influences on the sexual drive (libido) during early critical periods (psychosexual stages) result in enduring patterns of sexual expression during adulthood. Freud viewed adolescence as a time when early psychosexual patterns—particularly those associated with the Oedipus complex—are reactivated, possibly modified, and then confirmed as character types. Psychoanalytic theory has contributed probably more than any other 20th-century force to the reification of sexual types as character types: Homosexuals engaged in homosexual behavior because they had a relatively fixed underlying personality structure. Contemporary constructs of erotic identity derive from this intellectual current but are quite different in emphasis.

The reader may be surprised to know that Freud was "subversive in his uncensorious, neutral stance on the perversions, for he was convinced that to be fixated on early objects that had not been outgrown, whether this meant fetishism or homosexuality, was not a crime, not a sin, not a disease, not a form of madness or a symptom of decadence" (Gay, 1988, p. 149). For Freud, the term *perversion* was less an evaluation than a description of certain vicissitudes of the libidinal drive. He was particularly clear about not treating homosexuality as a sickness, sin, or illegal behavior (Downing, 1989; Lewes, 1988). For instance, he asserted that homosexuality should be no deterrent to someone becoming a psychoanalyst.

Despite Freud's views, many analysts from the 1930s to the 1960s became extremely negative in their valuation of sexual variation. In the conclusion of his landmark critique on the history of psychoanalysis and homosexuality, Kenneth Lewes (1988) writes that this erotonegative period of psychoanalysis demonstrated a "projection of analysts' own alienated impulses . . . coupled with an attack on homosexuals conducted with an intemperance, ferocity, and lack of empathy that is simply appalling in a discipline devoted to understanding and healing" (p. 239).

Lewes's critique of analytic theory involves a paradigm shift that revisions Freud from the perspective of the postwar gay and lesbian liberation movement. The essential paradigm shift, now widespread, holds that the problem is not homosexuality but homophobia and heterosexism. Thus the current official position of the "American Psychological Association urges all mental health professionals to take the lead in removing the stigma of mental illness that has long been associated with homosexual orientations" (Conger, 1975).

When Peter Blos introduced Erikson to Freud's circle in 1927, psychoanalysis was at the beginning of its most erotonegative phase. Although Erikson's work is free of the most virulent extremes, his assumptions (as the opening quotes demonstrate) are homophobic and heterosexist from the perspective of our current perspective. It is in this context that we must understand the paradox of his contribution: Erikson's emphasis on ego adaptations is part of a broader movement that peripheralizes sexuality within psychoanalytic theory and developmental psychology; he further peripheralizes homosexuality by labeling it pathological; and yet Erikson coined the construct of identity, and without this we might not talk about gay male or lesbian *identity* at all. The contemporary emphasis on the social construction of erotic identities is consistent with Erikson's deemphasis of drive theory but departs from his position that heterosexual genitality and offspring are essential for a healthy or normal life cycle.

Contemporary Models of Lesbian and Gay Identity

The paradigm shift from homosexual psychopathology to gay and lesbian identities resulted in a new array of research questions in an effort to study new (nonclinical) populations. An understanding of our current working models hinges on understanding the theoretical relationship between homophobia and gay and lesbian identities: They are, in large part, two aspects of a single construct. Without homophobia there is little motive to develop distinct gay and lesbian social structures and identities. For instance, few discriminations are made in northern Europe on the basis of sexual orientation, and patterns of socialization and identity are very similar for lesbians, gay males, and heterosexuals. Sexual identity as a construct of the ego parallels sexual identity as a social construct. In North America, lesbians and gay males usually learn to be homophobic before they discover they are sexually attracted to members of their own sex. It follows that revaluing homophobia is central to their developing a positive identity. Current developmental models of gay and lesbian identities are therefore models of how a person deals with homophobia and its sequalae.

Given Erikson's view that homosexuality is pathological, it is not surprising that the literature on lesbian and gay male identities—which in other respects is so indebted to Erikson—rarely credits his influence. A 1986 review located more than 100 research papers explicitly based on Erikson's identity construct, all of which sampled (usually presumptively) heterosexuals, and none of which addressed the issue of sexual orientation. The same review located some 15 research studies on the process of exploring and committing to a positive gay male or lesbian identity, none of which made explicit reference to Erikson's work (McConnell, 1986). This schism reflects the peripheralization of gay males and lesbians both academically and socially.

The initial models of gay and lesbian identities, which developed in the 1970s and early 1980s, generally eschewed psychoanalytic formulations in favor of sociological constructs such as role theory and deviance, or they were atheoretical or eclectic. However, in hindsight, many of these models are consistent with many of Erikson's ideas about adolescence. Most suggest a progression of stages, usually starting with the recognition of homoerotic fantasy in conjunction with homophobic values and a homophobic environment (foreclosure), progressing to a revaluation of the stigma (moratorium), and culminating with the acceptance of a positive gay male or lesbian identity and the establishment of nonhomophobic social networks (achievement).

Troiden's Model

Troiden (1989) has synthesized into one model the best from several recent models of gay male and lesbian identity. The caveats on his model are similar to those found for many other stage theories. For example, not all lesbians and gay males go through all stages or substages. Nor are the stages always traversed in the same order. Regressions can occur. Moderating influences may include the individual's degree of internalized homophobia, strengths and weaknesses of character, and environmental conditions. What follows is a synopsis of Troiden's four main stages: sensitization, identity confusion, identity assumption, and commitment. The author proposes links between Troiden's model and Erikson's.

Troiden's Stage 1: Sensitization

Sensitization occurs before puberty and is "characterized by feelings of marginality" (Troiden, 1989, p. 50). The individual is presumed by him- or herself and others to be heterosexual but feels different without yet having the cognitive constructs to start labeling this difference. In Erikson's terms, this represents foreclosure in a negative identity.

Troiden's Stage 2: Confusion

The stage of confusion starts when adolescents "begin to reflect upon the idea that their feelings, behaviors, or both could be regarded as homosexual" (Troiden, 1989, p. 52). In Erikson's terms, this marks the start of the moratorium. Troiden (1989, p. 55) observes that "lesbians and gay males typically respond to identity confusion by adopting one or more of the following strategies: (a) denial . . . (b) repair . . . (c) avoidance . . . (d) redefinition . . . and (e) acceptance."

- *Denial* is the attempt to block out homosexual thoughts and feelings.
- *Repair* involves an attempt to enlist professional aid to reorient to heterosexuality.
- *Avoidance* may take several forms: the avoidance of behaviors associated with homosexuality, the avoidance of heterosexual dating because it might betray nonresponsivenes, the avoidance of information about homosexual-

ity, the adoption of antihomosexual positions (i.e., reaction formation), immersion in heterosexual pursuits in the hope that homosexual feelings will go away, and, finally, escapism in drugs, fantasy, athletics (usually solitary), or academic achievement.

• *Redefinition* involves the individual rationalizing her or his homosexuality as a special case (a special person or circumstance such as drunkenness), a one-time occurrence, an adolescent phase, or bisexuality. Unlike a well-integrated bisexuality, the bisexuality of redefinition is a defensive strategy.

If adopted permanently, the above four strategies would result in identity diffusion, a negative identity, or both. They mark the uneasy, mostly unconscious transition from foreclosure in a negative (false heterosexual) identity, toward the open, relatively conscious exploration of the late moratorium stage.

The last strategy that Troiden includes in his *Confusion Stage* is *acceptance,* which simply means acceptance that the behavior may be homosexual. This marks the beginning of a true moratorium in which commitments are consciously set aside in favor of active exploration. Acceptance allows for progression to the next stage.

Troiden's Stage 3: Identity Assumption

In this stage, "homosexual identity becomes both a self-identity and a presented identity, at least to other homosexuals" (p. 59). Coming out to other gay men and/or lesbians involves adoption of a new set of peers, and a commitment to experiment with realistic and healthy adult roles. This is typical of Erikson's late moratorium: exploration and increasing commitment.

Troiden's Stage 4: Commitment

[Commitment] is indicated *internally* by (a) the fusion of sexuality and emotionality into a significant whole; (b) a shift in the meanings attached to homosexual identities; (c) a perception of the homosexual identity as a valid self-identity; (d) expressed satisfaction with the homosexual identity; and (e) increased happiness after self-defining as homosexual. It is indicated *externally* by: (a) same-sex love relationships; (b) disclosure of the homosexual identity to nonhomosexual audiences; and (c) a shift in the type of stigma-management strategies. (Troiden, 1989, p. 63)

Those with a positive identity use stigma-management strategies that are situational rather than rigid. They avoid self-defeating self-disclosure.

In Marcia's terms, Troiden's fourth stage represents identity achievement within the domain of sexual orientation. However, it also includes aspects of intimacy: "same-sex love relationships." I would object that while a positive identity may be a prerequisite for intimacy, same-sex love relationships may be based—for better or worse—on either a positive or negative identity. Also, while I would agree that sexuality and emotionality are integrated in this stage, Troiden's use of the term *fusion* overstates the case for most gay males. (See the later section on differences between lesbians and gay males.)

Cass's Stage of Identity Synthesis

Vivienne Cass (1990) has contributed a six-stage model that differs from but has many similarities to Troiden's 1989 model. I wish here only to draw attention to her useful distinction between identity commitment and a further stage of *identity synthesis.* In identity synthesis, "nonhomosexuals come [again] to be considered a significant reference group. There is less need to adhere to the gay community as a defense maneuver. . . . [T]he person gains a sense of well-being and peace" (Cass, 1990, p. 248). Continuity and flexibility are experienced temporally in how the inner self is presented to others and in the use of communities. The individual finds new pleasure in this.

Cass's (1990) stage of identity synthesis reminds us that for Erikson the contents (domains, identifications) of identity are in a sense only landmarks that allow us to describe the process of structuralization and integration that is ego identity proper. The similarities between Cass's last stage, identity synthesis, and Erikson's ideal of ego identity are readily apparent. Both involve a process of synthesizing identifications in different domains. Both involve adapting to available social roles to find a positive expression for these identifications. Operationalizing Cass's stage of identity synthesis for other domains—both erotic and nonerotic— would be a valuable refinement of our research instrumentation.

The Research Base

It is not this chapter's purpose to review the extensive research related to models of gay male and lesbian identities. However, a few comments may guide the reader who is unfamiliar with the literature. The rigorous research paradigms that have been used to address other stage theories (e.g., moral development, Piaget's work) have not been applied to Troiden's work. There are no longitudinal studies. Nor is there research designed to address the relationship of Troiden's model to Marcia's fourfold typology. However, Troiden's model draws explicitly on several previous models. These in turn are embedded in a nomological network of extensive research on (a) the age at which gay males and lesbians typically reach certain developmental milestones such as experiencing their first homoerotic fantasy and (b) the relationship between various markers of internalized homophobia and difficulty or delay in developing a positive gay identity (e.g., McConnell, 1986; McDonald, 1982; Troiden, 1989). Finally, many of the correlates of positive lesbian or gay male identities are similar to the correlates found for identity achievement in Marcia's sense (e.g., increased self-esteem and reduced anxiety). Given these generalities, I wish to address three particularly important areas of research on gay and lesbian identities: (a) prevalence, (b) extended moratorium, and (c) social sex role.

Prevalence

A study of 34,707 Minnesota public school students from grades 7 through 12 provides our best estimate of the prevalence and demographics of sexual orientation (Remafedi, Resnick, Blum, & Harris, 1992). Unlike previous studies, few differences in prevalence were found between males and females. A considerable number of adolescents struggle with sexual orientation: 25.9% were unsure of their orientation at age 12; the figure decreased to 8.9% at age 18. Between the ages of 12 and 18, the percentage of students who stated they were predominantly homosexual increased from 2.2% to 6.4%. But "less than one third of all subjects with predominantly homosexual fantasies, attractions, and/or behaviors actually described themselves as bisexual or homosexual" (Remafedi et al., 1992, p. 720). This suggests that a substantial incidence of gay males and lesbians have a negative or diffuse ego identity and that 6.4% probably underestimates the adult prevalence of gay males and lesbians.

Extended Moratorium

Gay males and lesbians typically have an extended moratorium when compared with their heterosexual peers. On average, both gay and heterosexual males experience their first same-sex sexual fantasies in their ninth year (Friedman & Stern, 1980). Self-designation as homo-sexual occurs later, at age 19 (McDonald, 1982) to 21 (Kooden et al., 1979). Finally, most gay males and lesbians achieve a positive accep-tance of their sexual identity only at age 24 (McDonald, 1982) to 28 (Kooden et al., 1979). It is not uncommon to encounter men and women who "came out" in their 30s, 40s, 50s, and even 60s. In contrast, Marcia (1980) concludes that most heterosexuals achieve a positive identity at approximately age 21.

The extended moratorium of gay males and lesbians reflects the struggle with homophobia and explains much of our psychosocial development. Few adolescents are equipped to tolerate prolonged am-bivalence regarding such a core identity issue as sexual orientation. Troiden's (1989) second and third stages—confusion and identity as-sumption—specify certain aspects of the extended moratorium. In my clinical work, a careful history often reveals struggles with denial, repair, avoidance, and redefinition. In addition, I frequently observe un-fortunate sequelae of these strategies. These are too complex to describe here, but two frequent variants are:

1. confusion may disintegrate into diffusion, anomie, aimless depression, or self-destructive behaviors; or
2. conversely, the individual may foreclose partway through his or her explo-ration and isolate sexuality from needs for love, intimacy, affection, and sociability.

Pleasurable homosexual sex is frequently the best antidote to inter-nalized homophobia because it confronts shame and guilt with a positive reality. But gay men who start exploring their sexual orientation through casual sexual encounters—which seem psychologically safe because they are isolated from the rest of their identity—may inadvertently establish a pattern of isolating their erotic life both externally and internally.

Social Sex Role

Asked about their childhood, lesbians report having felt more "mas-culine" than their heterosexual peers (35% to 9%), and gay males report having felt more "feminine" (Bell, Weinberg, & Hammersmith, 1981). Several studies on adults have found that gay males and lesbians rate themselves as more androgynous than their heterosexual peers (e.g.,

McConnell, 1986). Further, androgyny is correlated positively with self-esteem and positive attitudes toward homosexuality for gay men and lesbians. Indeed, for gay males, but not their heterosexual peers, femininity is positively correlated with masculinity, self-esteem, stability of self-concept, and internal locus of control (McConnell, 1986). These data indicate that, for many gay males and lesbians, achieving a positive identity involves integrating not only an alternative sexual orientation, but also a nontraditional social sex role. Clinically, I have observed that foreclosure on sex role may have unfortunate sequelae such as the adoption of rigid, dysfunctional, pseudoheterosexual sex roles in sex and romance. Dissatisfaction here is often projected on others, such as gay males or lesbians of nontraditional sex role.

Social sex role is one of many identity domains that have a reciprocal influence with the development of erotic identity. Religious beliefs, political values, and vocational choice are among the other domains that may be strongly impacted. Cass's stage of identity synthesis can be especially complex for lesbians and gay men.

Some Differences Between Lesbians and Gay Men

The relative invisibility of lesbians prompts me to include a section highlighting certain differences between lesbians and gay men. Studies on gay males far outnumber studies on lesbians. This represents institutionalized sexism. Gender strongly influences the coming-out process, sense of identity, and values. Lesbians face a double oppression. They often become aware of being oppressed as women before being aware that they are oppressed on account of their object choice. Thus many lesbians identify first as feminists and second as lesbians. There is a popular belief that because lesbianism is less "seen" it is easier for a lesbian to "pass," and that this makes her task of identity achievement easier. However, this invisibility is itself a measure of social oppression, which is often internalized as a denial of self. Mistaking invisibility as an advantage represents the repression of repression; in itself this becomes a barrier to a positive identity. Consider the paucity of role models for lesbian youths. Perhaps the most invisible of oppressed minorities, lesbians exist unseen within minorities defined by other criteria such as ethnicity, religion, and class.

Women tend to reach developmental milestones in Troiden's (1989) model at a later age than gay men. For instance, one major study (Bell et al., 1981) found that 77% of its gay, white male sample had an arousing physical same-sex encounter by 18—in contrast to 17% of the white lesbian sample. The reason for the slower development of erotic identity for lesbians is unclear. It could result from any combination of the following:

- male bias in establishing the milestones, many of which have to do with sexual experiences;
- the double oppression faced by lesbians;
- the enduring expectation for women of passivity rather than agency, which inhibits the exploration of alternative identifications;
- the economic disparity between men and women;
- that young lesbians, compared with young gay males, are far more re-stricted in their access to urban landscapes;
- that lesbians may need to deal with more complex residual pre-oedipal issues of separation because of their closer merger with the pre-oedipal mother (see Chodorow, 1978).

There is considerable controversy about whether heterosexual men and women embrace Erikson's stages of identity and intimacy in the same way (Marcia, 1980). Parallel issues are apparent for lesbians and gay males. Lesbians are more concerned with social attachments than are gay men (Jay & Young, 1977). For many, identity is as much or more concerned with a lesbian ethic as it is with erotic concerns. In contrast, gay men are often more concerned with sex and more frequently view sex and intimacy as separate issues. For gay males, the first same-sex experience is not usually in the context of a relationship, which is more typical for lesbians (Kooden et al., 1979; McDonald, 1982; Troiden, 1989). This parallels findings for heterosexuals. Lesbians more frequently self-identify in the context of emotional or romantic relationships, whereas men more fre-quently self-identify in the context of same-sex erotic contact (Troiden, 1989). Unlike lesbians, gay men often prefer open relationships in which fidelity does not mean monogamy. A survey of couples, which probably overrepresents monogamous couples because of sampling bias, found that 37% of gay male couples and 9% of lesbian couples have an agreement that sex outside the relationship is acceptable (Bryant & Demian, 1990). Moreover, the longer a gay male couple is together, the more likely they are to report an open relationship, whereas single gay males often report that the cause of previous breakups was extrarelational sex that was not agreed on beforehand (Bell & Weinberg, 1978).

Whether heterosexual or homosexual, parenting appears to be a more salient aspect of ego identity to women than men. Some would argue that this is essential for understanding how the relationship between intimacy and identity differs for men and women (see Chodorow, 1978).

The data presented in the above section emphasize aspects of lesbian identities that minimize the erotic. But Ferguson (1981) has pointed out there is perhaps a cart-before-the-horse problem with such interpretation. Ferguson observes that this type of data in itself reflects the more general repression of women's sexuality, and that the use of such data to define normative models of lesbian identities only reifies the repression of lesbian sexuality. At the least, Ferguson reminds us, there are many lesbian identities. It is an unwarranted projection to assume that sexuality plays the same role in the identities of lesbians as it does for others.

Lesbian and Gay Male Identities as Paradigms

Despite the many differences between lesbians and gay males, Troiden's (1989) model and Cass's (1990) stage of identity synthesis apply to both. Indeed, these models may be useful in studying other stigmatized identities, both erotic and nonerotic. In addition, the clinical insights gained from our understanding of the extended moratorium typical of lesbians and gay males may be useful in understanding other groups. I address sadomasochism (SM) and cross-dressing as examples in this section.

It is easy to forget that the reevaluation of homosexuality over the last 30 years is one of the most dramatic reversals in the history of mental health. Although the homosexualities are now accepted by most mental health workers, most other nontraditional erotic expressions remain pathological under the rubric of the American Psychiatric Association's *Diagnostic and Statistical Manual* (DSM-III-R) and psychoanalytic theory. It is as if we still view erotic orientation as a coin with two faces of desire (male or female), joined by the narrow border of bisexuality (male and female). But the coinage of eroticism is far more plastic. Among other dimensions of identification consider cross-dressing, activity-passivity, social sex role, SM, fetishism, bondage, cross-age preferences, and celibacy. These dimensions may combine into a veritable array of erotic identities.

The status of these erotic expressions is reminiscent of the status of homosexuality 30 years ago. Some of these atypical erotic expressions—most notably, SM and cross-dressing—have become the basis for sociosexual communities. These communities, like the research associated with them, remain stigmatized and peripheralized. Yet there is little if any well-designed double-blind research on nonclinical samples in the tradition of Hooker (1957) that addresses whether persons who have integrated these erotic identifications differ in psychological health. Available research often supports the null hypothesis: Persons of various erotic identifications do not differ in levels of psychopathology or optimal functioning.

In a study of 245 male practitioners of erotic SM, Spengler (1977) found that 70% would not change their "sexual disposition" if they could freely do so, which strongly suggests they had achieved a positive erotic identity. Less than 10% of Spengler's sample had sought psychotherapy. Mark Thompson (1991, p. xvi) introduces his anthology *Leatherfolk: Radical Sex, People, Politics and Practice* with the assertion that "by the late 1970s, what had once been clinically labeled as sadomasochism was often referred to as *sensuality and mutuality*." And "rather than keeping parts of the psyche distant and detached, [SM] can serve deep spiritual needs for wholeness and completion" (p. vii). Guy Baldwin's (1993) collected writings—indispensable for clinicians in this field—describe the gay leather scenes with the power, insight, and sensitivity of a master therapist and practitioner.

Peggy Rudd (1991) studied a nonclinical sample of 817 heterosexual male cross-dressers, many of whom found cross-dressing erotic. Rudd (1991, p. 34) found that most cross-dressers started with denial and experienced hostility, anger, fear, and guilt. Respondents in her sample began to move beyond these feelings and accept cross-dressing in their 30s, although self-acceptance was not universal until the men were in their 50s or 60s (pp. 123-124). This indicates a delayed and prolonged moratorium. Consistent with Troiden's model, self-acceptance occurred after self-labeling and typically involved socializing with other cross-dressers. Reevaluating their hypermasculine behavior often was important (an analog to reevaluating internalized homophobia for gay males and lesbians). Reframing the situation was critical to self-acceptance: seeing the problem as negative attitudes toward cross-dressing and not as cross-dressing itself.

This paradigm shift for erotic identity has important implications for clinical work and research. First, we must acknowledge that it does great harm to label conditions as pathological if they are not. When an erotic orientation such as cross-dressing, fetishism, sexual masochism, or sexual sadism involves consenting partners and does not cause marked distress for the individual, then it should not be listed as a disorder in future revisions of the DSM-III-R. When we model these erotic identities in the same manner as Troiden has done for the homosexualities, then we can make sense of the observation that for some persons a positive acceptance of a particular fetish, form of SM, or cross-dressing is a prerequisite rather than a barrier for intimacy.

Interventions and Specialization

Models can be helpful in understanding the development of erotic identities, but reality tends to be far more complex. Therapists must deal with particular people and must adapt their developmental models and techniques accordingly. Erikson's model of adolescent development is more useful as a theoretical perspective than it is for suggesting specific interventions. Lesbian, gay male, and other atypical erotic identities confront us deeply with the patriarchal and heterosexist assumptions of our society. These assumptions are so woven into the fabric of our culture that they often remain unconscious to the therapist, as does the countertransference.

An APA task force on psychotherapy with lesbians and gay men identified "17 themes illustrating biased, inadequate, or inappropriate practice" (Garnets, Hancock, Cochran, Goodchilds, & Peplau, 1991, p. 966). In many of the examples given by the task force, the therapist remained unaware of the bias. The task force called for the development of "guidelines for appropriate psychotherapy with gay male and lesbian clients and . . . that all psychologists receive adequate training" (p. 970). The task force recommends an excellent reading list in this area.

It seems to me that a therapist who works with clients of atypical erotic identities should:

1. be informed about the social construction of the patient's erotic community, both locally and in cross-cultural context;
2. in the course of their own therapy have carefully analyzed their own erotophobia, heterosexism, and sexism;
3. understand and have come to a radical critique of the traditional theories that give greater value to reproductive heterosexuality than other forms of eroticism;
4. have a clear developmental model of positive erotic identity;

5. feel comfortable in accepting atypical erotic and romantic feelings—both their own and the feelings of others toward them—and be aware of these in the transference and countertransference;

6. keep abreast of the extensive research and clinical literature in these and related areas, such as gay-affirmative therapy, social sex role, homophobia, sexual variance, and HIV illness; and

7. possess the therapeutic skills to help the patient along the path of identity synthesis.

In short, treating erotic identity issues requires specialization. For therapists who do not specialize, the best intervention is a referral.

Conclusions

Erikson's work revealed how ego identity depends on shifting social constructions that interact recursively with psychodynamic development. Identities are emergent. They are often deeply idiosyncratic. Erotic identities, because of the erotonegativism of our culture, are especially likely to have changing rather than fixed values and meanings. Identifications are just landmarks of the process Erikson calls ego identity. The central function of this process is to integrate various identifications into a healthy sense of self: a self with a pleasurable and conscious sense of continuity and community. The least favorable outcome of the research on Erikson's identity construct would be for our models to become Procrustean beds into which our patients must fit. The therapeutic goal is to create an environment that allows patients to explore safely their particular array of erotic identifications and determine for themselves how best to synthesize or abandon them.

References

Baldwin, G. (1993). *Ties that bind: The SM/leather/fetish erotic style.* Los Angeles: Daedalus.

Bell, A. P., & Weinberg, M. S. (1978). *Homosexualities: A study of diversity among men & women.* New York: Simon & Schuster.

Bell, A. P., Weinberg, M. S., & Hammersmith, S. K. (1981). *Sexual preference: Appendix.* New York: Simon & Schuster.

Bryant, S., & Demian. (1990). *Summary: Partners' national survey of lesbian and gay couples.* Seattle: Partners.

Cass, V. C. (1990). Homosexual identity formation. In D. P. McWhirter, S. A. Sanders, & J. M. Reinisch (Eds.), *Homosexuality/heterosexuality: The Kinsey Institute series* (pp. 239-266). New York: Oxford University Press.

Chodorow, N. (1978). *The reproduction of mothering: Psychoanalysis and the sociology of gender*. Berkeley: University of California Press.

Conger, J. (1975). Proceedings of the American Psychological Association Incorporated, for the year 1974: Minutes of the annual meeting of Council of Representatives. *American Psychologist, 30,* 620-651.

Downing, C. (1989). *Myths and mysteries of same-sex love*. New York: Continuum.

Erikson, E. (1950). *Childhood and society*. New York: Norton.

Erikson, E. (1968). *Identity, youth and crisis*. New York: Norton.

Ferguson, A. (1981, Autumn). Compulsory heterosexuality and lesbian existence: Defining the issues. *Signs, 7,* 158-172.

Foucault, M. (1978). *The history of sexuality* (Vol. 1). New York: Random House.

Friedman, R. C., & Stern, L. O. (1980). Fathers, sons, and sexual orientation: Replication of a Bieber hypothesis. *Psychiatric Quarterly, 52*(3), 175-189.

Gay, P. (1988). *Freud: A life for our time*. New York: Norton.

Garnets, L., Hancock, K., Cochran, S., Goodchilds, J., & Peplau, A. (1991). Issues in psychotherapy with lesbians and gay men. *American Psychologist, 46*(9), 964-972.

Halperin, D. (1990). *One hundred years of homosexuality*. New York: Routledge.

Hooker, E. (1957). Male homosexuality in the Rorschach. *Journal of Projective Techniques, 22,* 33-54.

Jay, K., & Young, A. (1977). *The gay report*. New York: Summit.

Kooden, H. D., Morin, S. F., Riddle, D. I., Rogers, M., Sang, B. E., & Strassburger, F. (1979, September). *Removing the stigma*. Washington, DC: American Psychological Association.

Lewes, K. (1988). *The psychoanalytic theory of male homosexuality*. New York: Simon & Schuster.

Marcia, J. E. (1980). Identity in adolescence. In J. Adelson (Ed.), *Handbook of adolescent psychology* (pp. 159-187). New York: John Wiley.

McConnell, J. H. (1986). Correlates of identity for homosexual and heterosexual young men. (Doctoral dissertation, California School of Professional Psychology, San Diego, 1986). *Dissertation Abstracts International, 86,* 17146.

McDonald, G. (1982). Individual differences in the coming out process for gay men: Implications for theoretical models. *Journal of Homosexuality, 8*(1), 47-60.

Remafedi, F., Resnick, M., Blum, R., & Harris, L. (1992). Demography of sexual orientation in adolescents. *Pediatrics, 89*(4), 714-721.

Rudd, P. J. (1991). *Crossdressing with dignity*. Katy, TX: PM Publishers.

Spengler, A. (1977). Manifest sadomasochism of males: Results of an empirical study. *Archives of Sexual Behavior, 6*(6), 441-456.

Thompson, M. (1991). *Leatherfolk: Radical sex, people, politics and practice*. Boston: Alyson.

Troiden, R. R. (1989). The formation of homosexual identities. In G. Herdt (Ed.), *Gay and lesbian youth* (pp. 43-73). Binghamton, NY: Harrington Park Press.

PART III

Curricular Interventions

8

Designing Curricular Identity Interventions for Secondary Schools

PHILIP H. DREYER

The purpose of this chapter is to outline ways in which educational environments and curricula can be structured to promote identity achievement in adolescents. Simply stated, curricula offered by schools and other traditional environments for youths—such as church youth groups, summer camps, and work settings—can be used to promote identity achievement and should be designed to do so. The chapter begins by presenting a rationale for a curriculum based on theories of identity formation, then reviews the research literature to urge a synthesis of work in the areas of adolescent cognitive development and identity achievement, and ends with a description and examples of some characteristics of an identity-enhancing curriculum. The discussion is framed by the educational reform movements of the past decade to argue that developmental psychologists, such as identity theorists, have much to offer the schools and that we must become more active in the public school reform movement.

A Theoretically Based Curriculum

One of the strongest advantages of identity theory is that it provides a theoretical basis for curriculum design that focuses on the developmental needs of the student rather than on the latest scholarly opinion of how

121

particular academic disciplines should be taught. The advantages to this approach are important for both teachers and students. For teachers who are well grounded in their academic field, it first provides a clear set of educational goals and objectives and clarifies the role that each academic subject plays in the larger development of the students. Second, it encourages crossdisciplinary teaching and gives teachers in different academic fields more ways to communicate with one another. And third, it helps explain why students react as they do to particular subject matters and suggests ways to make learning more meaningful and effective.

For students, it provides the opportunity to view school not as a series of obstacles to be overcome and a set of specific skills that may or may not be used but as a series of experiences leading to personal growth and a meaningful adulthood. It encourages them to assume responsibility for their own learning, it heightens feelings of self-determination, and it helps them feel that school and teachers are resources to be used rather than people to be worked around. In the end, a school that applies identity theory successfully should have more effective teachers, more successful students, and higher academic performance no matter how it is measured.

For most schools, adopting a theory to coordinate the curriculum is a difficult task. Teachers are wary of such attempts as encroachments on their independence. Organized teachers tend to react to such attempts politically in terms of the collective-bargaining agreement and the teaching contract. Nonorganized teachers tend to react philosophically, arguing in terms of academic freedom and the importance of their own fields. Unfortunately, both of these negative reactions miss the point that the psychosocial development of students is probably the most powerful element in the life of the school, whether teachers choose to admit it or not. Given this reality of student development, a school that takes advantage of what is known about how students think and feel is far more likely to be an effective school than one that does not.

Finally, adopting identity theory as a vehicle for organizing the curriculum does not mean lowering academic standards or abandoning the school to psychologists. On the contrary, adopting such a theoretical base requires the highest levels of academic preparation by teachers and a strict adherence to the latest advances in each academic field. Thus it ultimately adds a significant student-based dimension to the work of a well-trained and energetic faculty.

Identity Theory, Cognitive Development, and Educational Reform

Although the psychological theory about identity formation can be traced to the work of Erikson (1950, 1959, 1982), the most recent advances in the field have resulted from Marcia's (1966, 1980) description of identity as a set of statuses that are defined by the extent to which an individual has explored options for his or her life and has shown evidence of having made a commitment to an occupation and an ideology. Successful identity achievers in this framework are high in both exploration and commitment. Given this definition, identity formation in adolescents can be encouraged and promoted by surrounding them with educational environments that stimulate exploration and commitment.

This premise is compatible with other theories of development in which adolescence is characterized by the higher intellectual capabilities, such as formal operational logic (Inhelder & Piaget, 1958), analytical reasoning (Bruner, Goodnow, & Austin, 1956; Flavell, 1977), social cognition (Selman, 1980), moral reasoning (Gilligan, 1982; Kohlberg, 1984), and intellectual and ethical commitment (King, 1977; Kitchener, 1984; Kitchener & King, 1981; Perry, 1968). All of these approaches describe adolescent thinking as being characterized by increased abilities to think abstractly, consider different points of view when solving problems, and logically evaluate alternatives when searching for solutions to dilemmas. Identity theory builds on these notions of higher forms of intellectual reasoning, abstract thinking, and principled moral values to suggest that adolescents use these skills when testing hypotheses about personal identity in the real world. A key concept in cognitive development is the adolescent's ability to consider alternatives to the current reality, whereas a key concept in identity status research is the importance of the adolescent's exploratory activities in terms of such real-life issues as occupational choice and commitment to a religious and political ideology.

The linkage between research about intellectual development during adolescence and research about adolescent identity formation has yet to be systematically demonstrated. In both areas, good research indicates that adolescents make steady progress as a function of age or grade, but I am aware of no study that demonstrates parallel development in the two areas for the same subjects in the same setting. On both sides of this cognitive versus psychosocial discussion researchers have assumed that one side was related to the other, but few studies have actually shown a relationship between cognitive development and psychosocial development.

To briefly elaborate this point, there has been a great deal of research about how adolescents acquire what Piaget and Inhelder called "formal" operational thought. In their description of this process, for example, Piaget and Inhelder (Inhelder & Piaget, 1958) seemed to indicate that hypothetico-deductive reasoning developed at about the time of puberty as a result of a generalized interaction between the young person and his or her environment. Although the timing of the onset of this cognitive restructuring might vary by a few years as a result of cultural norms or handicapping condition, the nature of the final thought process itself was expected to be the same for most adolescents in most situations and to cut across all content areas. In 1972, however, Piaget revised this original formulation to say that such formal thought could appear in some content areas and not in others as a result of specific life experiences, such as work apprenticeships (Piaget, 1972). This expansion of Piagetian theory opened the door to the idea that the intellectual development of adolescents was neither inevitable (automatic) nor uniform across content domains and might depend on the specific life experiences of a particular individual.

By the early 1970s, researchers were commonly using Piagetian measures with adolescents and young adults to show what percentage of the tested group appeared to be formal operational and what work and educational settings were correlated with formal reasoning (Neimark, 1975). At the same time, a variety of studies tried to show that formal reasoning was related to specific types of experimental manipulations and educational curricula (Kuhn, 1979; Kuhn & Angelev, 1976; Kuhn & Brannock, 1977; Kuhn & Ho, 1977; Kuhn, Ho, & Adams, 1979). Thus a shift occurred in the research away from description and toward prescription and intervention.

A parallel change occurred in the research about the "moral" development of adolescents, as described by Lawrence Kohlberg. In the 1960s, Kohlberg (who was greatly influenced by Piaget) argued that moral development through his six stages seemed to occur as a result of normal experience. By the early 1970s, however, he had turned his attention to what he thought of as "moral education," or the development of specific lessons based on hypothetical moral dilemmas that could be used to stimulate directly higher levels of moral reasoning. With several collaborators, he devoted his energy to creating curricular materials for schools, prisons, and other settings in which young people and adults could be directly influenced (Colby & Kohlberg, 1987; Kohlberg, 1984; Lickona, 1976, 1991; Power, Higgins, & Kohlberg, 1989; Ryan & Lickona, 1992).

A third parallel track in this cognitive research can be seen in the work of William G. Perry, Jr., and his collaborators, who moved from describing "intellectual and ethical development" of college students in the 1960s (Perry, 1968) to descriptions of intervention programs for promoting student ethical growth and development in the 1970s and 1980s (King, 1977; Kitchener, 1984; Kitchener & King, 1981; Knefelkamp, 1982; Knefelkamp, Widick, & Parker, 1978). Again the shift was from early descriptions of development and toward the creation of academic and counseling programs that would promote development.

On the psychosocial side, the research has developed more recently and has remained more descriptive than prescriptive. Although Erikson's theoretical formulations were made in the 1950s and 1960s (Erikson, 1950, 1959, 1968), it was not until Marcia coined the notion of "identity statuses" that identity became a practical empirical construct (Marcia, 1966, 1980). Marcia's interview technique and operational definition of such content domains as occupation, religion, and politics provided a concrete way to measure an individual's identity status. Not long after, Adams introduced a paper-and-pencil measure of identity status that opened the possibility of collecting data from large numbers of subjects and subjecting the results to advanced statistical analysis (Adams, Bennion, & Huh, 1989).

With the availability of practical measuring tools, identity-status research has flourished in the last decade, with more than 200 studies being reported, many of which are described throughout this volume. Most of this research is descriptive, showing identity-status characteristics of different educational groups (Waterman, 1985), clinical groups (Arehart & Hull Smith, 1990; Bakken & Romig, 1989; Bilsker & Marcia, 1991), gender groups (Archer, 1989b; Jackson, Dunham, & Kidwell, 1990; Mellor, 1989), and ethnic groups (Phinney, 1989, 1992; Phinney & Alipuria, 1990; Raskin, 1989; Rotheram-Borus, 1989; Streitmatter, 1988). Many of the articles that discuss intervention strategies for enhancing identity development are found in one special 1989 volume of the *Journal of Adolescence* (see Archer, 1989a, 1989c; Marcia, 1989; Raskin, 1989; Waterman, 1989).

The closest the literature comes to a linkage between cognitive development and identity development is in research reported only recently. O'Connor and Nikolic (1990) found that a measure of egocentrism was correlated with measures of identity crisis, diffusion, and achievement but not with measures of formal operational thought. Berzonsky and colleagues compared identity status with measures of social cognition such as styles of personal problem solving and decision making (Berzonsky, 1989), personal-construct measures (Berzonsky & Neimeyer, 1988; Berzonsky, Rice, & Neimeyer, 1990), and need for cognition, openness to experience, and introspection (Berzonsky & Sullivan, 1992). Finally, Boyes and Chandler (1992) studied the relationship of measures of identity status with what they termed *epistemic doubt* in young people of high school age who were classified as either *concrete* or *formal* operational to show relationships among formal operational thought, epistemic doubt, and moratorium- and achievement-identity statuses.

As this brief review indicates, research is needed that systematically tests the relationship between the intellectual changes associated with adolescence and the achievement of a personal identity. Until we have such research, the link between the two remains only a reasonable assumption. What are needed are answers to the following questions:

1. How do cognitive and psychosocial (identity) development relate to and influence each other?
2. In the sequence of development, is one of these two areas more important than the other? In other words, is one necessary for the development of the other?
3. Will development in one of these areas promote development in the other?
4. Can programs be designed to foster the development of these areas?

Although this research agenda is long and may take years to complete, our dilemma as psychologists and educators is that we do not have the time to wait for the answers to these questions, because the need for educational reform in the United States is profound. Whether or not we feel completely ready, we must take what limited theory and data we have now and begin to consider how to implement them at the school level.

The urgency of the educational agenda for U.S. schools has been overwhelmingly documented in the past decade. Beginning with the 1983 report of the National Commission on Excellence in Education, *A Nation at Risk: The Imperative for Educational Reform,* and the 1986 report of the National Governors' Association, *Time for Results: The*

Governors' 1991 Report on Education, there have been scores of reports, studies, books, and calls to action to improve schools. In his summary of this literature, Bacharach (1990) refers to these educational reforms as coming in two waves. In the first wave, reforms were the many attempts to raise standards of academic achievement, increase certification requirements for teachers, and create a system of national achievement tests that all students would take. The second wave of reforms can be traced to calls by the Children's Defense Fund (1984) and the Committee for Economic Development (1985, 1987) for more investment in the country's children. Included in the second wave of reforms have been calls for the renewal of teacher-education programs (Holmes Group, 1986) and the many efforts to "restructure" public schools to include more local decision making and involvement by parents and community members (Hawley, 1990).

What is missing in most of these reports and calls for educational reform is discussion of the psychosocial needs of children and youth. There are discussions of the need to strengthen families, improve the safety and physical health of children and youth, and make schooling more relevant to the economic needs of students; however, little attention is paid to the psychosocial development of children and adolescents and virtually no mention of the term *identity*. See, for example, the report of the National Education Goals Panel (1992). Education policy makers seldom get involved with psychosocial issues, and when they do they often encounter amusement if not ridicule. A useful example of this can be found in the work of California Assemblyman John Vasconcellos, who generated a great deal of public discussion in the 1980s about how schools might improve student self-esteem. Public hearings were held around the state, study panels were created to take advantage of research and clinical experience, and reports were written (Mecca, Smelser, & Vasconcellos, 1989). The public response to this activity was mixed at best, and the self-esteem projects in California became the subject of satirical jokes on late-night television and lampooning in a series of "Doonesbury" cartoon strips. In the end, most of the effort withered for lack of funds before it was ever seriously implemented.

The message of the educational reform movement of the 1980s for those of us who claim to be developmental psychologists is that we have a long way to go just to get the issue of identity formation on the agenda for discussion. Because the burden of proof is on us, we must be realistic about our claims and design plans for classroom practice that not only are informed by theory and research but also are sensitive to the realities of the public schools and the curricular needs of students. In this spirit, the rest of this chapter suggests concrete applications of theories of identity formation to the realities of the curriculum presented to adolescents by secondary schools.

Characteristics of an Identity-Enhancing Curriculum

The process of identity formation in school begins with the feeling on the part of the student that his or her schoolwork represents an investment of his or her own feelings and talents. It is crucial that students assume ownership over their own work and feel it to be personally expressive. An effective curriculum thus offers students reasonable choices of assignments and forms of expression and encourages each student to choose those tasks that seem to be not only the most interesting and fun but also the most meaningful. Assignments that require students to repeat age-old lessons in traditionally rote ways may effectively promote discrete skills, such as vocabulary enrichment or the ability to factor quadratic equations, but they do little to foster identity formation.

In addition to these issues of exploration of ideas and alternative behaviors, identity formation in school fosters commitment to oneself as a whole person who can work effectively in some socially acceptable occupation, be faithful to other persons, and be optimistic about the future. To form true commitments, a person must be able to take risks and have the confidence that the decisions one makes to work at a particular occupation, care for a particular individual, or believe in a particular set of ideas will make life more meaningful and personally rewarding. Thus identity achievement in the sense of both exploration and commitment requires not only knowledge and careful thought, but also courage and will.

An effective educational curriculum thus is more than a set of cognitive lessons and skill practices. It offers chances to take risks, learn from one's mistakes, and be surrounded by sensitive people who care not only about the subject matter at hand but also about each student and his or her ability to act in a confident and willful fashion.

Specific suggestions for the implementation of identity theory can be organized around the following four assertions:

1. An identity-enhancing curriculum promotes exploration, responsible choice, and self-determination by students.

A central aspect of the identity-achievement process is the consideration of alternative ways of acting, thinking about the self, and understanding the world. In fact, it is the ability of adolescents to think abstractly and logically in formal ways that provides the intellectual basis of the so-called identity crisis. Overwhelmed by logical possibilities and reasonable alternatives to the present reality of one's life, the adolescent sometimes loses his or her sense of self and becomes distracted by the host of apparent role possibilities and confused by the many ideas and ideologies that seem attractive. One key to successful identity achievement is thus being able to control the process of exploration so that the youth is able to make reasonable decisions and arrive at firm commitments in such areas of life as occupation, religion, and politics without being overwhelmed by the multitude of possibilities or the magnitude of the decision-making task.

To do this, the young person must be able to understand the alternatives, evaluate each one systematically, and feel a sense of personal control over the decisions that he or she makes. Each of these elements—knowledge, critical thinking skills, and a sense of self-determination—is important to identity achievement. Most schools stress the first two without giving enough emphasis to the third, and it is the focus on self-determination that distinguishes and personalizes the identity-enhancing school environment.

Self-determination requires giving students choices and letting them follow through to their logical conclusions. For instance, when assignments are given to fulfill course requirements, students can be allowed to choose from among several options offered by the teacher or to suggest their own method for meeting the course requirements. By offering choices created by the teacher, immature students are discouraged from wasting time; by allowing students to suggest their own choices, mature students are encouraged to express their own needs and particular skills. In this way, even "bad" choices become useful lessons in understanding one's own limits and talents.

A favorite example of giving students choices in assignments comes from a young history teacher in Chicago who assigned his students to learn about the so-called Chicago school of architecture by visiting famous buildings in the city and interviewing people who worked or lived in the buildings. Students were given a list of appropriate buildings, a set of interview questions, and a guide for the report they were to write when their visit was completed. Although most students visited the nearest building on the list and spent five minutes with the elevator operator, two young men in the class went to a large downtown department store, talked their way into the president's office, and spent several hours with the president touring the building and examining the 100-year-old original architectural plans that were being used for the restoration of the building. When students returned to class to report on their experiences, it became clear that everyone had learned much about architecture and their community, although for these two young men the lesson included exposure to the world of big business—which excited them more than anything else.

A famous example of the power of giving students choices in their academic work is the success of the Foxfire Project that was begun by a young English teacher in Rabun Gap, Georgia, in the late 1960s. Frustrated by his students' lack of interest in the traditional English curriculum, Eliot Wigginton and his high school class decided to write a local newspaper as an exercise in journalism. Students were asked to go into the community to find material for stories, and many returned with interviews and accounts of how local handicrafts were made. Soon these stories and descriptions of the work of local craftspeople became popular reading, and the class newspaper was sold publicly, eventually becoming a series of best-selling books (Wigginton, 1972). The students in the original class formed a corporation and used the profits from the books to buy the school, pay their own teacher, and eventually create a historical village for the preservation of mountain crafts.

A third example of the power of choices is the enthusiasm and excellence that is displayed by students who participate in science fairs. Although science fairs are highly structured, the choice of research topics is open, and students become deeply involved in a project of their choosing, conducting research, analyzing results, and presenting findings in a professional manner before a panel of expert judges.

The success of all of these cases is to be found in the students' control over their own work in a structured environment. Thus they can explore intellectually challenging issues under the guidance of a teacher and can claim ownership over their exploration and its results. What is learned is different for each student and takes on long-lasting significance to the extent that the learning becomes part of the individual's identity. Even "failed" lessons become useful, in this sense, because by learning what skills and interests a person does not have the search for identity is narrowed and becomes more clearly focused on the final commitment.

2. An identity-enhancing curriculum promotes role-playing and social interaction across generations.

Adolescence involves expanded opportunities to play new social roles. "Normal" adolescents begin experimenting with new role behaviors, which they usually see as exciting opportunities to grow up and act like adults. For example, an adolescent girl may begin working as a baby-sitter or newspaper carrier. She may also begin studying computers and foreign languages in school. At her church or synagogue, she goes through a formal confirmation or bat mitzvah that allows her to share in adult ceremonies and tasks. At home, she may find herself being expected to take a greater share in housekeeping tasks. She and her friends may be encouraged to join a social or school activity group. She may begin to date. In each social role, she is expected to demonstrate different social skills, knowledge, and attitudes. She is also expected to be consistent across these roles and in control of herself at all times.

This multiplicity of roles, with their separate behaviors, sources of knowledge, and attitudes, offer the youth both opportunities for new growth and self-expression as well as opportunities for confusion and loss of identity (Gilligan, Lyons, & Hanmer, 1989). The problem for the adolescent, then, is how to maintain consistency of action and thought across these diverse situations. For most youths, this continuity is achieved through a process of role experimentation and interaction with others. The adolescent self—the identity—comes to be understood as a result of trial and error as the individual slowly decides which roles do and do not fit his or her true self. As identity is slowly achieved, the individual comes to feel that he or she is the same person no matter which role is being acted out at a particular time or in a particular situation.

The ultimate resolution of the identity question for most youths concerns the question of occupational choice. "What will my career be?" is usually the best answer to the question "Who am I?" Experimentation with different jobs and work roles thus becomes a key activity for most adolescents.

A curriculum that is organized around principles of identity theory encourages the learner to go far beyond the normal role of passive student and to consider each subject as a possible vocation. All courses can promote exploration of vocational choice, because in all courses the student can role-play what it is like to be a mathematician, historian, literary critic, teacher, engineer, astronomer, foreign language expert, photographer, botanist, and so on. Teachers should understand this and ask students to think about how they feel about being, for example, a mathematician, not just how they like mathematics. The issue is not only the discrete academic skills the student learns in any particular course, but also the opportunity to role-play what it is like to be a professional in that field. Teachers should encourage such role-playing, even though it may be full of fantasy and unrealistic behaviors, putting the emphasis on the student's experience in the role and its potential meaning for future work.

A second way in which schools can encourage role continuity in students is by responding caringly and compassionately to individuals. Teachers, counselors, administrators, and other school personnel can serve as powerful models and significant others for students, and often the teacher's actions and responses to student behaviors come to define the meaning of the student's behavior. A student who is deeply involved with science may be called a "nerd" by uncaring classmates, but an interested teacher's encouragement and help can be powerful influences on that student's willingness to explore and to consider a commitment to science. Teachers should try to understand each student as a whole person with a complex life and dreams that extend far beyond the classroom.

The challenge is thus responding to each student as a whole person, which means taking the time to learn something about each student and being compassionate about his or her life. It also means encouraging each student to be his or her best self and to be optimistic about the future, no matter what the student's performance in a particular class may be.

3. An identity-enhancing curriculum promotes the student's understanding of time and how the past is related to the present.

One intellectual attribute of the identity-achievement process is the ability to understand time, particularly as it relates to one's sense of how the past, present, and future are connected. In a practical sense, time involves the answers to the questions "Who was I?" "Who am I?" and "Who will I become?" Being confident and comfortable with the answers to these questions is one of the hallmarks of identity achievement.

The answers to these questions involve two different time contexts: historical time and personal time. *Historical time* is that of one's family ancestors and the cultural past. As adolescents become aware that they are members of a larger group with social, cultural, and historical dimensions, they must reconcile their own places in their group's collective memories and traditions. An African-American youth, for example, confronts the reality that black people in the United States have been the victims of centuries of slavery, oppression, and racial discrimination. For this youth, one identity problem is to understand and come to terms with this history. He or she must reach a point of personal understanding of what this cultural past means personally in the present so that he or she can move on to a viable sense of a personal future.

Personal time refers to a person's own experiences since he or she was born or to chronological time. In that sense, each person has a unique set of childhood experiences and memories out of which grows his or her sense of self. At adolescence the individual must reconsider those particular childhood experiences to achieve a sense of continuity between the way he or she was as a child and the way he or she is as an adolescent. For example, someone born with a cleft palate may have undergone many painful operations and visits to doctors as a child and may have acquired a lowered self-esteem because of the birth "defect." Having reached adolescence, he or she must adjust these childhood experiences and memories to fit his or her present reality as a mature, independent young adult who is no longer a small and helpless child.

Although one often experiences a sense of crisis in confronting both cultural and personal past, the important issue in achieving an identity is reaching a point of personal understanding: The way one experiences the self in the present is consistent with and an outcome of the way it was experienced in the past. In other words, adolescents must realize that they are not different people than they were as children; instead, they are the same people expanding their understanding of belonging to a family cultural group.

School can be a powerful environment for students trying to deal with these issues of continuity in time, and a few examples from the secondary school curriculum illustrate the point.

First, social studies classes can become places to learn about one's own cultural and familial past—who one's ancestors were and what a family's cultural roots are. To accomplish this, the teacher must be able to respond to the demographic characteristics of the class by providing course materials related to the history of the ethnic groups present and by being sensitive to the role that different ethnic groups have played. Thus the issue in what is commonly called "multicultural" education is not only that all students need exposure to the diversity of peoples in the world, but also that people of different cultural heritages experience history differently and tend to learn whatever is most relevant for their own sense of who they are. For this reason, students need information not only about other groups in order to learn toleration and respect but also about themselves in order to achieve a sense of personal identity.

The curricular issue here is not so simple as it may first appear. For instance, what ethnic group should a teacher use to organize the material in a course? In U.S. history, quite different courses emerge when the instructor chooses to focus on one group's perspective rather than on another's, while courses that offer a smattering of each group's experience often become disjointed and confusing. For example, most teachers organize historical material from the perspective of the dominant ethnic group in the class, emphasizing its cultural history and heroes as subjects for identification by students. This gives the course a consistent focus and point of view but excludes students who are not members of the majority group.

In the history of California, for instance, a European-American version would focus on the participants in the Gold Rush of 1849, the shipping and rail magnates of the late 19th century, and the people from the Midwest who migrated to California in the 1930s. A course taught from this perspective provides European-American students with many opportunities for identity exploration. The same course taught from the Spanish point of view might emphasize the early priests who built missions along the Pacific coast; the Spanish businessmen who established large ranchos, founded Los Angeles, and governed for almost 300 years; and the Mexican-American immigrants of the past century who have provided much of the labor necessary to build the state's economy. Such a course would offer many opportunities for identification by Latino students.

Both versions of California's history are valid—as would be an Asian version, a women's version, and an American Indian version—but they are quite different courses that provide not only different views of history but also different psychosocial experiences for students. Thus the curricular issue is a matter of not simply course content and presentation but also developmental purpose.

No matter what the cultural emphasis of a particular course, students will try to understand it within the context of their own cultural experience. If their cultural group is highly represented in the course, then they will look for sources of positive identification, but if their group is not represented or is represented negatively, then they will view the course as irrelevant at best and alienating at worst. Consider, for example, how a Sioux student might react to the story of Custer's "Last Stand" at the battle of the Little Bighorn if the incident were reported only as a "massacre" of several hundred U.S. Cavalry troopers by several thousand belligerent American Indian warriors. In response to the identity questions "What is my past?" and "Who are my people?" the Sioux student is left with negative answers: "My people were wild and violent and led by a man named Crazy Horse." Or perhaps, "My people were weak and easily pushed around by the white soldiers until they caught the cavalry in a surprise attack with overwhelming numbers." For this Sioux youth, these lessons are negative and disconfirming, leaving him or her with no positive sense of a personal past and little hope for a personal or cultural future.

Second, perhaps the most fundamental issue of the continuity of time deals with the issues of birth and death, and here the science curriculum offers abundant opportunities for adolescents to consider who they are and what life means. No student in ninth grade picks up a scalpel to begin the frog dissection without realizing that this was a living organism and that he or she is participating in the destruction of life. For adolescents struggling with issues of sexuality and the creation of life, which are largely ignored by schools, dissecting a frog with the encouragement of the school can present a challenge to one's self-concept and raise serious concerns about the meaning of life itself. Teachers who consider such experiences as merely lessons in science and laboratory technique run the risk of failing to meet the psychosocial needs of their students.

Third, mathematics classes can provide many opportunities for testing personal continuity across time, because mathematics is one of the most consistent experiences students have over time in school. What and how one did in first- and second-grade arithmetic relates directly to what and how one does in high school algebra, because both involve computation, mathematical reasoning, and playing the role of mathematician.

One difficulty in students' mathematics experiences as seen from an identity point of view is that unpleasant experiences from elementary school years often have a long-lasting negative influence on the high school student trying to deal with algebra and geometry (Paulos, 1988). If a student had a difficult struggle with arithmetic in the lower grades and was made to feel incompetent by insensitive teachers and parents, that student is likely to have an especially hard time during high school because he or she will face the challenge of algebra with little self-confidence, no matter what the actual state of his or her computational skills. So the algebra teacher faces a dual problem: (a) planning a systematic course of study in algebra and (b) helping students relate their past experiences in arithmetic in positive ways to the present study of algebra. Currently the failure rates of students in high school mathematics classes and the declining enrollment of women students in third- and fourth-year math classes seem to indicate that teachers are not succeeding with either aspect of this challenge.

The case of the loss of women students from advanced math classes is particularly serious, because high school math is a gateway subject for any technical or scientific career. The reasons given for women's lack of interest in mathematics in high school vary greatly, but there is a growing consensus among mathematics education researchers that most girls who give up on math and science do so in the seventh and eighth grades—that is, before they get to high school. From an identity point of view, many of these girls apparently cannot synthesize their early experiences in arithmetic with their current study of mathematics in such a way as to commit themselves to a viable future in a mathematically oriented occupation. The issue may be neither girls' mathematical aptitude nor their skill level but their identity diffusion about who they have been as young students, who they are now as high school students, and who they may become in a highly technological world that continues to send out mixed messages about opportunities for women.

4. An identity-enhancing curriculum promotes self-acceptance and positive feedback from teachers and counselors.

The awareness that one has continuity across situations and in time must be accepted and acknowledged by others if identity achievement is to be successful. In other words, the perception that one has of self must be agreed on and approved by such significant others as parents, teachers, and friends. If the girl who was a baby-sitter, a student of computers, an adult churchgoer, and a friend to her classmates at school should settle on an identity based on being a student and future businesswoman, then this identity must be acknowledged by others who share and support her self-perception. If others do not—for instance, if her parents see her as finishing her education at high school and then marrying a man and becoming a homemaker—then she will most likely experience a continuing form of identity crisis. In short, achieving identity can only be done within a person's particular social and historical setting, where the individual's awareness of self-sameness and continuity is understood and accepted by the larger society.

Next to parents, teachers represent the most powerful adult significant others that most adolescents encounter on a regular basis. For this reason, teachers' responses to the various roles that adolescents experimentally play have unusual power to aid or interfere with identity formation. A positive response from a teacher to a student's essay about the need to save whales, for example, can reinforce the student's sense of herself or himself as both a competent writer and an informed citizen. The best teachers always take the student's search for personal meaning seriously by treating the student with respect and as a competent individual whose exploratory behavior may not always be error-free or successful but whose need for acceptance and reassurance is legitimate. Ultimately this positive feedback that teachers provide about a student's overall well-being is more important than any subject matter skill they teach.

Conclusion

These four characteristics of an identity-enhancing curriculum are intended to help start the discussion of how school curricula can be reorganized to promote more directly student identity achievement. They are not by any means intended to be a complete list; they are, however, suggested ways in which the psychosocial development of students can be understood within the traditional instructional sequence.

The need for educational reform in U.S. public schools is clearly recognized. What remains to be seen is whether developmental psychologists, such as identity theorists, will play a role in that reform or will retire to the world of abstract research and individual clinical practice. The contention of this chapter is that identity theory has a great deal to offer the schools and that we as developmental psychologists need to accept the burden of proof and become active members of the educational reform movement.

References

Adams, G. R., Bennion, L., & Huh, K. (1989). *Objective measure of ego identity status: A reference manual* (2nd ed.). Logan: Utah State University, Department of Family and Human Development.

Archer, S. L. (1989a). Adolescent identity: An appraisal of health and intervention. *Journal of Adolescence, 12,* 341-343.

Archer, S. L. (1989b). Gender differences in identity development: Issues of process, domain and timing. *Journal of Adolescence, 12,* 117-138.

Archer, S. L. (1989c). The status of identity: Reflections of the need for intervention. *Journal of Adolescence, 12,* 345-359.

Arehart, D. M., & Hull Smith, P. (1990). Identity in adolescence: Influences of dysfunction and psychosocial task issues. *Journal of Youth and Adolescence, 19,* 63-72.

Bacharach, S. B. (1990). *Education reform: Making sense of it all.* Boston, MA: Allyn & Bacon.

Bakken, L., & Romig, C. (1989). Adolescent ego development: Relationship to family cohesion and adaptability. *Journal of Adolescence, 12,* 83-94.

Berzonsky, M. D. (1989). Identity style: Conceptualization and measurement. *Journal of Adolescent Research, 4,* 268-282.

Berzonsky, M. D., & Neimeyer, G. J. (1988). Identity status and personal construct systems. *Journal of Adolescence, 11,* 195-204.

Berzonsky, M. D., & Sullivan, C. (1992). Social-cognitive aspects of identity style: Need for cognition, experiential openness, and introspection. *Journal of Adolescent Research, 7,* 140-155.

Berzonsky, M. D., Rice, K. G., & Neimeyer, G. J. (1990). Identity status and self construct systems: Process X structure interactions. *Journal of Adolescence, 13,* 251-263.

Bilsker, D, & Marcia, J. E. (1991). Adaptive regression and ego identity. *Journal of Adolescence, 14,* 75-84.

Boyes, M. C., & Chandler, M. (1992). Cognitive development, epistemic doubt, and identity formation in adolescence. *Journal of Youth and Adolescence, 21,* 277-304.

Bruner, J. S., Goodnow, I. J., & Austin, G. A. (1956). *A study of thinking.* New York: John Wiley.

Children's Defense Fund. (1984). *American children in poverty.* Washington, DC: Author.

Colby, A., & Kohlberg, L. (1987). *The measurement of moral judgment.* New York: Cambridge University Press.

Committee for Economic Development. (1985). *Investing in our children: Business and the public schools.* Washington, DC: Author.

Committee for Economic Development. (1987). *Children in need: Investment strategies for the educationally disadvantaged.* Washington, DC: Author.

Erikson, E. (1950). *Childhood and society.* New York: Norton.

Erikson, E. (1959). Identity and the life cycle. *Psychological Issues,* Issue 1, Monograph 1.

Erikson, E. (1968). *Identity: Youth and crisis.* New York: Norton.

Erikson, E. (1982). *The life cycle completed.* New York: Norton.

Flavell, J. H. (1977). *Cognitive development.* Englewood Cliffs, NJ: Prentice-Hall.

Gilligan, C. (1982). *In a different voice.* Cambridge, MA: Harvard University Press.

Gilligan, C., Lyons, N. P., & Hanmer, T. J. (1989). *Making connections: The relational worlds of adolescent girls at Emma Willard School.* New York: Emma Willard School.

Hawley, W. D. (1990). Preparing students from today's families for tomorrow's cognitive challenges. In S. B. Bacharach (Ed.), *Education reform: Making sense of it all* (pp. 213-233). Boston: Allyn & Bacon.

Holmes Group. (1986). *Tomorrow's teachers*. East Lansing, MI: Author.

Inhelder, B., & Piaget, J. (1958). *The growth of logical thought from childhood to adolescence*. New York: Basic Books.

Jackson, E. P., Dunham, R. M., & Kidwell, J. S. (1990). The effects of gender and of family cohesion and adaptability on identity status. *Journal of Adolescent Research, 5,* 161-174.

King, P. M. (1977). The development of reflective judgment and formal operational thinking in adolescents and young adults. *Dissertation Abstracts International, 36,* 7233-A.

Kitchener, K. S. (1984). A longitudinal study of moral and ego development in young adults. *Journal of Youth and Adolescence, 13*(3), 197-211.

Kitchener, K. S., & King, P. M. (1981). Reflective judgment: Concepts of justification and their relationship to age and education. *Journal of Applied Developmental Psychology, 2,* 89-116.

Knefelkamp, L. (1982). Faculty and student development in the 80's: Renewing the community of scholars. In H. F. Owens, C. H. Witten, & W. R. Bailey (Eds.), *College student personnel administration* (pp. 373-390). Springfield, IL: Charles C Thomas.

Knefelkamp, L., Widick, C., & Parker, C. A. (1978). *New directions in higher education: Applying new developmental findings*. San Francisco: Jossey-Bass.

Kohlberg, L. (1984). *The psychology of moral development: The nature and validity of moral stages*. New York: Harper & Row.

Kuhn, D. (1979). The significance of Piaget's formal operations stage in education. *Journal of Education, 161,* 34-50.

Kuhn, D., & Angelev, J. (1976). An experimental study of the development of formal operational thought. *Child Development, 47,* 697-706.

Kuhn, D., & Brannock, J. (1977). Development of the isolation of variables scheme in experimental and "natural experiment" contexts. *Developmental Psychology, 13*(1), 9-14.

Kuhn, D., & Ho, V. (1977). The development of schemes for recognizing additive and alternative effects in a "natural experiment" context. *Developmental Psychology, 13*(5), 515-516.

Kuhn, D., Ho, V., & Adams, C. (1979). Formal reasoning among pre- and late adolescents. *Child Development, 50,* 1128-1135.

Lickona, T. (1976). *Moral development and behavior: Theory, research, and social issues*. New York: Holt, Rinehart & Winston.

Lickona, T. (1991). *Educating for character: How our schools can teach respect and responsibility*. New York: Bantam.

Marcia, J. E. (1966). Development and validation of ego identity status. *Journal of Personality and Social Psychology, 3*(5), 551-558.

Marcia, J. E. (1980). Identity in adolescence. In J. Adelson (Ed.), *Handbook of adolescent psychology* (pp. 159-187). New York: John Wiley.

Marcia, J. E. (1989). Identity and intervention. *Journal of Adolescence, 12,* 401-410.

Mecca, A. M., Smelser, N. J., & Vasconcellos, J. (1989). *The social importance of self-esteem*. Berkeley: University of California Press.

Mellor, S. (1989). Gender differences in identity formation as a function of self-other relationships. *Journal of Youth and Adolescence, 18,* 361-376.

National Commission on Excellence in Education. (1983). *A nation at risk: The imperative for educational reform.* Washington, DC: Government Printing Office.

National Education Goals Panel. (1992). *The national education goals report 1992.* Washington, DC: Government Printing Office.

National Governors' Association. (1986). *Time for results: The governors' 1991 report on education.* Washington, DC: Government Printing Office.

Neimark, E. D. (1975). Intellectual development during adolescence. In F. D. Horowitz (Ed.), *Review of child development research* (Vol. 4, pp. 541-594). Chicago: University of Chicago Press.

O'Connor, B. P., & Nikolic, J. (1990). Identity development and formal operations as sources of adolescent egocentrism. *Journal of Youth and Adolescence, 19,* 149-158.

Paulos, J. A. (1988). *Innumeracy: Mathematical illiteracy and its consequences.* New York: Hill & Wang.

Perry, W. G., Jr. (1968). *Forms of intellectual and ethical development during the college years—a scheme.* New York: Holt, Rinehart & Winston.

Phinney, J. (1989). Stages of ethnic identity development in minority group adolescents. *Journal of Early Adolescence, 9,* 34-49.

Phinney, J. S. (1992). The multigroup ethnic identity measure: A new scale for use with diverse groups. *Journal of Adolescent Research, 7,* 156-176.

Phinney, J. S., & Alipuria, L. L. (1990). Ethnic identity in college students from four ethnic groups. *Journal of Adolescence, 13,* 171-183.

Piaget, J. (1972). Intellectual evolution from adolescence to adulthood. *Human Development, 15*(1), 1-12.

Power, F. C., Higgins, A., & Kohlberg, L. (1989). *Lawrence Kohlberg's approach to moral education.* New York: Columbia University Press.

Raskin, P. M. (1989). Identity status research: Implications for career counseling. *Journal of Adolescence, 12,* 375-388.

Rotheram-Borus, M. J. (1989). Ethnic differences in adolescents' identity status and associated behavior problems. *Journal of Adolescence, 12,* 361-374.

Ryan, K., & Lickona, T. (Eds.). (1992). *Character development in schools* (2nd ed.). Washington, DC: Council for Research in Values and Philosophy.

Selman, R. (1980). *The growth of interpersonal understanding.* New York: Academic Press.

Streitmatter, J. L. (1988). Ethnicity as a mediating variable of early adolescent identity development. *Journal of Adolescence, 11,* 335-346.

Waterman, A. (1985). Identity in adolescence: Processes and contents. *New directions for child development.* San Francisco: Jossey-Bass.

Waterman, A. S. (1989). Curricula interventions for identity change: Substantive and ethical considerations. *Journal of Adolescence, 12,* 389-400.

Wigginton, E. (1972). *The Foxfire book.* Garden City, NY: Doubleday.

9

A Working Curriculum
for Gender Roles

KAREN GREENLAW BIERI
MINDY BINGHAM

Gender is a component of self-definition that provides direction and meaning or imposed restrictions by self and others. Gender roles as defined by one's culture establish patterns of behavior that construct and constrain the individual and form the foundation of family structure. These roles vary by race, age, class, sexual orientation, ethnicity, and geographic area. Each generation is socialized by its institutions, parents, teachers, significant others, the same and opposite sexes, and media.

As used in this chapter, *gender curriculum* refers to a course of study that assists the individual in determining a sense of self in the context of family and society. The purpose of this chapter is to explore what is being done in the area of gender curriculum as well as what needs to be done. The Choices and Challenges curriculum, the exemplar for this chapter, will address the problem of role stereotyping.

The Situation

During adolescence, the parameters of adult roles are defined. The decisions made with regard to career, marriage, and children will have profound implications for the rest of life and are responsible for fixing

141

men's and women's place in society. By early adolescence, we see that girls and boys place different emphasis on the relationship and career areas of their lives. Boys' identities are believed to revolve around their work and career plans, while girls' identities focus on their relationships. This has dire economic consequences for females and emotional and stress-related consequences for males.

Historically, schools have done little to help adolescents learn about gender roles and life planning. Counselors bogged down with heavy case loads rarely have time to discuss the connection of curriculum decisions to life satisfaction and economic security. Nor is there time to discuss how to combine work and family life. Students fulfilling graduation requirements may have little time for life-planning classes that may or may not be offered.

Despite some cultural advances, role stereotyping is still one of our most constricting dilemmas. We would like to believe that the barriers and discriminatory practices have been removed from our culture and that women can have careers of their choice and that men can be more involved fathers (LaRossa, 1992). Numerous authors point out that this is not the case in the family, school, workplace, research, legal system, and field of science. Much of what needs to be done requires deeper changes in socialization than saying that opportunities are available to all and that the law prohibits discrimination. Habits continue long after broad beliefs have changed. Thus it is necessary to have more complete and comprehensive changes in the areas of internal environment, structures, and core gender belief systems that undermine the new messages before the opportunities will become available to all (Brush, 1991).

The traditional family and career choices are no longer viable for the majority of the population. The family is in transition to greater diversity in structures resulting from divorce, separation, desertion, remarriage, single parenthood, same-sex unions, and teenage pregnancy. The hectic pace of daily life and the need for multiple-career families to meet difficult economic times, fulfill life satisfaction, and achieve the American dream of home ownership compound the difficulties.

Divorce alone has had a profound cultural impact. It taxes our finances, shakes our emotions, and reorganizes gender-role activities. No one seems to divorce easily. No one seems prepared to deal with the changes in the nuclear family structure with its multiple losses and gains in relationships. Divorce alone may well introduce the single-parent family to poverty (Firebaugh, 1991).

Gender Concerns for Males

The main identity concern for males concerns the role of family provider and its impact on the quality of life in a rapidly changing society. Current economic facts of life jeopardize the traditional male role. Males are truly caught in a double bind. They risk not meeting human needs when they live their stereotyped role. Brannon (1976) identified four themes of stereotyped male role behavior: (a) the need to be different from women—no sissy stuff; (b) the need to be superior to others—the big wheel; (c) the need to be independent and self-reliant—the sturdy oak; and (d) the need to be more powerful than others, through violence if necessary—give 'em hell. Males have integrated the lessons of childhood that taught them to repress their inner thoughts and fears. It becomes burdensome for males to orally express the inner life and its feelings of vulnerability (Rubin, 1992). Unchecked, traditional sex-role behaviors are associated with a shorter life expectancy of as much as seven years. Harrison, Chin, and Ficarrotto (1992) support a "profound cultural revolution" in which the male sex role "ceases to be defined as opposite to the female role."

Males need to be supported in accepting the attitudes and behaviors that have been traditionally labeled as feminine (Block, 1984; Thompson, 1991). They need to learn to accept their vulnerability, show fear and sadness, ask for support, be gentle, be nurturant, be cooperative, be communicative, and use nonviolent means to resolve conflict. If we accept that human development is relational, then we must say that males have been disadvantaged (Surrey, 1991). New ways need to be found to balance the needs of family, career, and self. These concerns run parallel to the concerns for females.

Gender Concerns for Females

Females face an identity process that is both complex and confusing. Both Archer (1985b) and Tavris and Baumgartner (1983) found that girls could easily identify disadvantages in being female but had difficulty finding advantages. Somehow girls pick up the message that they are less important than their brothers. This feeling can lead to loss of self-esteem, teen pregnancy, poor performance in school, and an unrealistic or apathetic attitude toward the future.

Today's girls do not necessarily plan to avoid the pitfalls their mothers experienced, and they may not even know that they are there (Friedan, 1986). They may not realize that the traditional family makes up only 6% to 12% of all American families. Some will attempt the superwoman life without realizing the cost involved. Some will not plan for the expected 25 years of work and the 19 years of living alone (Vetter, 1985). If a woman stays single to obtain needed career education, she risks becoming an "old maid." If she becomes skilled in a nontraditional trade, she risks alienation. She may maintain her female identity (nurturant help-mate and parent) and forego preparation for her career or its implementation (Archer, 1989).

Girls tend to perceive the formation of values, goals, and beliefs in the context of relationships (Archer, 1990) and make career decisions in conjunction with family, marriage, and societal expectations. Therefore, females tend to select service jobs, while males select technological jobs (Erb, 1983). Mathematics is a critical factor in career selection (Lantz & Smith, 1981). Females need to be socialized to mathematics as a significant course of study leading to potential financial independence. The childbearing role affects values, beliefs, goals, and societal expectations and has complex behavioral consequences. With a 50% divorce rate, females may find themselves head of a single-parent household in poverty. In 1985, the typical female worker earned 24% to 45% less than the average male. A decision to have a child before being financially independent brings with it a high potential for poverty. Poverty may not be a consideration in the mind of the adolescent, but in reality it is a distinct possibility.

Childbearing and sexuality affect other areas of life. There are approximately 1.2 million teen pregnancies, with 500,000 births annually (Dryfoos, 1990). Before reaching age 18, one of every four girls will be sexually abused, with only 10% of these sexual assaults ever being reported (Archer, 1990). Girls are torn between the values of home and career (Archer, 1985a) and receive little support or counseling. All girls face pressure to focus on physical attractiveness, intimacy (reassessing the importance of academic achievement compared to intimacy), and family and peer relationships and values (developing skills to communicate individual values and request support) (Archer, 1990). In a society in which doing is rewarded (grades, athletic achievement, excellence in careers, and so forth), girls can justifiably be classified as disadvantaged because of their potential as childbearers.

Identity Development

Gender identity incorporates a "fundamental, existential sense of one's maleness or femaleness, an acceptance of one's gender as a social-psychological construction that parallels acceptance of one's biological sex" (Spence, 1984). The basic sense of female identity and development is based on self in the world and self in relation, while males push for independence and separation (Josselson, 1987). Gilligan (1982) states that females define themselves by what they are and in their relationship to others, while males define themselves in terms of what they do. Females appear to be more influenced by relationships, support, and approval than are males (Dryfoos, 1990).

Adolescents are usually in the identity statuses of diffusion or foreclosure (Archer, 1989). Neither status provides sufficient skills for the ongoing process of identity formation. As readiness occurs, intervention should be able to stimulate exploration and commitment so that adolescents move toward moratorium and achievement statuses. It is hoped that the individual will move toward personally expressive commitments by the increasing awareness of self and others and by experiencing exploration, separation, and individuation. A healthier and more satisfying life can be created through conscious choices and reflective compromises based on individual values made in a supportive environment.

If we believe that healthy identity requires the exploration of options, commitment to choices, the integration of new choices to previous decisions and vigilance to ongoing life changes, then we need to support curriculum that assist adolescents in obtaining these skills. Little psychological or physical evidence supports gender stereotyping. Because current definitions of gender role damage individuals, relationships, and society, it is imperative that we move beyond the belief that we have made dramatic changes to the reality of changing behaviors (Basow, 1980). Because gender roles are learned, they can be unlearned and redefined. By helping adolescents explore who they are, what they want, and where they are going, we can affect the formation of healthy identity development.

Based on research with adolescents, Adams (1990) and Archer (1985c) advise parents to select a curriculum and school that encourages debate, discussion, and analysis. Adams advises moderation in independent behavior, in giving and receiving all things, and also suggests that parents maintain strong communication, companionship, and affection without smothering the adolescent. Dryfoos (1990) recommends individualized instruction, early identification, and community-wide multiagency approaches.

The purpose of intervention is to provide youths with the skills needed to meet changing conditions so that they can form and redefine their selves (Archer, 1989). Psychologists identify the developmental tasks of adolescents to include the search for self-definition, the search for personal values, acquiring problem-solving and decision-making competencies, gaining social interaction skills, becoming emotionally independent of parents, achieving a balance between achievement and acceptance by peers, and experiencing a variety of behaviors, attitudes, and activities (Dryfoos, 1990).

Curricula Goals and Description

Bingham, Stryker, and Edmondson (Bingham, Edmondson, & Stryker, 1983, 1984; Bingham & Stryker, 1990) have written five texts[1] with community or teacher guides that explore self-awareness and life planning and have been utilized by more than half a million students in 50 states, Canada, Australia, the Netherlands, and foreign-based U.S. schools. The precareer awareness training known as Choices and Challenges, followed by the career and life-planning information in Career Choices and More Choices can guide the participants toward a fulfilling life. The curricula encourage students to:

- give serious thought to career choice,
- learn to live a balanced life,
- live the life of their choosing,
- strive for equal partnership in marriage,
- be more attentive to their relationships,
- choose to sacrifice neither career for the sake of family nor family for the sake of career, and
- find a true sense of self instead of a stifling stereotype.

Career Choices, More Choices, and Changes all offer additional curricula for self-emergence and definition. More Choices covers the need to plan family and careers with the understanding that the day only has 24 hours. Discussed in the journal are career and vocational opportunities from the point of view of part-time work, flexibility of work hours, hourly rates for various careers, and the importance of viewing selection in relationship to other life interests. Changes is the curriculum with additional budgetary information and a new chapter that deals with the impact of change. This text has been rewritten for the adult woman and is designed to work with Mother and Daughter Choices programs[2] or by itself. Career Choices is designed to help adolescents establish and consolidate their identity and combine action with their vision in order to achieve their life of choice. Career Choices can stand alone or be incorporated into many disciplines, notably language arts.

In the curricula, students see how their own expectations for the future may be self-limiting. The curricula is therapeutic and preventative by providing the individual with the experiences of questioning, confirming, and altering attitudes, behaviors, and knowledge. Whether in a group setting or individually, the participant has the opportunity to see the self in relation to others and to experience life in a fact-finding manner while reflecting on new awareness.

The Choices and Challenges curricula encourage participants to look at cultural messages by exploring fairy tales, television, advertising, and the words of significant others. Self-awareness and exploration are encouraged through activities that provide an opportunity for students to project into the future starting with today and concluding with age 60 by completing a chart that identifies where they live, their jobs and major activities, and their significant others. Students will refer back to this lesson for the purpose of evaluating choices and making new commitments.

Females discuss careers that both men and women select and how those selections affect salary, power, and control. Males explore balancing their lifestyles by looking at shared parenting, economic roles, and the health hazards of the male lifestyle.

Students explore the financial ramifications of life plans by evaluating a corresponding budget. They relate career choices to lifestyle dreams. It is hoped that when students see the high cost of living, they will reevaluate their financial needs and career choice. Individual values are assessed and applied to career, family, and life-activity goals. Through role-playing, interviews, and simulation activities, students explore the life-altering decision of parenting. Skills in assertiveness and decision making are emphasized throughout the curricula.

Uses and Limitations

It is difficult for any one curriculum to fulfill the needs of all adolescents. Adding culturally specific information would deepen the program's acceptance. Low-income individuals would feel more comfortable if broader financial parameters were included. Additional skills in managing stress would enhance the program. These areas could be included with a combination of workshops, speakers, and resources materials. The artwork is geared to middle-class children. Sexuality per se is not covered in depth and could be added (with parental support) or coordinated with other school or community programs. The journaling aspects and personal quality of the texts make it especially appealing. The texts become prized personal possessions.

The curricula have been used with many different populations and in many different formats. Penelope Paine, educational services director of Advocacy Press/Girls Incorporated of Santa Barbara, indicates that schools are incorporating Choices and Challenges into the ninth-grade freshman orientation program, home economics, career planning, alternative education, teen parenting program, family-life program, and existing curriculum with the support of guidance counselors. In the junior high school, home economics and guidance programs are typical locations. In vocational education programs, Choices and Challenges is being offered as a precareer awareness course through a multidisciplinary approach. Paine states that Career Choices is being infused into core curricula.

Parent-education programming could run simultaneously with Choices and Challenges classes or as periodic classes. We know the difficulty of effecting change when the adolescent must return to an environment that may be rigid or run by traditional family concepts. We know that parents are the first and primary teachers of core knowledge and that they continue to have power and influence in the child's life (Kenkel & Gage, 1983; Marini, 1978). Parent and teacher support can be significant influences for females' career choice (Farmer, 1985).

Rigorous research has not been done on the Choices curricula in its many forms. Longitudinal studies are needed to determine effectiveness. We do have anecdotal findings, evaluative information from Oregon and New Jersey, results from an evaluation of the Mother and Daughter Choices programs completed by the University of California at Santa Barbara, and interesting information from various surveys.

At San Marcos High School in San Diego County, California, 150 of 692 females students became pregnant during the 1983-84 academic year. A sex-education class was in place. One year after Choices was added as an intervention curriculum, there were only seven pregnancies. In Oregon, when 400 students were asked to evaluate the Choices and Challenges program, 85% stated that they felt it was very important. They documented increased self-awareness, career awareness, and decision-making skills. They noted that they learned the realities of what it takes to get a job, budgeting, and the importance of mathematics and science. This comprehensive program uses a multidisciplinary approach and outside resources.

New Jersey has more than 100 trained facilitators and has been funded through the State Department of Education, Division of Vocational Education, the American Association of University Women (AAUW), and currently by the Geraldine Dodge Foundation. The AAUW has used the Choices journals as a statewide project since 1986. Mother and Daughter Choices and Choices were the two formats followed. To date, more than 500 teenaged women have completed the program. Group and individual participant evaluations have indicated a desire to continue the program, viewing it as an experience of high value. Everyone appears to have different favorite lessons, with some finding certain lessons boring and others identifying the same lesson as the most interesting. The most and least favorite lesson was the budgeting chapter. Many found it depressing. Participants noted increased interest in mathematics and science.

Bieri has utilized Choices and Challenges in a high school in New Jersey. Four sections were offered for 18 weeks each. As a result, two female students changed academic schedules to reflect new career goals. One abrasively behaving male changed to a newly learned assertive behavior. Another male who initially felt he did not belong in this class stated, "I'm glad I stayed. I have so much in common with my classmates but I never knew it." Ten students purchased their own journals. Three students did not wish the class to end because it helped them stay focused on themselves and what they were doing. More than two thirds of the class decided that they would wait until they were financially able to have children. Some thought that parenthood was not right for them. One female student was surprised that she and her boyfriend had different values. Four students "eyed" a male classmate just as he had done to them and were pleased that he was somewhat embarrassed at the role reversal even though he stated, "It doesn't bother me." Bieri's students indicated that they valued the program. After completing the 18-week course, a ninth-grade female wrote:

> Not only is it fun, but it is very informative. Along with preparing myself for the future, it has helped me deal with the present. Learning how to see things in a different perspective was interesting. Before this class I had no idea of the direction of my future, now I have a career, life, and family goal, which should be exciting as I am trying to fulfill those goals. This class also made me less insecure, not to go along with whatever happens, but to do something about it. I think the one, most important thing I got out of this class was the valuable ability to think logically about what is going on around me. Also dealing with everything, because I've learned that just because I have a problem, time does not stop. I am much more careful with relationships, now that I've realized the mistakes I made. I feel, that of any course I could ever take, I got the most out of Choices and Challenges.

Denise D. Bielby and C. Lee Harrington, sociologists from the University of California at Santa Barbara, completed a program evaluation of the Mother and Daughter Choices project. Data were collected regionally and supplemented with findings at the national level. The report looked at attitudinal changes, confidence in gender-role performance, educational aspirations, life plans, and related issues for mothers and daughters. Their findings indicate that a girl's perceptions of efficacy in her roles of wife, parent, and worker increased significantly. Almost all participants felt that the mother-daughter relationship was enhanced, although they were already fairly progressive in their gender-role attitudes. Girls became more realistic in their educational aspirations. As with New Jersey participants, budgeting was the most and least favorite lesson. Bielby and Harrington found that 50% of all girls felt that participation in the Choices program had significantly altered their lives. Nearly 84% of participating mothers reported that their own lives would have been significantly altered if the program had been available to them. Approximately 97% of the participating mothers would recommend "without reservation" the Choices program to a close friend and would join a women's service organization that worked for women's rights.

The mother and daughter format has been completed in several programs, including mother and son, father and daughter, and father and son. Linda Wagner, the national coordinator for the program has found that mother and son is more effective in the seventh and eighth grades.

She found that the mothers wanted to dominate the conversation and that sexuality, dating, passive-aggressive behavior, and "Being a Man Isn't Always Easy" were not well handled. In father and daughter programs, the fathers wanted to fill out the mathematics problems and had difficulty discussing passive behavior. The girls blamed themselves, while the fathers blamed external forces. According to Wagner, the father and son programs easily dissolved into "macho stuff," with a refusal to discuss "Being a Man Isn't Always Easy." Wagner believes that to enhance communication, male groups should be smaller in number and female groups should be larger. In female groups, she noted, women tell all in 10 minutes, while men objectify without getting personal.

Other Curricula

What else is being offered in gender curricula? Some schools infuse career information in academic and elective classes and offer career days, college fairs, or opportunities to shadow a local businessperson. Health classes may incorporate family-life education (marriage and parenting) with sex education, including physical and mental health. Mandatory family-life classes are being taught by physical education or health teachers who may or may not want to teach these subjects and who have no educational background to provide a quality program. There are, of course, many youth development programs such as the Association of Junior Leagues' Teen Outreach program (a teen-pregnancy prevention program), the sex-equity programs such as Achieving Sex Equity Through Students (ASETS) and Gender and Ethnic Expectations and Student Achievement (GESA) that address many gender issues. There are also curricula available such as the *Life Planning Education Program,* which focuses on career preparation and sexuality. Published by the Center for Population Options, this program uses activities from the Choices texts.

Conclusions

If both sexes continue to depend on females for the care of the home and family, and females continue to depend on males for their financial security (Tittle, 1981), then we can expect the economic and life satisfaction crises we are now experiencing to continue. We can expect poverty or dependency to be the typical consequence of divorce for women and children. We can expect males and females to be in conflict or submission over roles and to experience a lack of intimacy in their relationship because of shortages in energy, time, and communication. We can also expect females to continue to be confused as they attempt to sort out their conflicting roles in a world that now requires them to be financially independent. According to Okin (1989), a just society must include women and their points of view as well as men and their points of view, thereby providing the same opportunities to develop capacities, participate in political power, influence social change, and be secure physically and economically. She states that if justice and reciprocity do not exist in the family, then our children will be hindered in becoming people. The sharing of roles will create the opportunity for understanding the viewpoints of others. This understanding may eliminate careless sexual behavior, the need for single-parent nurturance of children, and unequal incomes and it may enhance identity development and the broadening of human experience (Okin, 1989).

The future will require the cooperation of men and women (Miles, 1989), making it essential to understand the history of how male and female roles were determined. Thompson (1988) proposes a move from gender roles to two systems of human interaction shared by men and women. The private primal system is the changing institution of the family. The public and workplace arena is characterized by group process, hierarchy, and control. The problem in our society is that we have failed to make a commitment to assisting youths in understanding the importance of life planning for all individuals regardless of their childbearing role.

Using this type of curricula enables the students to experience personal power in the design of their lives. The positive feedback indicates that this type of program fills an important role in the lives of males and females. Offering gender curricula while attentively looking for the teachable moment seems to be the wisest of choices.

Longitudinal studies are needed to clarify, quantify, and qualify our final achievements. A joint coalition is needed to truly affect youths, one in which the curriculum creators, practitioners, researchers, and youths design reliable methods and language for evaluating identity formation in its complexity. The final analysis will come from the individuals' evaluation of the quality of their lives. Let us hope that the work we do today provides sufficiently for those who are ready for our efforts.

Notes

1. All Choices texts (*Choices, More Choices, Challenges, Changes, Career Choices,* and teachers' guides) can be obtained through Academic Innovations, 3463 State Street, Suite 230, Santa Barbara, CA 93105; (805) 967-8015.

2. Mother and Daughter Choices was originally funded in 1987 by the Lilly Endowment, Inc., of Indianapolis, Indiana.

References

Adams, G. A. (1990). *Certain environmental factors aid teens in identity growth* [Machine-readable data file, Utah State University, producer, PENN pages No. 085071651]. University Park: Pennsylvania State University.

Archer, S. L. (1985a). Career and/or family: The identity process for adolescent girls. *Youth & Society, 16,* 289-314.

Archer, S. L. (1985b). Identity and social roles. In A. S. Waterman (Ed.), *Identity in adolescence: Processes and contents* (pp. 79-100). San Francisco: Jossey-Bass.

Archer, S. L. (1985c). *Reflections on earlier life decisions: Implications for adult functioning.* Paper presented at April meeting of Society for Research in Child Development, Toronto, Canada.

Archer, S. L. (1989). The status of identity: Reflections on the need for intervention. *Journal of Adolescence, 12,* 345-359.

Archer, S. L. (1990). Females at risk: Identity issues for adolescents and divorced women. In C. Vandenplas Holper & B. P. Campos (Eds.), *Interpersonal and identity development: New perspectives* (pp. 87-102). Porto, Portugal: Instituto de Consulta Psicologica, Formacao e Desenvolvimento.

Basow, S. (1980). *Sex role stereotypes: Traditions and alternatives.* Belmont, CA: Brooks/Cole.

Bingham, M., & Stryker, S. (1990). *Career choices: A guide for teens and young adults. Who am I? What do I want? How do I get it?* Santa Barbara, CA: Able.

Bingham, M., Edmondson, J., & Stryker, S. (1983). *Choices—A teen woman's journal for self-awareness and personal planning.* Santa Barbara, CA: Advocacy Press.

Bingham, M., Edmondson, J., & Stryker, S. (1984). *Challenges—A teen man's journal for self-awareness and personal planning.* Santa Barbara, CA: Advocacy Press.

Block, J. H. (1984). *Sex identity and ego development.* San Francisco: Jossey-Bass.

Brannon, R. C. (1976). No "sissy stuff": The stigma of anything vaguely feminine. In D. David & R. Brannon (Eds.), *The forty-nine percent majority* (p. 12). Reading, MA: Addison-Wesley.

Brush, S. G. (1991). Women in science and engineering. *American Scientist, 79*(5), 404-419.

Dryfoos, J. G. (1990). *Adolescents at risk.* New York: Oxford University Press.

Erb, T. O. (1983). Career preferences of early adolescents. *Journal of Early Adolescence, 3*(4), 349-359.

Farmer, H. S. (1985). The role of typical female characteristics in career and achievement motivation. *Youth & Society, 16,* 279-314.

Firebaugh, F. M. (1991). Families in transition: A global perspective. *Journal of Home Economics, 83*(3), 44-50.

Friedan, B. (1986). *The second stage.* New York: Summit.

Gilligan, C. (1982). *In a different voice.* Cambridge, MA: Harvard University Press.

Harrison, J., Chin, J., & Ficarrotto, T. (1992). Men and health: Body and mind. In M. Kimmel & M. Messner (Eds.), *Men's lives* (pp. 271-285). New York: Macmillan.

Josselson, R. (1987). *Finding herself.* San Francisco: Jossey-Bass.

Jourard, S. (1971). *The transparent self.* New York: Van Nostrand Reinhold.

Kenkel, W. F., & Gage, B. A. (1983). *Sex role attitudes among high school seniors: Views about work and family roles* (ISR report). Ann Arbor: University of Michigan.

Lantz, A. E., & Smith, G. P. (1981). Factors influencing the choice of nonrequired mathematics courses. *Journal of Educational Psychology, 73*(6), 825-837.

LaRossa, R. (1992). Fatherhood and social change. In M. Kimmel & M. Messner (Eds.), *Men's lives* (pp. 521-535). New York: Macmillan.

Marini, M. M. (1978). Sex differences in the determination of adolescent aspirations: A review of research. *Sex Roles, 4*(5), 723-753.

Miles, R. (1989). *The women's history of the world.* New York: Harper & Row.

Okin, S. M. (1989). *Justice, gender and the family in the United States.* New York: Basic Books.

Rubin, L. (1992). The approach-avoidance dance. In M. Kimmel & M. Messner (Eds.), *Men's lives* (pp. 335-340). New York: Macmillan.

Spence, J. T. (1984). Masculinity, femininity, and gender-related traits: A conceptual analysis and critique of current research. *Progress in Experimental Personality Research, 13,* 84.

Surrey, J. L. (1991). Relationship and empowerment. In J. V. Jordan, A. G. Kaplan, J. B. Miller, I. P. Stiver, & J. L. Surrey (Eds.), *Women's growth in connection* (pp. 162-180). New York: Guilford.

Tavris, C., & Baumgartner, A. I. (1983, February). How would your life be different if you'd been born a boy? *Redbook,* pp. 92-95.

Thompson, C. (1991). We should reject traditional masculinity. In K. Thompson (Ed.), *To be a man—In search of the deep masculine* (pp. 4-10). Los Angeles: Jeremy P. Tarcher.

Thompson, P. (1988). *Home economics and feminism: The Hestian synthesis.* Prince Edward Island, Canada: Home Economics Publishing Collective.

Tittle, C. (1981). *Careers and family: Sex roles and adolescent life plans.* Beverly Hills, CA: Sage.

Vetter, L. (1985). Stability and change in the enrollment of girls and young women in vocational education: 1971-1980. *Youth & Society, 16,* 335-356.

10

Identity and the Career
Counseling of Adolescents

The Development of Vocational Identity

PATRICIA M. RASKIN

During adolescence, as in adulthood, the course of vocational development parallels other developmental systems. Just as the adolescent is
unsure of religious, ideological, and sexual aspects of identity, so
vocational choice is unclear. Developmental stage is also related to
self-concept and personality. Indeed, Super (1984), Ginzberg, Ginsburg,
Axelrad, and Herma (1951), Gottfredson (1981), Gribbons and Lohnes
(1968, 1982), and Knefelkamp and Slepitza (1976) described their
theories as explicitly developmental, while Tiedeman (1961) and his
associates (Dudley & Tiedeman, 1977; Peatling & Tiedeman, 1977;
Tiedeman & Miller-Tiedeman, 1984) credited Erikson specifically for
their theoretical approaches—that is, there are sequential enumerated
stage-specific vocational-development tasks. Jepsen (1984) has reviewed
the literature explicating the vocational developmental perspective, and
Gelso and Fassinger (1992) have summarized these various approaches
as addressing "the implementation of the self-concept as the individual
moves through developmental stages defined by particular life roles"
(p. 279). Others have specifically addressed the issue of the interaction
between vocational development and other aspects of the emerging self,

calling for a paradigm that incorporates the dynamic interactional perspective. Vondracek, Lerner, and Schulenberg (1983) described dynamic interaction as incorporating "a recognition of the fact that complex, multidirectional relations exist between an individual and [his or her] context, and that changes in one of the multiple sources of development . . . will influence changes in all others" (p. 187). Grotevant (1987) suggested that identity formation occurs in at least four social contexts: culture and society, family, peers, school and work. Furthermore, the individual characteristics of personality, cognitive ability, and current identity interact with these contexts, which are themselves shaped by individuals' choices. Taken together, both individual characteristics and social contexts influence and are influenced by the identity-formation process within, between, and among identity domains (occupation and ideology).

The purpose of this chapter, then, is to bring together some of what is known about identity formation, especially in the occupational domain, and its potential relationship to career counseling.

The Vocational Tasks of Adolescence

Exploration and Tentative Choice

From a vocational developmental point of view, the task of adolescence is not identity formation per se, but exploration and tentative choice. Until recently, only Jordaan (1963) focused on the exploratory process, but he did so in the context of making occupational choices rather than forming identity. Grotevant (1987) has drawn the connection, suggesting further that exploration as an element of identity formation is probably gradual and more relational than has been thought. Once exploration is conceived of in this way, it is easier to see the interaction between exploration and commitment. Exploratory behavior yields information about the work environment, the work itself, work-related interpersonal relationships, and the self in relation to work, including one's abilities, interests, and values. The more successful these early forays are into the world of work, the more likely they are to lead to certainty about an occupation and also a confidence in one's ability to get information, do the work, and succeed; this creates a sense of self-efficacy that is likely to result in the capacity to make first tentative and then firmer commitments. (For instance, see Berzonsky, Rice, & Neimeyer, 1990; Blustein, Ellis, & Devenis, 1989.)

Gender, Ethnicity, and Class

Gender

Erikson (1956) made the point that occupational choice was perhaps the most salient feature of an adult (male's) identity, and that confusion and doubt in this realm is particularly unsettling. Seen in this light, the unanswered questions about gender, ethnicity, and identity become more explicit. Do girls have different experiences in school and at work than boys? Despite girls' perceptions, when compared with boys' perceptions, that their paid work is more psychologically meaningful, girls tend to be paid less and to be seen as having less-complex jobs, even when this observation is questionable (Mortimer, Finch, Owens, & Shanahan, 1990). Do girls then, as Archer (1989) suggested, engage in the identity-formation process in the occupational domain differently than boys? In a case narrative, Archer (1989) demonstrated the dilemma: A young woman choosing a nontraditional major may not be deciding in the occupational domain alone; such a choice might result in a sense of interpersonal isolation that also spans the political, sex-role, and family and career domains.

Ethnicity

Do adolescents of color experience the world of work similarly to white adolescents? There is evidence that they do not, at least when given "standard" career maturity measures (Omvig & Thomas, 1977; Smith & Herr, 1972; Westbrook, Cutts, Madison, & Arcia, 1980). Westbrook and Sanford (1991) obtained similar findings. It is clear that African-American adolescents develop in a much more complex environment than do white adolescents, and Rotheram-Borus (1989) went so far as to suggest that identity-focused interventions with these adolescents might address this component of identity formation rather than other domains.

Class

There is no doubt that the historically disenfranchised view the occupational opportunity structure with somewhat more cynicism and perhaps a healthy skepticism about the importance of "career" to their lives. Newlan and Haase (1982) pointed out that when daily survival is at stake, future orientation is meaningless. Yet the consideration of occupational alternatives remains important to the achievement of identity and must be attended to in all adolescents. A considerable amount of research on the vocational development of white middle-class adolescents has been conducted, including at least three long-term longitudinal studies (Ginzberg et al., 1951; Gribbons & Lohnes, 1982; Jordaan & Heyde, 1979). Each researcher has identified specific tasks whose completion leads to "satisfactory" occupational choice. (As the quotes indicate, the term is hard to define. Researchers have defined career satisfaction in a variety of ways, using a variety of measures.) Jordaan (1963) has demonstrated the relation between early occupational exploration and later career satisfaction, while other researchers have focused on vocational maturity (Crites, 1978), style of decision making (Pitz & Harren, 1980), level of aspiration (Nafziger, Holland, Helms, & McPartland, 1974), commitment (Blau, 1988; Gottfredson, 1981), and nonpsychological variables to account for occupational choice and satisfaction. Blustein, Ellis, and Devenis (1989) explored the sequence and means by which career commitment occurs. Although little empirical research has been done on the relationship between identity formation and career development (Harmon & Farmer, 1983), some evidence suggests that such a relationship exists (Archer & Waterman, 1993; Blustein, Devenis, & Kidney, 1989; Fannin, 1979; Munley, 1975; Savickas, 1985). Indeed, Berzonsky and Neimeyer (1988), although not explicitly investigating this relationship, did find that information-oriented self-exploration was relevant to identity formation. There are no data to suggest that these findings are applicable to populations with more constricted opportunity. It is likely that true individual occupational choice can occur only when an array of potentially and equally attractive options exists. The implicit but unwarranted assumption of this research is that occupational choice occurs at all levels of socioeconomic status. As Hamilton and Powers (1990) noted, however, "Working-class youth do not choose careers; they find jobs" (p. 246). As we think about career interventions, it would serve us well to consider those designed specifically for non-college-bound adolescents as well as our traditional clientele.

Other Factors Related to Vocational Identity

Buehler (1933, in Super, 1957), Super (1957), and Gottfredson (1981) specifically addressed the importance of self-concept to vocational choice, suggesting that what one chooses for one's life's work is a reflection of

self-awareness, self-esteem, and deeply held values. Roe (1956) believed that unconscious motivation drives career choice and that individuals choose careers to satisfy id and ego demands in a sublimated
way. Parsons (1909), Holland (1966), and their followers have posited
that when personality types are matched with occupations congenial to
those types, career satisfaction is more likely than when there is a
mismatch of type and occupation. It is important to note that although
vocational identity formation is an aspect of identity formation as a
whole, individual and environmental variables quite independent of this
psychosocial process may account for much of the variance in occupational choice and commitment.

Vocational Interventions

Because it has been shown that there are variables that can be related
to career choice and satisfaction, it makes sense to see if one can design
interventions based on these findings that might improve the quality of
individual career choice and subsequent work-derived satisfaction. As
Herr and Cramer (1988) have observed, however, little of this basic
research has been sufficiently replicated or diversified to result in the
development of systematic models of intervention. When forms of
career assistance have been developed and evaluated, however, these
materials and techniques have seemed promising. The Guided Career
Exploration Program (Super & Bowlesbey, 1979) is an example of a
structured intervention designed specifically to enhance exploration.
According to Holland, Magoon, and Spokane (1981), "The beneficial
effects are due to the common elements in these divergent treatments:
(a) exposure to occupational information; (b) cognitive rehearsal of
vocational aspirations; (c) acquisition of some cognitive structure for
organizing information about self, occupations, and their relations; and
(d) social support or reinforcement from counselors or workshop members" (p. 285). Spokane and Oliver (1983) were able to document these
observations in a metaanalysis, and Blustein, Ellis, and Devenis (1989)
found that a career-development intervention did result in lower scores
on a tendency to foreclose scale. It can be seen that each element is
represented in the process of forming identity: Without occupational
information no exploration, no future projection can occur. The active
acquisition of data, trying out occupational roles, and expressing intentions

are key elements of moratorium, the essential crisis needed to at least consider committing to an occupational identity.

The Identity-Status Model as a
Career-Counseling Intervention

Within a developmental framework it is thus useful to consider the identity-status paradigm for assessment and intervention purposes. The model allows the counselor to determine not only the presence or absence of doubt and commitment, but also the cognitive process that has occurred to date. One can see, for instance, whether an adolescent has not yet begun or has apparently completed a choice process and the degree of comfort with either uncertainty or commitment. At the same time, one also can gather substantive data about the amount, realism, and nature of the occupational information held by the client—an important aspect to answering the questions basic to vocational counseling: Why does this client need my help in choosing a career? How much does he or she know already? What is it about this particular time and context in the client's life that is suggesting that now is the right time to get help?

It is important to note, however, that for this model to be effective in career development, counselors must be knowledgeable about vocational psychology. Even though the identity-status model is designed to assess psychological process, its usefulness as an intervention is tied to the substantive content of that process. Counselors need to be able to discriminate between the need to give vocational information, to elicit exploratory behavior on the part of the client, to do specific vocational assessment, and to help the client increase self-awareness. It is in the two counseling formats, individual and group, that the potential for using what we know about identity status becomes most feasible. Professional counselors are trained to think in developmental ways, are focused on individual differences, and are skilled in the communication techniques that would facilitate the use of identity-status instruments in both individual and group counseling formats.

Preadolescence

For the moment, let us assume that the most likely context for career counseling occurs within the school. In elementary school, little career counseling per se is done. Interventions are systemwide secondary preventions (Caplan, 1964). Occupational information is typically infused into the curriculum, and the goals of career guidance tend to be focused on helping students acquire a sense of industry (Vondracek, 1993) and learn that (a) understanding one's strengths, values, and preferences is the foundation for education and occupational choices; (b) goal attainment requires planning; (c) they have the competence to choose and achieve educational and occupational goals; (d) change occurs and that it may have implications for future options; and (e) problem-solving skills and personal decision-making skills are similar (Herr & Cramer, 1988). Little individual career counseling is systematically undertaken, but guidance personnel might get involved in some group process that takes place in the classroom. At this level, the foundation is laid for future exploration and commitment, although it is rare that seriously considered lifelong choices are made at this time.

Junior High or Middle School

Differences among individuals are great in this age group. Some seventh graders look like their sixth-grade peers, whereas others mature early and more nearly resemble their high school peers. Certainly the differences between seventh and ninth graders are profound, and physiological changes seem to occur almost overnight in some boys and girls. In the cognitive domain, these early adolescents are more able to understand relationships and abstractions than they were before. In the social domain, the need to belong, conform, and solidify same-sex relationships predominates. Career-guidance goals for this group of students can include (a) understanding decision-making skills, (b) learning to cope with transition, (c) becoming informed about and prepared for alternative and vocational choices, (d) relating personal interests to occupational areas, (e) learning conflict management, (f) attaining realistic self-understanding, and (g) learning to manage work and leisure (Herr & Cramer, 1988). Career education continues to be infused into the curriculum, but group counseling per se becomes more likely. Counselors are sometimes invited into the classroom specifically to address the goals of learning about decision making and getting occupational information. Individual counseling also becomes more common because students must make crucial educational decisions (such as science versus nonscience) as early as the eighth grade. At this level, career counselors need to be well informed about intergroup differences and the differential messages sent to girls and children of color regarding expectations of performance and success.

Group Interventions

"Group counseling and classroom discussion groups help children begin exploring their ambitions and dreams; to discover their own similarities and differences; to enlarge their repertoire of human relation skills; and to adapt to [an] ever-enlarging environment" (Ohlsen, Horne, & Lawe, 1988, p. 251). Although it is possible that middle school students can be assigned to any of the four identity statuses in the occupational domain, it is likely that students in the middle school would modally be classified as precrisis diffuse or foreclosed. At this age, students need to be reassured that wherever they are in their individual development, their questions are relevant, and they need to be encouraged to seek occupational information to help them with later decision making. Aspects of the identity-status interview in a group can be used to model questioning and data gathering as well as to facilitate peer relationships in the exploration of those questions. Marcia (1989) has suggested that adults provide safety, structure, facilitation, and some direction in groups, while peers provide reality and relevance.

Individual Interventions

The meaning of past crisis. It is unlikely that "crisis" or an active decision-making period has much current meaning in this age range. Junior high school students have not really had the opportunity to try out occupational roles, or even to observe many directly. We note, however, that there is great variability among early adolescents in the amount of thinking done about work roles or aspects of occupational identity. Thus in assessing past crisis, it is important to remember that although responses may be simplistic in the younger adolescents, four of the five criteria used in assessing crisis are present: knowledgeability, activity, consideration of alternative potential identity elements, and emotional tone. Desire to make an early decision is not realistic in this age group because implementation still seems quite distant (Archer, in Marcia, Waterman, Matteson, Archer, & Orlofsky, 1993).

The meaning of present crisis. For middle school students, crisis in the occupational domain can be observed when a career seems attractive but others also look interesting. Archer (in Marcia et al., 1993) is careful to delineate the difference between alternative foreclosed options and real decision-making activity. Experts in career development suggest that what is most crucial for this age group is engaging in as much exploration as possible, although there can be many forms of exploration. To meet the criterion of present crisis, there has to be some evidence of activity occurring in more than one occupational or educational arena. Present crisis can often be seen in eighth grade, when curriculum tracking occurs. In that case, desire to make an early decision may be present, so that all five criteria may be applied.

The meaning of commitment. According to Archer (in Marcia et al., 1993), six criteria are used to ascertain the presence of commitment: knowledgeability, activity, emotional tone, identification with significant others, projection into one's personal future, and resistance to being swayed. In junior high school, the clearest case for commitment can be found in the foreclosed individual who is firmly convinced that his or her parent's occupation is the one and only one of interest. It is important to remember that direct experience with the occupation is not a necessary criterion, because true exposure to adult career forms is unlikely to have occurred at this juncture. Baby-sitting, for instance, does not truly represent a career in either child care or education; delivering newspapers does not represent journalism, although working on the school newspaper might. Nevertheless, all three activities "count" toward the assessment of commitment.

The intervention. The goal of the intervention at this point in an individual's educational and occupational development is to open doors. Students who begin as precrisis diffuse are in a good position to explore themselves and the world of work, while those who can be assessed as still foreclosed can be assisted in exploring arenas not yet considered. It is not unusual to find junior high school boys who know all there is to know about baseball, dinosaurs, ant farms, or the solar system. Each boy can say with confidence that he is going to enter a career relevant to those interests, and yet we know that as they all mature, they might come to different conclusions. The key here is to encourage exposure to a more varied world without denigrating the beloved activity, for it is in that activity that the sense of competence, mastery, and self-esteem now rest. Creative interventions may initially involve the exploration of occupations that are ancillary to the area of interest, providing a natural extension of the exploration.

Senior High School

In these grades, students continue to vary enormously with respect to physical, social, and emotional maturity; and they also begin to vary with respect to their work experiences, career development, and need for career counseling. Some students will be selecting the next phase of their education, others will be choosing postsecondary technical training, while others will be entering the labor force full-time. Military service, marriage, financial constraints, and opportunities are factors that might be considered within the context of career choice, and the realities of our society's opportunity structure begin to play an increasingly important role in the student's life. Goals for career guidance in the senior high school are likely to include specific planning and gaining an increasing awareness of life roles, and career exploration is likely to include more experiential elements and opportunities for reality-testing than in the prior years. At the same time, choices begin to have more consequences as well. Choosing one kind of college or university might preclude certain post-graduate opportunities, while failing to make choices also becomes more consequential. There is evidence to suggest (Waterman, 1985) that identity activity at this juncture can be quite sophisticated. By high school, individual counseling sessions are expected. Counselors become actively involved in helping with post high school planning, and they continue to play an active role in the classroom. Many adolescents are in active crisis by this time, nervous about ruling out options but aware that some preliminary choices may have that effect. Goals of counseling at this level are to help students test reality, obtain information, engage in self-assessment, and do some preliminary planning.

Group Interventions

By this time, most students have been sufficiently exposed to career information and guidance services that the question of tentative occupational choice has been raised. Some students will still be precrisis diffuse or foreclosed, but many will be classified as moratorium or even achieved. Group counseling with this age group can help students define meaningful goals, increase self-understanding, identify opportunities, improve interpersonal skills, and develop the self-confidence necessary to explore and take risks in the occupational realm.

Individual Interventions

The meaning of past crisis. By this time, it is conceivable that individuals have met the criteria for the presence of past crisis. Previous foreclosed choices may have been called into question, and there may have been some anxiety or at least some focused future-oriented thought associated with educational decisions made in junior high school.

The meaning of present crisis. By one's sophomore year, a fair amount of attention and energy is devoted to self-assessment. The external performance pressures generated by standardized testing, the selection decisions necessary for further education and training, and the focus on peers and competition provide ample stimulation for a true period of moratorium. All five criteria for current crisis can be expected to be present, and the level of complexity is much greater than at earlier periods.

The meaning of commitment. Commitment in high school looks more like adult commitment than at any previous developmental stage. Whether an aspect of foreclosed or achieved identity, commitment tends to be based on some real information, and exploration appropriate to the adult form of the occupation is present. An awareness of the fact that alternatives have been permanently jettisoned can be expressed, although in some cases one wonders whether the individual truly understands the impact of narrowing one's options at this point in life.

The intervention. Although there are some careers that require early commitment, such as dance, music, and athletics, it is usually appropriate to engage in further focused exploration based on interests and abilities. It is not premature to commit to further education, but it may be premature to specialize beyond broad areas of interest. Choosing to go to an art school rather than a university with an art department, or a nursing diploma rather than a degree program, ought to be the result of an extensive and thoughtful exploration, because it is so difficult to change course once one has embarked on such specialized training. The intervention, therefore, with those who are foreclosed might be to test the limits of the commitment.

Students who can be categorized as moratorium need to be helped to obtain relevant occupational information and experience, and they must be supported in the postponement of decision, despite discomfort, until sufficient data are obtained. Individuals in the moratorium status are easily influenced (Donovan, 1975; Josselson, 1973; Radin, 1978), and because indecision is uncomfortable, they can sometimes be seduced into making premature career choices that sound good and postpone action. For example, a high school senior might say that she is going to be a lawyer but she has neither actively chosen prelaw as a college major nor has any true understanding of the substance of the preparation. But because the path to a legal career is clear, there is enormous appeal for the undecided student.

Precrisis diffuse students can be helped to raise appropriate questions because inactivity in this period can result in poor choice or career events that may occur by default. The status assignment of postcrisis diffusion to a high school student would be unusual and probably diagnostic. High school students are not normally apathetic about their futures, and thus it would be important to rule out depression, substance abuse, or another pathology in students so categorized (Donovan, 1975; Josselson, 1973; Radin, 1978; Raskin, 1989).

Those students who are identity-achieved can best be supported by the encouragement of continued awareness of other career options, as well as experience in the chosen occupation. It is important, for instance, for those high school students who have selected direct-delivery health care occupations to have real "hands on" experience with patients at this point, even if it is not paid work. The classification, in fact, of identity achievement at this age is somewhat unusual and slightly suspect, although possible.

College

In college, counselors continue to play an active role, although they are less likely to be directly involved in classes. Students may be assigned to counselors or faculty members for academic advisement; career planning and placement centers are likely to offer group career-planning sessions, and it is not unusual for workshops or career seminars to be offered by residence hall staffs and student organizations. Peer counseling is usually available, and these student counselors are at least trained in communication skills. There are three primary choice points during the college years, although individuals may seek career counseling at any point in their individual experience. The first opportunity students have to make vocational decisions is on entry. Counseling center staffs regularly "test" freshmen (e.g., give interest and value inventories, personality measures, and sometimes aptitude tests) as part of an orientation program designed to help incoming students become familiar with the campus and its services; testing specifically introduces them to advisors. In many cases, students see counselors until they choose a major, at which point advisement devolves onto academic faculty. The second choice point occurs during the last semester of the sophomore year. By this time, students are expected to declare majors if they have not already done so and to begin to narrow educational goals. The third point occurs at the beginning of the senior year, when students participate in on- and off-campus placement activities or apply to graduate or professional schools. The goals, then, for career guidance in college can be summarized as helping students (a) select major fields of study, (b) become more skilled at self-assessment and self-analysis, (c) understand the world of work, and (d) become skilled at decision making (Herr & Cramer, 1988).

Group Interventions

By late adolescence, all of the identity statuses are represented in the occupational domain. Representation in the moratorium status tends to increase, especially at choice points, as does identity achievement. One way to use the identity-status paradigm is to form heterogeneous status groupings for discussion. Here is an instance where students who are more advanced along the developmental continuum can assist those who are less advanced, not necessarily in making occupational decisions but by being articulate about the process. The identity-status interview could be given by group members to one another, and the scoring manual might be presented thereafter for discussion. Group counseling sessions and psychology classes are appropriate formats for this kind of intervention, because it is wise to ensure the presence of trained professionals in these groups.

Individual Interventions

The meaning of past crisis, present crisis, and commitment. Although not all college students have actively thought about their careers by this time, a large proportion of them have. College students are capable of articulating both the process and substance of this activity, and one can see by the comfort level whether it is in the recent past or still present. In a longitudinal study of college students, Waterman and Goldman (1976) found, however, that if a crisis had occurred in the freshman year, it was sometimes forgotten by the senior year. Moratorium is never more clear than in college students. Options are available, and decisions have to be made. One has to be careful, however, to look for active data seeking; mere indecision does not constitute present crisis. When students are committed to a career, they can describe it accurately and articulate how their interests, abilities, and values coincide with the occupation's requirements; it seems clear that the student has thought about how his or her self-concept can be implemented at work.

The intervention. It is unlikely that college counselors will see committed students for career counseling for other reasons than early academic advisement, placement, and assistance with graduate school. But when an external event threatens the committed position (e.g., a foreclosed premed student fails chemistry), the counseling approach needs to include a period of mourning for the "lost" career because it often represents an unwanted separation from a parental object. In these circumstances, counselors need to help clients mourn as they explore careers that are related to the original goal as well as careers that might develop from subsidiary interests (e.g., medical journalism as well as direct-delivery health care occupations).

Moratorium students can be assisted in much the way as high school students, although college often provides a richer environment for exploration. In college, students who are classified in this status may become intensely involved in a subject taught by a particularly engaging professor. It is not unusual to see a student make an apparently overnight decision when this happens. Although a healthy skepticism about the quality of the decision is not unwarranted, it is also possible that part of the appeal of the subject matter is that it just "clicks," bringing about a consolidation of previously nonintegrated career elements, even though this cannot be clearly articulated by the student.

Both pre- and postcrisis diffusion students need help with motivation before a good career decision can be made. Counselors need to explore the nature of the inhibition here and to assess how career issues interact with other aspects of the student's life. Once again, diffusion in the occupational realm should not be underestimated as a diagnostic indicator, especially for postcrisis diffusion.

Community Organizations

It is important to note that although the majority of organized career interventions take place in school, the larger local community can be attentive to the need for such interventions as well. Early jobs have been found to play a role in vocational development (Jordaan & Super, 1974; Super & Overstreet, 1960). In 1973, the President's Science Advisory Committee noted that when young people are excluded from the workplace, deficits in learning from elders might occur, and the committee suggested that the community is an appropriate setting to help young people make the transition to adulthood. Greenberger and Steinberg (1986) concluded that student employment might not assist in these ways, but Hamilton and Powers (1990) suggested that school-sponsored cooperative education and employment in a family business might. Volunteer work—in a social service capacity, for example—can have a similar effect, as can experience-based career education (e.g., "shadowing") and mentoring (Hamilton & Powers, 1990). Libraries, youth programs (such as those organized by local "Y"s), and religious organizations sometimes provide contexts within which both formal and informal career counseling can occur. Public libraries maintain career information files at the very least and thus become excellent sources for occupational information, while youth programs, churches, and synagogues as gathering places for teenagers provide natural arenas for the informal discussion of life after school. The workplace also is a potentially good source of career information, although the quality of these data tend to be highly variable. Community employment is primarily a middle-class phenomenon (Greenberger & Steinberg, 1986). Government-sponsored interventions (secondary preventions) might assist at-risk youth with vocational development as well.

Conclusion

For the most part, helping professionals who engage in vocational counseling at all levels at least say they are developmentally focused. Because the identity-status paradigm is based on a comprehensive developmental theory (Erikson, 1968; Marcia, 1980; Waterman, 1982), it may help to sharpen that focus and promote dynamic interactional thinking in career counseling especially in work with adolescents. The structure of the interview is such that it can be used as an assessment device in addition to standard vocational batteries to enhance both counselor and client understanding of the role of vocational development in the client's internal and external worlds in a nonthreatening informative way. As Archer (1989) has noted, sophisticated identity has been correlated with desirable psychological variables. If the purpose of identity intervention (Archer, 1989; Waterman, 1989) is to enhance youths' ability to become conscious of, develop, and refine their sense of self, choice, and commitment in all domains, then career counseling is certainly appropriate. The work environment, broadly conceived, tends to dominate most of our waking moments, and sometimes our occupational identity is seen as *the* defining characteristic of the self. We have known for some time that it is possible to engage in interventions that result in greater maturation and increased psychological differentiation (Mosher & Sprinthall, 1971; Sprinthall & Mosher, 1969, 1971), and, as is becoming clear in the literature, interventions do have the potential to influence and be influenced by their target populations. Career counseling is first and usually tertiary prevention, but when applied in a school system, it also can be seen as secondary. Marcia (1989) has pointed out that psychologists are usually not good at influencing social policy, but education is always under scrutiny in this country. Perhaps career counselors in their role as education professionals using sound career-counseling principles can subtly influence primary prevention as well.

References

Archer, S. L. (1989). The status of identity: Reflections on the need for intervention. *Journal of Adolescence, 12,* 345-359.

Archer, S. L., & Waterman, A. S. (1993). *Identity activity among college and working youth.* Unpublished manuscript.

Berzonsky, M. D., & Neimeyer, G. J. (1988). Identity status and personal construct systems. *Journal of Adolescence, 11,* 195-204.

Berzonsky, M. D., Rice, K. G., & Neimeyer, G. J. (1990). Identity status and self-construct systems: Person × structure interactions. *Journal of Adolescence, 13,* 251-263.

Blau, G. L. (1988). Further exploring the meaning and measurement of career commitment. *Journal of Vocational Behavior, 32,* 284-297.

Blustein, D. L., Devenis, L. E., & Kidney, B. A. (1989). Relationship between the identity formation process and career development. *Journal of Counseling Psychology, 36*(2), 196-202.

Blustein, D. L., Ellis, M. V., & Devenis, L. E. (1989). The development and validation of a two-dimensional model of the commitment to career choices process. *Journal of Vocational Behavior, 35,* 342-378.

Caplan, G. (1964). *Principles of preventive psychiatry.* New York: Basic Books.

Crites, J. O. (1978). *Theory and research handbook for the Career Maturity Inventory.* Monterey, CA: CTB/McGraw-Hill.

Donovan, J. M. (1975). Identity status and interpersonal style. *Journal of Youth and Adolescence, 4*, 37-55.

Dudley, G. A., & Tiedeman, D. V. (1977). *Career development: Exploration and commitment*. Muncie, IN: Accelerated Development.

Erikson, E. H. (1956). The problem of ego identity. *Journal of the American Psychoanalytic Association, 4*, 56-121.

Erikson, E. H. (1968). *Identity: Youth and crisis*. New York: Norton.

Fannin, P. M. (1979). The relation between ego-identity status and sex-role attitude, work-role salience, atypicality of major and self-esteem in college women. *Journal of Vocational Behavior, 14*, 12-22.

Gelso, C. J., & Fassinger, R. E. (1992). Personality, development, and counseling psychology: Depth, ambivalence, and actualization. *Journal of Counseling Psychology, 39*(3), 275-298.

Ginzberg, E., Ginsburg, S. W., Axelrad, S., & Herma, J. (1951). *Occupational choice: An approach to a general theory*. New York: Columbia University Press.

Gottfredson, L. S. (1981). Circumscription and compromise: A developmental theory of occupational aspirations. *Journal of Counseling Psychology, 28*(6), 545-579.

Greenberger, E., & Steinberg, L. (1986). *When teenagers work: The psychological and social costs of adolescent employment*. New York: Basic Books.

Gribbons, W. D., & Lohnes, P. R. (1968). *Emerging careers*. New York: Teachers College Press.

Gribbons, W. D., & Lohnes, P. R. (1982). *Careers in theory and experience: A twenty-year longitudinal study*. Albany: State University of New York Press.

Grotevant, H. D. (1987). Toward a process model of identity formation. *Journal of Adolescent Research, 2*(3), 203-222.

Hamilton, S. F., & Powers, J. L. (1990). Failed expectations: Working-class girls' transitions from school to work. *Youth & Society, 22*(2), 241-262.

Harmon, L. W., & Farmer, H. S. (1983). Current theoretical issues in vocational psychology. In W. B. Walsh & S. H. Osipow (Eds.), *Handbook of vocational psychology* (Vol. 1, pp. 39-77). Hillsdale, NJ: Lawrence Erlbaum.

Herr, E. L., & Cramer, S. H. (1988). *Career guidance and counseling through the life span: Systematic approaches* (3rd ed.). Glenview, IL: Scott, Foresman.

Holland, J. L. (1966). *The psychology of vocational choice*. Waltham, MA: Blaisdell.

Holland, J. L., Magoon, T. M., & Spokane, A. R. (1981). Counseling psychology: Career interventions, research, and theory. *Annual Review of Psychology, 32*, 279-300.

Jepsen, D. A. (1984). The developmental perspective on vocational behavior: A review of theory and research. In S. D. Brown & R. W. Lent (Eds.), *Handbook of counseling psychology* (pp. 178-215). New York: John Wiley.

Jordaan, J. P. (1963). Exploratory behavior: The formation of self and occupational concepts. In D. Super, R. Starishevsky, R. Matlin, & J. P. Jordaan (Eds.), *Career development: Self-concept theory* (pp. 42-78). New York: College Entrance Examination Board.

Jordaan, J. P., & Heyde, M. (1979). *Vocational maturity during the high school years*. New York: Teachers College Press.

Jordaan, J. P., & Super, D. E. (1974). The prediction of early adult vocational behavior. In D. F. Ricks, A. Thomas, & M. Roff (Eds.), *Life history research in psychopathology* (Vol. 3, pp. 108-130). Minneapolis: University of Minnesota Press.

Josselson, R. L. (1973). Psychodynamic aspects of identity formation in college women. *Journal of Youth and Adolescence, 2,* 3-52.

Knefelkamp, L. L., & Slepitza, R. (1976). A cognitive-developmental model of career development: An adaptation of the Perry scheme. *Counseling Psychologist, 6*(3), 53-58.

Marcia, J. E. (1980). The process of adolescence. In J. Adelson (Ed.), *Handbook of adolescence* (pp. 159-187). New York: John Wiley.

Marcia, J. E. (1989). Identity and intervention. *Journal of Adolescence, 12,* 401-410.

Marcia, J. E., Waterman, A., Matteson, D., Archer, S., & Orlofsky, J. (1993). *Ego identity: A handbook for psychosocial research.* New York: Springer Verlag.

Mortimer, J. T., Finch, M. D., Owens, T. J., & Shanahan, M. (1990). Gender and work in adolescence. *Youth & Society, 22*(2), 201-223.

Mosher, R. L., & Sprinthall, N. A. (1971). Psychological education: A means to promote personal development during adolescence. *Counseling Psychologist, 2*(4), 3-82.

Munley, P. H. (1975). Erik Erikson's theory of psychosocial development and vocational behavior. *Journal of Counseling Psychology, 22,* 314-319.

Nafziger, D. H., Holland, J. L., Helms, S. T., & McPartland, J. M. (1974). Applying an occupational classification to the work histories of young men and women. *Journal of Vocational Behavior, 5,* 331-345.

Newlan, B., & Haase, A. (1982). The school counselor, Puerto Rican youth and preparation for work. *Journal of Career Education, 9,* 115-122.

Ohlsen, M. M., Horne, A. M., & Lawe, C. F. (1988). *Group counseling* (3rd ed.). New York: Holt, Rinehart & Winston.

Omvig, C. P., & Thomas, E. G. (1977). The relationship between career education, sex, and career maturity of sixth- and eighth-grade pupils. *Journal of Vocational Behavior, 11,* 322-331.

Parsons, F. (1909). *Choosing a vocation.* Boston: Houghton Mifflin.

Peatling, J. H., & Tiedeman, D. V. (1977). *Career development: Designing self.* Muncie, IN: Accelerated Development.

Pitz, G. F. & Harren, V. A. (1980). An analysis of career decision-making from the point of view of information-processing and decision theory. *Journal of Vocational Behavior, 16,* 320-346.

President's Science Advisory Committee, Panel on Youth (1973). *Youth: Transition to adulthood.* Chicago: University of Chicago Press.

Radin, J. J. (1978). *An exploratory study of personality development during early adulthood: Ages 23 to 29* (Dissertation #7822986 01800). Ann Arbor, MI: University Microfilms International.

Raskin, P. M. (1989). Identity status research: Implications for career counseling. *Journal of Adolescence, 12,* 375-388.

Roe, A. (1956). *The psychology of occupations.* New York: John Wiley.

Rotheram-Borus, M. J. (1989). Ethnic differences in adolescents' identity status and associated behavior problems. *Journal of Adolescence, 12,* 361-374.

Savickas, M. L. (1985). Identity in vocational development. *Journal of Vocational Behavior, 27,* 329-337.

Smith, E. D., & Herr, E. L. (1972). Sex differences in the maturation of vocational attitudes among adolescents. *Vocational Guidance Quarterly, 20,* 177-182.

Spokane, A. R., & Oliver, L. W. (1983). The outcomes of vocational intervention. In W. B. Walsh & S. H. Osipow (Eds.), *Handbook of vocational psychology: Vol. 2. Applications* (pp. 99-136). Hillsdale, NJ: Lawrence Erlbaum.

Sprinthall, N. A., & Mosher, R. L. (1969). *Studies of adolescents in the secondary school.* Monograph 6. Cambridge, MA: Center for Research and Development, Harvard Graduate School of Education.

Sprinthall, N. A., & Mosher, R. L. (1971). Voices from the back of the classroom. *Journal of Teacher Education, 22*(2).

Super, D. E. (1957). *The psychology of careers.* New York: Harper & Row.

Super, D. E. (1984). Career and life development. In D. Brown and L. Brooks (Eds.), *Career choice and development: Applying contemporary theories to practice* (pp. 192-234). San Francisco: Jossey-Bass.

Super, D. E., & Bowlesbey, J. (1979). *Guided career exploration.* New York: Psychological Corporation.

Super, D. E., & Overstreet, P. L. (1960). *The vocational maturity of ninth-grade boys.* New York: Teachers College Press.

Tiedeman, D. V. (1961). Decision and vocational development: A paradigm and its implications. *Personnel and Guidance Journal, 40,* 15-20.

Tiedeman, D. V., & Miller-Tiedeman, A. (1984). Career decision-making: An individualistic perspective. In D. Brown & L. Brooks (Eds.), *Career choice and development: Applying contemporary theories to practice* (pp. 281-310). San Francisco: Jossey-Bass.

Vondracek, F. W. (1993). Promoting vocational development in early adolescence. In R. M. Lerner (Ed.), *Early adolescence: Perspectives on research, policy, and intervention* (pp. 277-292). Hillsdale, NJ: Lawrence Erlbaum.

Vondracek, F. W., Lerner, R. M., & Schulenberg, J. E. (1983). The concept of development in vocational theory and intervention. *Journal of Vocational Behavior, 23,* 179-202.

Waterman, A. S. (1982). Identity development from adolescence to adulthood: An extension of theory and a review of research. *Developmental Psychology, 18,* 341-358.

Waterman, A. S. (1985). Identity in context of adolescent psychology. In A. S. Waterman (Ed.), *Identity in adolescence: Processes and contents* (pp. 5-24). San Francisco: Jossey-Bass.

Waterman, A. S. (1989). Curricula interventions for identity change: Substantive and ethical considerations. *Journal of Adolescence, 12,* 389-400.

Waterman, A. S., & Goldman, J. A. (1976). A longitudinal study of ego identity development at a liberal arts college. *Journal of Youth and Adolescence, 5*(4), 361-369.

Westbrook, B. W., Cutts, C. C., Madison, S. S., & Arcia, M. (1980). The validity of the Crites model of Career Maturity. *Journal of Vocational Behavior, 16,* 249-281.

Westbrook, B. W., & Sanford, E. E. (1991). The validity of Career Maturity attitude measures among black and white high school students. *Career Development Quarterly, 39,* 199-208.

11

Curricula Focused on Behavioral Deviance

RANDALL M. JONES

In view of the dangerous potentials of man's long childhood, it is well to look back at the blueprint of the life stages and to the possibilities of guiding the young of the race while they are young. . . . [T]he child is at no time more ready to learn quickly and avidly, to become bigger in the sense of sharing obligation and performance than during this period of development. He is eager to make things cooperatively, to combine with other children for the purpose of constructing and planning, and he is willing to profit from teachers and to emulate ideal prototypes.

Erik Erikson (1963, p. 258)

Historically, efforts to prevent or delay the onset of various youth-related problem behaviors have netted less than acceptable results. The adage "History repeats itself" is clearly confirmed when one traces the evolution of prevention approaches that have been applied to adolescent substance use, teen pregnancy, school dropout rates, and academic underachievement. For each specific behavior, prevention efforts have evolved in similar fashion (and yielded similar results at each phase). Rather than look to any of several existing theories for guidance, our habitual approach to dealing with undesirable behaviors has been mostly emotional, reactive, and unsuccessful. With a century of failed effort behind us, perhaps it is time to consider a theoretical alternative.

174

Erikson's psychosocial theory seems particularly appropriate for explaining and understanding adolescent problems because many undesirable behaviors emerge during the second decade of life—that is, concurrently with Erikson's fifth stage, the identity crisis.

When Does an Ounce of Prevention Equal a Pound of Cure?

The answer to the question "When does an ounce of prevention equal a pound of cure?" is "When both sides of the equation equal zero." In other words, when—*and only when*—a course of action is effective in delaying, deterring, or significantly altering the natural progression of an undesirable event. Such has not been the case when dealing with adolescent problem behaviors. Indeed, efforts to prevent or intervene in adolescent problem behaviors seem to evolve with each (non-validating) program evaluation. Decades of failed effort (e.g., escalating rates of teen pregnancy, substance use, and school dropout) have literally forced individuals who work with youths to examine critically popular assumptions, beliefs, and techniques available for "preventing" undesirable behavior. Similar to Kuhn's (1970) description of "pre-revolutionary" periods for scientific advances, the prevention field is cluttered with a variety of competing philosophies and hardworking, dedicated, and hopeful campers who are craving a revolution, as well as a theoretical framework capable of providing guidance and suggesting tools to prevent youth-related problems. Although most of these camps continue to disseminate information about harmful consequences from various problem behaviors, there is an apparent shift toward cognitive, skill-based strategies that are designed to fortify or strengthen the individual.

Cognitive and skill-based prevention approaches are supported by recent studies that have established a relationship between identity development and adolescent substance use (Jones & Hartmann, 1988), substance abuse (Jones, Hartmann, Grochowski, & Glider, 1989), and motivations for substance use (Christopherson, Jones, & Sales, 1988). Findings from these studies indicate that the identity-status paradigm shares substantial variability with adolescent initial and continued use of substances. In general, diffused adolescents (who lack commitment and have not experienced meaningful exploration) are three to five times (depending on the substance) more likely to use and abuse substances than are foreclosed adolescents (who have adopted commitments from significant authority figures). Furthermore, the reasons and motivations for use and abuse among diffused youths are distinctly different than those for adolescents who are classified as foreclosed, achieved, and moratorium. Conceivably, cognitive, skill-based approaches may prove worthwhile in deterring risky or health-compromising behaviors by providing skills and experiences that are necessary for:

1. internalizing resistance strategies that are primarily externally based among foreclosed youths, without jeopardizing existing commitments;
2. structuring psychosocial exploration to minimize the likelihood of risky or health-compromising commitments among adolescents who are experiencing moratorium;
3. inducing crisis (moratorium) or exploration among diffused adolescents and structuring these activities to minimize risky or health-compromising commitments; and
4. serving to solidify commitments among achieved adolescents by increasing awareness of the relationship between risky and health-compromising behaviors and attainment of goals.

The identity and substance use relationships support interventions that foster a healthy transition during the identity "crisis." This speculation is supported by Erikson's writings and a growing body of research concerning risk and resiliency.

Lessons From the Past

Historically, efforts to curtail adolescent problem behavior (e.g., chemical abuse, school dropout, and teen pregnancy) have evolved in similar fashion. Concern with "preposterous" behavior initially gives birth to various mechanisms for monitoring behavioral trends. A series of correlational studies simultaneously links these behaviors to social phenomena that inherently connote negative or threatening images. Teenage sexual behavior, for example, has been linked to sexually transmitted diseases (STDs) and escalating pregnancy rates (Holmbeck, Waters, & Brookman, 1990); the latter are associated with higher rates of infant mortality, divorce, foster care, welfare support (DiBlasio & Benda, 1990), and so on. Likewise, adolescent chemical use and abuse has been correlated with school dropout rates, homicide, suicide, a plethora of criminal activities (Newcomb & Bentler, 1988), and the like. Thus, through a process of association, specific behaviors are deemed undesirable and unacceptable. Such behaviors are swiftly recognized as problems worthy of intervention.

Once a behavior attains problem behavior status, institutions that are closest to the problem, socially responsible, and politically controllable are called on to intervene. Finally, selected institutions adapt their own tools and resources to affect the problem. In the case of adolescent problem behavior, schools currently use their expertise in education by adapting contemporary pedagogy to address youth-related problems.

First-Generation Prevention and Intervention Programs

For most youth-related problems, initial stages of prevention have targeted religion or the home as the most appropriate institution for intervention. Once a behavior has obtained problem behavior status, our emotional and reactive approach has involved moral appeal or legal sanction. The primary strategy at this level entails public retribution and moral objection. For example, alcohol consumption achieved problem behavior status at the turn of the century, and initial prevention and intervention approaches used moral objection—alcohol use was portrayed as evil—and prohibition followed. A similar process is evident for a wide variety of youth-related behaviors that are viewed as undesirable and unacceptable (e.g., drug use and premarital sexual activity).

Second-Generation Prevention and Intervention Programs

When moral appeal and legal restraint fail to curb rising trends, prevention and intervention strategies take on new form. The second round of activity has historically involved some form of education. Purely educational prevention approaches have successfully increased knowledge, often meeting or exceeding expected criteria. And yet increases in knowledge have had little or no effect on the behaviors in question (Tobler, 1986). Substance use and abuse, adolescent sexual activity, and school dropout continue to rise despite successful educational interventions (i.e., empirical evidence of increased knowledge). Apparently, knowledge of the harmful consequences of chemical use and abuse does not curtail adolescent use of licit and illicit substances; knowledge of the harmful consequences of unprotected sexual activity does not ensure that youths will use safeguards when expressing their emerging sexuality; and knowledge of the undesirable consequences of dropping out of school does not motivate adolescents to take full advantage of the educational system.

Obviously, this dilemma has raised doubts about the utility of traditional educational approaches to adolescent problem behavior. These doubts do not concern the choice of the school as the most appropriate institution for intervening in these problems; they instead concern the type of education or information that is being disseminated within school-based prevention and intervention programs.

At this juncture, it is instructive to note that preventive interventions into adolescent problem behavior are generally nonextant; instead, each of several youth-related problems has fostered its own specialized prevention regimen, even though similarity in process outweighs all difference in content. After all, what sense is there to teaching adolescents about the devastating consequences of unprotected sexual activity if the goal is to dissuade them from consuming illicit substances?

Prompted by a lack of observable behavior change (i.e., stable or increasing adolescent sexual activity, stable or increasing adolescent substance use, and stable or increasing dropout rates), educational prevention approaches are gradually being supplanted with cognitive skill-based approaches. These strategies incorporate similar content, technique, and objectives to address a plethora of adolescent problem behaviors. Professionals who are using cognitive skill-based approaches to prevent adolescent sexual behavior, chemical use and abuse, or school dropout are dancing in arenas that are clearly more similar than different.

Third-Generation Programs

The focus on the effects and consequences associated with each type of adolescent problem behavior is gradually being complemented with educational strategies that enhance coping, problem-solving, and decision-making skills. Commercial chemical-abuse prevention curricula echo this sentiment with titles such as *Choices and Challenges*; *Choices, Learning to Say No*; *Clear Choices*; *Consider the Consequences*; *Deciding*; *Deciding About Drugs*; *Decisions About Drug Use*; *Drinking, Driving, and Deciding*; *Health Choices*; *Making Smart Choices About Drugs*; *Social Thinking and Reasoning*; *Stanford D-E-C-I-D-E Drug Education Curriculum*; and *Thinking, Changing, and Rearranging*. Despite notable variation across these curricula, a common goal is introducing participants to new, presumably more effective ways of problem solving, decision making, and coping.

Use of cognitive interventions is not novel within substance abuse prevention efforts; they are increasingly evident in programs that target a wide range of behaviors, including school dropout and adolescent sex. Activities within various curricula are structured to provide students with opportunities to practice new skills, typically using situations or problems associated with a particular problem behavior (content) as examples.

Although direct evidence—that is, an empirical link connecting cognitive interventions to measurable changes in problem behavior—that supports the utility of this approach within chemical-abuse prevention programs is rare (until recently, few program evaluations considered strength and integrity of implementation as relevant to outcome; e.g., Crippen, 1983; Schaps, DiBartolo, Moskowitz, Palley, & Churgin, 1981), the potential benefit of cognitive approaches for intervening in adolescent substance use is unambiguously apparent in two related literatures: (a) studies that have established links between identity development and substance use and (b) studies that have linked identity development to cognitive style.

Identity Development

According to Erikson (1963, 1968) identity development involves an integration of past identifications with present competency and future aspiration, which results in a sense of self founded in experience and association with significant others. Marcia (1966) conceived four identity statuses that represent varying levels of crisis and commitment. The bulk of identity research conducted during the past two decades has used either self-report (e.g., Adams, Shea, & Fitch, 1979; Grotevant & Adams, 1984) or interview (e.g., Marcia, 1966) measures that are modeled on Marcia's statuses. Adams and Jones (1983) summarize the statuses as follows:

> An individual who has *achieved* an identity has made a self defined commitment following a period of questioning and searching (crisis). An individual who is currently engaged in this questioning and searching process is defined

as being in a state of *moratorium*. *Foreclosed* persons have accepted parental values and advice without question or examination of alternatives. Individuals who are *diffused* show no sign of commitment nor do they express a need or desire to begin the searching process. (p. 249)

Identity Development and Substance Use

Several studies have examined adolescent substance use within the identity-status paradigm. Jones and Hartmann (1988) reported that frequencies of substance-using adolescents among diffused respondents were consistently higher than estimates for the moratorium and achieved youths; in addition, foreclosed adolescents reported the lowest frequencies of experience. Controlling for age and in comparison with their foreclosed peers, diffused adolescents were twice as likely to have tried cigarettes and alcohol, three times as likely to have tried marijuana, four times as likely to have tried inhalants, and five times as likely to have tried cocaine. In a related effort (Jones et al., 1989), the identity statuses were used to discriminate chemically dependent adolescents from a matched sample of normals (high school students). Four of eight subscales combined to differentiate 98% of the abusing adolescents from nonabusing respondents. In both studies, users and abusers were significantly less mature than "normals" as evidenced by lower scores on measures of achievement and moratorium, as well as higher scores on the foreclosure subscales.

A third study (Christopherson et al., 1988) revealed that motivations for drug use also varied with identity status. In response to the question "Why do people your age use alcohol or drugs?" diffused adolescents cited boredom and stress as primary reasons; for these youths, alcohol and drug use was viewed as a means of coping—that is, self-medication for a meaningless existence. As predicted from the identity-status paradigm, the modal response for achieved adolescents was "To recreate and have fun with friends," for moratoriums, "curiosity." Foreclosures described alcohol use in the context of family get-togethers, tradition, and celebration.

Cognitive Style and Identity Development

Findings that relate cognitive style (i.e., preferred strategies for problem solving, decision making, coping, etc.) to the identity statuses mirror and help to explain the identity and substance use and abuse relationships already discussed. Berzonsky (Berzonsky, Rice, & Neimeyer,

1990) differentiates cognitive strategy (an integrated collection of behaviors and cognitive responses) and identity status on the basis of
process versus outcome:

> [T]he statuses function as different types of self-theorists. Self-explorers,
> Achievers and Moratoriums, were characterized as *information oriented,*
> scientific theorists who actively seek, process, and evaluate information
> before solving problems and making decisions. Foreclosures were described
> as *norm-oriented,* dogmatic theorists who look to significant others, including
> parents, for normative expectations and prescriptions. Diffusions were por-
> trayed as *avoidance-oriented, ad hoc* theorists who delay and procrastinate
> as long as possible. (pp. 252-253)

These (identity) status-specific cognitive qualities have been supported in the literature. Read, Adams, and Dobson (1984) reported status
differences in social influence behavior among females. Achieved females
were most likely to interact in an orally aggressive, nondeceptive
fashion, whereas foreclosed females were observed to exhibit a greater
degree of manipulation. Moreover, foreclosures and diffusions were
likely to restrict their attention focus, thus excluding or ignoring relevant information.

Grotevant and Adams (1984) reported a positive relationship between
identity achievement and self-directed or confronting problem-solving
strategies. Foreclosures relied on other-directed problem solving strategies, and diffused respondents tended to avoid (repress) personal
problems altogether.

According to Berzonsky et al. (1990):

> [T]he statuses differ in the way they process, structure, and utilize self-relevant
> information. For example, [diffusions] have been found to avoid coping with
> problems and to have a restricted attentional focus. Foreclosures possess rigid
> belief systems and are intolerant of ambiguity. Also, [foreclosures] have been
> found to have problems establishing a self-selected perspective within which
> conflicting sources of information can be synthesized. (p. 252)

In summary, positive relationships between a diffuse cognitive style
and identity diffusion ($r = .62$; Berzonsky, 1988), in conjunction with
studies that have reported greater frequencies of substance use and
abuse among adolescents who score high on measures of identity
diffusion (Christopherson et al., 1988; Jones & Hartmann, 1988; Jones
et al., 1989), provide indirect support for third-generation prevention

approaches designed to reduce or eliminate adolescent chemical use and abuse, involvement in unprotected sexual activity, and school dropout (i.e., cognitive interventions to promote coping, problem-solving, and decision-making skills). This approach seems particularly appropriate for diffused adolescents who are characterized by "no attachment, no meaningful exploration and experimentation, no subsequent commitment, no commitment, no identity" (Marcia, 1983, p. 221). Diffused adolescents demonstrate low cognitive integrative complexity (Slugoski, Marcia, & Koopman, 1984), restrict their attention focus in interpersonal interactions (Read et al., 1984), and tend to avoid facing personal problems, opting to rely on other-directed problem-solving strategies (Grotevant & Adams, 1984). Diffused adolescents who participate in activities designed to enhance problem-solving, decision-making, and coping strategies thus will likely benefit most.

Capitalizing on Developmental Differences
to Maximize Intervention Effectiveness

The literature on resilient children, or those who "recover from or adjust easily to misfortune or sustained life stress" (Werner, 1984, p. 68), echoes Erikson's (1963, 1968) theoretical notions about the early stages of psychosocial development. According to Erikson (1959), the central task of Stage 1 involves establishing a basic sense of trust or an adaptive balance of trust to mistrust. Resolution of this stage is thought to evolve from strong mother-infant attachments during the first year of life. "The firm establishment of enduring patterns for the balance of basic trust over basic mistrust is the first task of the budding personality and therefore first of all a task for maternal care" (Erikson, 1959, p. 9); "mothers create a sense of trust in their children" (Erikson, 1959, p. 63). Descriptive accounts of resilient children (Werner, 1984) also highlight early adult-child relations:

> More of the resilient children had received a great deal of attention from their primary caretakers during the first year of life (as judged by public health nurses and social workers who observed in the home) than did the children of alcoholic parents who later developed serious coping problems. (p. 37)

Resilient children also had "at least one caregiver from whom they received lots of attention during the first year of life" (Werner, 1984, p. 69). Clearly, the resilient children described by Werner were in situations conducive to successful negotiation of Stage 1 in Erikson's paradigm.

Erikson's Stage 2 (autonomy versus shame and doubt) becomes salient during the second and third years of life when the individual "gets ready to stand on his feet more firmly, the infant delineates his world as 'I' and 'you,' 'me' and 'mine' " (Erikson, 1959, p. 67). Resilient children appear to have resolved the second stage; they are frequently described as having pronounced autonomy (Murphy & Moriarty, 1976), and they "seek out novel experiences, lack fear, and are quite self-reliant" (Werner, 1984, p. 69).

Stage 3 (initiative versus guilt) becomes paramount during the fourth and fifth years. During this stage, the child "seems to be, as it were, self-activated; he is in the free possession of a certain surplus of energy that permits him to forget failures quickly and to approach what seems desirable (even if it also seems dangerous) with undiminished and better aimed effort" (Erikson, 1959, p. 75), particularly as he masters the skills associated with language, movement, and imagination. Seemingly on track,

> resilient children often find a refuge and a source of self-esteem in hobbies and creative interests. . . . Such activities . . . gave them a reason to feel proud. Their hobbies, and their lively sense of humor, became a solace when things fell apart in their lives. (Werner, 1984, p. 69)

Stage 4 (industry versus inferiority) is salient during the elementary school years (ages 6 through 12). According to Erikson (1959), "The child now wants to be shown how to get busy with something and how to be busy with others" (p. 82). Children in this stage of development focus on either feeling competent as they learn and do well or feeling inferior if they fail. Werner (1984) notes that:

> in middle childhood and adolescence resilient children are often engaged in acts of "required helpfulness." . . . [M]any adolescents took care of their younger siblings. . . . [S]ome managed the household when a parent was ill or hospitalized. . . . [O]thers worked part time after school to support the family. . . . [R]esilient children are apt to like school and to do well in school. . . . Even if they are not unusually talented, they put whatever abilities they have to good use. (Werner, 1984, p. 70)

Clearly, characteristics of the resilient children described by Werner and others parallel Erikson's notions of healthy psychosocial development.

Werner's (1984, 1986) observations suggest that resilient children possess the same developmental qualities that Erikson deemed necessary for successful resolution of identity issues, namely, a balanced sense of trust versus mistrust, autonomy versus shame and doubt, initiative versus guilt, and industry versus inferiority. Parallels between resiliency and adaptive psychosocial development, in conjunction with the substance-by-identity relationships reported above, provide indirect support for cognitive-based, social-skill prevention and intervention approaches. In other words, the literature on so-called resilient children clearly suggests that psychosocially healthy children may be inoculated against the pressures involved with substance use and associated at-risk behaviors; and research that examines substance use via the identity-status paradigm indicates that psychosocially advanced adolescents are less likely to use and abuse substances. Moreover, psychosocially advanced adolescents (the achieved and moratorium identity statuses) who do report occasional substance use presumably do it for reasons that are quite different from their diffused peers.

Erikson (1959, 1963, 1968) maintains that successful resolution of the first four developmental issues facilitates the resolution of Stage 5 (identity crisis) during adolescence and young adulthood. Conversely, inadequate or faulty resolution of the earlier stages will likely impede identity development as well as resolution of subsequent developmental stages (namely, Stage 6, intimacy versus isolation; Stage 7, generativity versus stagnation; and Stage 8, integrity versus despair).

Baumrind and others (Baumrind, 1987; Baumrind & Moselle, 1985) have speculated that early substance use or abuse may impede adolescent development, "including impairment of attention and memory; developmental lag in cognitive, moral, and psychosocial domains, amotivational syndrome; consolidation of diffuse or negative identity; and social alienation and estrangement" (Baumrind, 1987, p. 103). Does substance use or abuse impede normal psychosocial development? Or is nonadaptive psychosocial development conducive to a higher likelihood of substance use? Either way, Erikson's theoretical notions and Werner's description of resilient children suggest that participants in early (elementary) prevention efforts and later (secondary) intervention efforts would likely benefit from a psychosocial approach.

A Dilemma for Schools

As mentioned early on, schools have been tasked as the social and political institution that is (a) closest to the problem, (b) socially responsible, and (c) politically controllable. Willingly or not, educators are being forced to provide surrogate parenting to children who come from families that are unwilling or unable to fulfill developmental functions. Instrumental tasks that were traditionally served by the family are now commonplace in the classroom, including values clarification, social-skills training, sex education, chemical-abuse prevention, education concerning AIDS and STDs, and so on. The ability of schools to address these problems continues to be scrutinized on the basis of escalating rates of adolescent problem behavior.

Unfortunately, most school personnel lack appropriate training to implement these programs, some personnel are simply resistant (after all, this is not their job), and facilities are ill-equipped to fulfill traditional family roles in fostering healthy psychosocial development. At best, schools may be an effective arena in which to teach today's students parenting skills and responsibilities that are necessary for effective parenting of their own children, thus sacrificing immediate results with the hope of seeing positive outcomes in future generations of students. Likewise, prevention efforts would likely benefit by including a parenting component (for parents) that focused on assisting children with tasks that form the foundation for healthy psychosocial development. Erikson's (1963) blueprint provides a valuable source of information for developing such an intervention.

Prevention, Intervention, and Future Programs

By acknowledging that normal development and problem behavior may share a reciprocal relationship, important insights as to why previous school-based prevention approaches have been less than optimal in affecting specific problem behaviors become apparent. Most, if not all, school-based prevention and intervention strategies have thus far targeted specific, isolated behaviors as the problem (e.g., substance use, academic underachievement, school dropout rates, teen sexual behavior, and adolescent pregnancy), and the foci of these prevention and intervention efforts reflect this bias. If these behaviors are construed as symptoms of one or more underlying developmental issues rather than the issue, then exclusive focus on symptoms rather than issues would partially explain previous failure. If future prevention and intervention strategies were to view specific behaviors as symptomatic of developmental maladjustment, the foci of these programs would likely target developmental issues and expect reduction or elimination of specific behaviors as a side effect of the developmental intervention.

By making general rather than idiographic assumptions about etiology and motivation, is it any wonder that we have yet to witness notable decreases in youth-related problems? The key perhaps lies in matching intervention and prevention approaches to specific psychosocial deficiencies at the individual level. This perspective has at least two advantages over previous approaches that have applied one intervention to a wide range of underlying issues. First, and perhaps most important, it seems likely that a majority of students may not need any prevention or intervention at all! "Why fix it if it's not broken?" After all, the number of adolescents who progress from occasional or experimental substance use to abuse, and the number of teen pregnancies in relation to the number of adolescent females are both relatively small. From this perspective, one could argue that ongoing blanket efforts dilute scarce resources by providing programs to students who are not likely to benefit because they did not need a program in the first place. School-based prevention and intervention efforts probably would be more beneficial if specific high-risk populations received the bulk of available resources. Second, the psychosocial blueprint developed by Erikson (substantiated by empirical data) provides important insights for identifying these high-risk populations as well as a means of tailoring efforts to address known deficiencies.

Implications for Prevention at the Elementary School Level

Schools are currently targeted as the social and political institution that is closest to the problem, socially responsible, and politically controllable. Perhaps we should reconsider this choice. Even though parents and families are less socially responsible and harder to control in a political sense (when compared to schools), they are undeniably closer to the problem. Prevention participants would likely benefit from the inclusion of a parenting component (for parents) that focused on assisting children with tasks that form the foundation for healthy psychosocial development. Erikson's (1963) blueprint provides a valuable source of information for developing such an intervention. Erikson (1963) attaches the relevance of Stages 1 through 3 to the preschool years, and the importance of Stage 4 with the formal schooling years, up through the onset of puberty (when Stage 5 becomes salient). "Many a child's development is disrupted when family life has failed to prepare him for school life, or when school life fails to sustain the promises of earlier stages" (1963, p. 260).

Implications for Prevention and Intervention at the Secondary School Level

The promotion of healthy psychosocial development would appear to be a viable strategy for preventing adolescent problem behavior. By reducing the incidence of identity diffusion during adolescence, we may expect to see a reduction in adolescent chemical use and abuse, as well as reductions in school dropout rates, adolescent pregnancy, the transmission of STDs, and related behavior. Current strategies that promote problem solving, decision making, and coping may affect diffused and foreclosed adolescents by providing them with competencies that are conducive to a healthy psychosocial moratorium. This approach may affect moratorium adolescents by providing a structured experience in which to refine these skills, helping to resolve issues and solidify commitments. Finally, for achieved adolescents, cognitive strategies may reinforce and strengthen commitments that were made before exposure to these programs. These outcomes are purely speculative at this point and will continue as such until program evaluators examine the strength and integrity of various interventions (i.e., assessing relationships between change in problem-solving, decision-making, and coping skills; change in identity development and status and cognitive strategy; and change in adolescent problem behavior).

Beyond this, we must confront questions about how one becomes diffused in the first place. For Erikson (1959, 1963, 1968), faulty resolution of the first four stages is a key factor. Accordingly, preadolescents who have not successfully resolved issues pertaining to trust versus mistrust, autonomy versus shame and doubt, initiative versus guilt, and industry versus inferiority are likely candidates for identity diffusion during adolescence. To reduce identity diffusion during adolescence, we will need to foster healthy resolution of the crises that precede Stage 5.

To construct psychosocial interventions that reduce the likelihood of diffusion during adolescence, research is needed to identify stage-specific characteristics of the identity statuses. In other words, research is needed to identify which aspects of trust versus mistrust, autonomy versus shame and doubt, initiative versus guilt, and industry versus inferiority define each of the four identity statuses. According to Erikson (1963), identity achievement should be characterized by a balance across all four of these psychosocial qualities—that is, moderate levels across each of the four qualities that precede the identity crisis. This scenario may apply to the moratorium status as well. Foreclosures and diffusions, on the other hand, may be characterized by an imbalance across the four psychosocial qualities. For example, it is conceivable that the profile for foreclosed adolescents is characterized by abnormally high levels of trust (submission to authority) and industry (hardworking) and abnormally low levels of autonomy (lack sense of self) and initiative (lack creativity in problem solving and decision making). Diffused adolescents may be abnormally low on levels of trust, initiative, and industry; and they may be abnormally high on levels of autonomy. Following documentation of psychosocial differences across the identity statuses, appropriate interventions can be constructed to address known psychosocial deficiencies in order to reduce the frequency of identity diffusion during adolescence; this would then lead to reductions in adolescent chemical use and abuse, school dropout rates, teen pregnancy, the transmission of STDs, and related problem behavior.

References

Adams, G. R., & Jones, R. M. (1983). Female adolescents' identity development: Age comparisons and perceived child-rearing experience. *Developmental Psychology, 19,* 249-256.

Adams, G. R., Shea, J., & Fitch, S. A. (1979). Toward the development of an objective assessment of ego-identity status. *Journal of Youth and Adolescence, 9,* 223-237.

Baumrind, D. (1987). A developmental perspective on adolescent risk taking in contemporary America. In C. E. Irwin, Jr. (Ed.), *Adolescent social behavior and health* (pp. 93-125). San Francisco: Jossey-Bass.

Baumrind, D., & Moselle, K. (1985). A developmental perspective on adolescent drug abuse. *Advances in Alcohol and Substance Abuse, 4,* 41-67.

Berzonsky, M. D. (1988). Self-theorists, identity status, and social cognition. In D. K. Lapsley & F. C. Power (Eds.), *Self, ego, and identity: Integrative approaches* (pp. 243-262). New York: Springer Verlag.

Berzonsky, M. D., Rice, K. G., & Neimeyer, G. J. (1990). Identity status and self-construct systems: Process × structure interactions. *Journal of Adolescence, 13,* 251-263.

Choices and challenges. (1986). Tampa, FL: C. E. Mendez Foundation.

Choices, learning to say no. (1989). Palatine: Illinois Renewal Institute.

Christopherson, B. B., Jones, R. M., & Sales, A. P. (1988). Diversity in reported motivations for substance use as a function of ego-identity development. *Journal of Adolescent Research, 3,* 141-152.

Clear choices. (1988). Tampa, FL: C. E. Mendez Foundation.

Consider the consequences. (1985). Princeton, NY: FLI Learning Systems.

Crippen, D. R. (1983). Substance use-abuse and cognitive learning: Suggested approaches to viable drug education programs. *Journal of Instructional Psychology, 2,* 74-82.

Deciding. (1972). New York: College Board Publications.

Deciding about drugs. (1987). Chicago: Society for Visual Education.

Decisions about drug use: Adolescents issues curricula. (1982). Boston: Judge Baker Guidance Center.

DiBlasio, F. A., & Benda, B. B. (1990). Adolescent sexual behavior: Multivariate analysis of a social learning model. *Journal of Adolescent Research, 5*(4), 449-466.

Drinking, driving, and deciding. (1983). Seattle: Comprehensive Health Education Foundation.

Erikson, E. H. (1959). Growth and crisis of the healthy personality. In G. S. Klein (Ed.), *Psychological issues* (pp. 185-225). New York: International Universities Press.

Erikson, E. H. (1963). *Childhood and society* (2nd ed.). New York: Norton.

Erikson, E. (1968). *Identity: Youth and crisis.* New York: Norton.

Grotevant, H. D., & Adams, G. R. (1984). Development of an objective measure to assess ego identity in adolescence: Validation and replication. *Journal of Youth and Adolescence, 13,* 419-438.

Health choices. (1985). City Center, MN: Hazelden Educational Materials.

Holmbeck, G. N., Waters, K. A., & Brookman, R. R. (1990). Psychosocial correlates of sexually transmitted diseases and sexual activity in Black adolescent females. *Journal of Adolescent Research, 5*(4), 431-448.

Jones, R. M., & Hartmann, B. R. (1988). Ego identity: Developmental differences and experimental substance use among adolescents. *Journal of Adolescence, 11,* 347-360.

Jones, R. M., Hartmann, B. R., Grochowski, C. O., & Glider, P. (1989). Ego identity and substance use: A comparison of adolescents in residential treatment with adolescents in school. *Personality and Individual Differences, 10*(6), 625-631.

Kuhn, T. S. (1970). *The structure of scientific revolutions.* Chicago: University of Chicago Press.

Making smart choices about drugs. (1987). Dominguez Hills, CA: Laurel Park Publishing.

Marcia, J. E. (1966). Development and validation of ego-identity status. *Journal of Personality and Social Psychology, 3,* 551-558.

Marcia, J. E. (1983). Some directions for the investigation of ego development in early adolescence. *Journal of Early Adolescence, 3*(3), 215-223.

Murphy, L., & Moriarty, A. (1976). *Vulnerability, coping and growth from infancy to adolescence.* New Haven, CT: Yale University Press.

Newcomb, M. D., & Bentler, P. M. (1988). *Consequences of adolescent drug use: Impact on the lives of young adults.* Newbury Park, CA: Sage.

Read, D., Adams, G. R., & Dobson, W. R. (1984). Ego-identity, personality, and social influence style. *Journal of Personality and Social Psychology, 46,* 169-177.

Schaps, E., DiBartolo, R., Moskowitz, J. M., Palley, C. S., & Churgin, S. (1981). A review of 127 drug abuse prevention program evaluations. *Journal of Drug Issues, 11,* 17-43.

Slugoski, B. R., Marcia, J. E., & Koopman, R. F. (1984). Cognitive and social interactional characteristics of ego identity status in college males. *Journal of Personality and Social Psychology, 47,* 646-661.

Social thinking and reasoning (STAR). (1988). Irvine, CA: Irvine Unified School District, Guidance Projects Office.

Stanford D-E-C-I-D-E drug education curriculum. (1981-83). Palo Alto, CA: Project Pegasus.

Thinking, changing, and rearranging. (1981). Eugene, OR: Timberline Press.

Tobler, N. S. (1986). Meta-analysis of 143 adolescent drug prevention programs: Quantitative outcome results of program participants compared to a control or comparison group. *Journal of Drug Issues, 16,* 537-568.

Werner, E. E. (1984). Resilient children. *Young Children, 40,* 68-72.

Werner, E. E. (1986). Resilient offspring of alcoholics: A longitudinal study from birth to age 18. *Journal of Studies on Alcohol, 47,* 34-40.

PART IV

The Interface of Identity and Intimacy for Intervention

12

Identity: A Precursor to Intimacy

GERALD R. ADAMS
SALLY L. ARCHER

Erik Erikson (1968) viewed the process of identity formation as being closely associated with social living. At birth, each individual has a predisposition to respond to the expectations of the social environment. Further, society is perceived as being organized around a series of culturally defined psychosocial turning points, each requiring a developmental response to stage-specific social expectations. The responses can be either positive or negative resolutions. Most important, these resolutions contribute to an accumulating series of ego strengths that booster identity formation. For example, the classic turning points and stage resolutions—trust versus mistrust, autonomy versus shame, initiative versus guilt, industry versus inferiority, and identity versus role confusion—are thought to be the major developmental challenges of childhood and adolescence. Intimacy versus isolation, generativity versus stagnation, and integrity versus despair are central to adult development.

Each of the first four stages makes a substantial precursory contribution to the fifth stage of identity resolution. During infancy, experience with trustworthy caregivers and a sense of mutuality with others provides the basis for an adolescent to search for self-chosen loves and incentives. Autonomy contributes to the development of courage and a sense of independence. Initiative provides a sense of purpose and the promise of fulfillment. Industry provides the basis for mastery and skill development. Each ego strength in turn provides the foundation for identity formation during adolescence.

Identity formation itself is viewed by Erikson as being resolved in either active or passive form. The passive form is generally viewed as acceptance of an unmitigated form of role confusion (diffusion) or a foreclosed acceptance of others' choices, recommendations, or expectations. The active form is volitional in nature, with searching, self-selection, and psychological integration central processes underlying identity formation.

For Erikson, a healthy personality is based on an active form of identity formation. Identity development based on active mastery of the environment, autonomous and independent functioning, and congruence between what one wants to be and acceptance by significant others of what one is and plans to become are foundational ingredients to positive identity formation.

The importance of identity formation to social life is seen in the theorized association between identity and intimacy. Although Erikson views identity formation as a central developmental task of adolescence, its major importance to adulthood is reflected in its foundational implications for the formation of intimate social relationships. Erikson suggests that the resolution of identity is a precursor to the ability to formulate and maintain intimacy. In referring to intimacy, he defines it as a sharing or fusing of identities. Further, he proposes that intimacy involves a capacity to make commitments to others and to maintain the ethical strength to abide by commitments, even in the face of tempting and desirable alternatives. Without an active form of identity, the individual is thus thought not to possess the necessary components of a healthy personality and is unable to make commitments to others or to abide ethically by commitments made. Put another way, fulfillment of intimacy requires a sense of shared identities. By implication, one might assume that active-based shared identities are more likely to result in greater depth of relationship commitment and intimacy. Thus identity formation is proposed to be a necessary precondition for the formation of intimate, long-term, social relationships.

In the remainder of this chapter, we shall briefly define how identity and intimacy typically have been operationalized, and we will selectively summarize some of the evidence testing the association between identity and intimacy. Three comparative models of the identity-intimacy association and their gender-specific implications will be detailed and evaluated. The chapter will conclude with a discussion of the implications for socialization.

The Operationalization and
Measurement of Identity and Intimacy

Identity

A multitude of operationalizations of identity formation have been proposed with corresponding measurement development. (See Marcia, Waterman, Matteson, Archer, & Orlofsky, 1993, for the most recent review.) Two general operational strategies have been most commonly used: the ratio-scale score technique and the status classification. Following Erikson's assumptions that the fifth stage of identity development and its corresponding outcome can be judged as a ratio of positive to negative resolutions, several scholars have either used a ratio score (e.g., Hawley, 1988) or have reserve-weighted negative resolution items and generated a single positive-resolutions score (e.g., Rasmussen, 1964). Regarding status classifications, Marcia's (1966) operationalization of the identity-status paradigm has been widely used. In this chapter, identity diffusion and foreclosure will represent passive forms of identity, and moratorium and identity achievement will represent active forms.

The strength of the ratio or scale score technique is that identity is based on a continuum, making the score readily usable in all forms of data analysis. The weakness is that the conceptual meaning of the gradations remains obscure, wherein passive and active forms of identity are confounded. The strength of the status classification is that one is aware of the nature of the passive or active form of identity. The weakness is that individuals are classified into statuses that may categorically oversimplify the complexity of the individual's identity formation. A compromise between these two systems has been offered by Grotevant and Cooper (1981), in which both identity status classification and ratings of the exploration and commitment are derived from clinical interview data. (See Marcia et al., 1993, for a review of the reliability, validity, and application of the status-classification technique.)

Intimacy

Because intimacy is not addressed previously in this book, its operationalization and measurement will be detailed more specifically here than will identity. Intimacy has been conceptualized in numerous ways. In some research strategies, intimacy is contrasted with isolation (e.g.,

Constantinople, 1969). In other techniques, low intimacy is equated to some unspecified level of isolation (e.g., Rosenthal, Gurney, & Moore, 1981). Several scholars have used indirect assessments of intimacy through the measurement of personality characteristics that are based on social relationships. For example, Yufit (1969) has used such characteristics as need for affiliation or nurturance to assess intimacy, with withdrawal, rejection, abasement, and aggression used to assess isolation. Others have used assessments of ratings of intimacy, disclosure, quality, satisfaction, initiation, and meaningfulness of social interactions in same-sex and opposite-sex social contacts (e.g., Craig-Bray & Adams, 1986). Still others have used assessments of semistructured interviews and intimacy status or relationship-maturity rankings (e.g., Orlofsky, Marcia, & Lesser, 1973; Paul, White, Speisman, & Costos, 1989). The latter techniques are based on notions of successive stages in intimacy formation. We shall elaborate with a description of several such stage-ranking techniques.

Modeled after the identity-status paradigm, Orlofsky et al. (1973) conceptualized several forms of intimacy-isolation resolutions. A semistructured interview is scored using the criteria of (a) the extent of involvement with male and female friends, (b) the degree of enduring commitment in loving relationships, and (c) the depth and quality—as reflected in openness, communication, mutual caring, and quality—of friendship and loving relationships. Scored interviews result in the classification of one of five intimacy statuses. The *isolate* is a withdrawn and marginally involved person with few or no personal relationships. The *stereotyped* individual has conventional or superficially stereotyped relationships that are based on a low degree of communication or closeness. The *pseudointimate* holds commitments but lacks depth (as seen in shared feelings) in his or her relationship(s). The *preintimate* has developed depth and closeness but has not entered into an enduring and committed relationship. The *intimate* status is reserved for individuals who have formed deep relationships that include enduring commitment. Substantial evidence has been provided for the validity of these statuses and elaborations thereof (see Orlofsky, 1993).

A separate but parallel strategy for assessing intimacy has been based on criteria of individuality, perspective taking, and mutuality (White, Speisman, & Costos, 1983). Using a family relationship interview and an intimacy interview, Paul and colleagues (1989) have assessed the affect, cognition, and behavior of parental, same-sex, and opposite-sex peer relations and have derived one of three categories of relationship maturity. The *self-focused* person primarily uses simple processes of self-individuation, manifests poor perspective taking, and shows little involvement in social relationships with others. The *role-focused* person emphasizes mostly stereotyped and socially acceptable forms of relationships. The *individuated-connected* person manifests a sense of individuality within an attachment context that reflects the capacity to be mutual, sensitive, and empathic with others. Paul and colleagues (1989) provide evidence showing that greater relationship maturity is associated with greater capacity for communion (versus agency), blends of masculinity and femininity (androgyny), and higher ego-development functioning.

Most recently, Archer and student colleagues (Archer et al., 1989) have devised an intimacy status-classification system for use in romantic relationship contexts. In this scheme, three broad classes are defined with subclassifications. The *casual* class consists of isolated individuals, immature casual playboy or playgirl types, and mature casuals who show signs of depth in intimacy without expectations of seriousness. The *traditional* class is characterized by persons who seek, want, or are participating in relationships in which commitments are desired and expected. Relationships are characterized by conformity to gender stereotypes, external expectations versus internal or self-regulated ego mechanisms, and relatively immature defense mechanisms. Finally, the *intimate* class represents individuals who are seeking or maintaining a romantic relationship represented by mutuality, interdependence, acceptance of others for who they are as individuals, openness, and self-disclosure.

The substantial strength of the status or relationship maturity ranking is that each assumes there is a gradation in the depth and quality of intimacy in which lower ranks or statuses are less mature or socially desirable than higher ones. Further, the rankings are highly comparable between measurement systems. The isolate, self-focused, and casual classifications represent a marginally involved, socially immature, and self-focused individual. The stereotyped, pseudointimate, role-focused, and traditional relationship person is characterized by a conformity-focused, external bound, and highly dependent person. Preintimate, intimate, and individuated-connected persons are self-individuated but interdependent persons who are capable of reciprocal mutuality. The primary weakness of such systems is that with the exception of the system formulated by Orlofsky et al. (1973; also Orlofsky, 1993), relatively little published evidence of the validity of the gradations and their developmental process is currently available. However, most systems are just now emerging and are based on strong conceptualizations. Strong reliability and validity evidence thus is likely to be forthcoming.

The Association Between Identity and Intimacy

The basic assumption that identity and intimacy are conceptually linked developmental constructs has been tested primarily through two research strategies. The first strategy has concurrently assessed identity and intimacy constructs and established their correlated association. The second strategy has used short-term longitudinal designs and assessed identity at one point in time and intimacy at another. This strategy adds a temporal association to the assessment of the relationship between identity and intimacy. Identity has been primarily measured through clinical interview and self-report ratings. Intimacy has been assessed using indirect and direct measures. Intimacy has been indirectly assessed through the measurement of psychological characteristics that are associated with social functioning (e.g., nurturance, affiliative needs, and so forth) and behavioral assessments of the quality and satisfaction of social interactions. Direct assessments of intimacy have included clinical assessments of rank-order intimacy statuses. Because direct assessments of intimacy are judged to be the stronger research strategy, we shall only briefly and selectively review the findings for indirect measurement techniques to afford space for a discussion of several studies that have included direct assessments of identity and intimacy.

Personality and Behavioral Characteristics

All of the indirect measurements of intimacy have been concurrently measured with identity-status assessments. A selective summary of findings for personality, perceived social living, and family relationships are summarized in Table 12.1. Comparisons are made between passive (diffused and foreclosed) and active (moratorium and achieved) forms of identity.

The following general portrait or impression emerges from these findings. Identity is associated with a wide range of constructs that indirectly assess social relationships elements that are connected to the likelihood of establishing and maintaining intimacy. Passive forms of identity are associated with lesser psychosocially mature personality characteristics that reflect a protective (repression or denial-based) psychological profile. Passive identity is correspondingly associated with low self-esteem, undifferentiated sex-role development, mistrust, and defensive concern about deprivation. Further, such individuals reflect an alienated personal life, where few interpersonal commitments are made and ineffective social behaviors such as demanding, interrupting, and domineering behavior are commonly used with others. Individuals with passive identities are also likely to manifest poor social adjustment, contribute to low family affection, and fail to assist in providing a sense of integration or communion in their family life.

In contrast, active identity is associated with a humanistic and compassionate personality style that includes consistent ethical behavior and an ability to process and use extensive social information within social relationships. An active identity is accompanied by a complex ego that has the capacity to analyze, share, and compare the psychological selves of the individual and partners. Such individuals hold high self-esteem and perceive their relationships to be based on secure attachments. The formation of an active identity appears to be associated with a blending of self-individuation, a sense of mastery, and personal independence with that of interpersonal relatedness reflected in effective social behaviors that enhance others' well-being and individual choices in values and behaviors that are selected out of personal interest versus conformity to social expectations. Such individuals are open to personal expression and support such expression in their social relationships, provide for and encourage affectionate relationships, and also highly value independent self-expression. The self is presented and treated as unique but also grounded in a sense of union or communion with others.

In one of the few actual studies of behavioral indices of intimacy, Craig-Bray and Adams (1986) categorized the ego-identity status of approximately 300 college students and selected an equal proportion of males and females who were in the four identity statuses. These subjects then kept daily behavioral diaries of their social interactions and assessed their perceived quality, satisfaction, influence, and so forth. Among many complex findings it was observed that for women an active identity was associated with higher perceived quality of social interactions, more depth in intimacy, and greater social involvement. However,

Table 12.1 Intimacy Linked Psychological and Behavioral Characteristics Correlated With Passive and Active Identity Formation

General Construct	Form of Identity	Associated Characteristics
Personality		
Mallory (1989)	Passive	Avoids close relationships, not warm, not dependable, represses conflict of impulses
	Active	Warm, compassionate, ethically consistent, maintains close relationships
Read, Adams, & Dobson (1984)	Passive	Restricted insight and limited analytic ability
	Active	Able to process extensive social information; high self-esteem
Orlofsky & Frank (1986)	Passive	Focus on trust and mistrust, nurturance and deprivation, compliance and rebellion
	Active	Focus on blending individuation and relatedness, mastery, independence, competition
Ginsburg & Orlofsky (1981) and Adams & Shea (1979)	Active	Postconformist ego development
Kroger (1985)	Active	Secure attachment
Lamke & Abraham (1984)	Active	Higher levels of both masculinity and femininity
Orlofsky (1993)	Passive	Undifferentiated sex-role orientation, low self-esteem

this finding was not observed for men, possibly because of a lesser ability to accurately discern and assess their daily social interactions, although this suggestion is based more on conjecture than any immediate fact derived from the study.

Identity and Intimacy Statuses

Orlofsky et al. (1973) completed the seminal test of the proposed association between identity and intimacy statuses. In this investigation, 53 college men were assessed using an identity and intimacy interview. Passive identity (diffusion and foreclosure) was correlated

Table 12.1 Continued

General Construct	Form of Identity	Associated Characteristics
Social Living		
Donovan (1975)	Passive	Few interpersonal commitments; isolation, social disorganization, alienation; unsure; interpersonally inhibited sexual impulses
	Active	Appropriate self-confrontations; socially mobile; capable of probing and expressing feelings; socially active
Read, Adams, & Dobson (1984)	Passive	Frequent use of demanding, interrupting, and dominance behaviors
	Active	Frequent use of positive feedback, enhancement of others
Carlson (1986)	Passive	Low social adjustment
Archer (1985)	Active	Liberated orientation focusing on individual choices, irrespective of societal conventions
Family Relationships		
Willemsen & Waterman (1988)	Passive	Lack of family interaction
Cooper, Grotevant, Moore, & Condon (1984)	Active	Individuated and family relationships
Adams (1985)	Passive	Low family affection
	Active	High companionship in family

with stereotypical and superficial relationships. Active identity was associated with greater intimacy capacity. As expected, diffused respondents were the most isolated, and identity-achieved were the most intimate. Additional studies using both male and female respondents reported similar concurrent associations between identity and intimacy statuses (e.g., Craig-Bray, Adams, & Dobson, 1988; Hodgson & Fischer, 1979; Kacerguis & Adams, 1980; Tesch & Whitbourne, 1982).

Each study supports the assumption that an active form of identity, with identity achievement specifically, is predictive of greater intimacy capacity. However, in each investigation some diffusions were capable of intimacy. Thus while the developmental association between identity and intimacy is supported, the association is not perfect.

However, the findings from these investigations are limited. In all cases, the samples were college subjects who were selected through voluntary participation from either psychology or social science courses. The subjects thus were not representative of any given population. Indeed, some might argue that students enrolled in psychology (or even other social sciences) are a unique group who are specifically interested in psychological and social relationship functioning. The findings thus may be highly unique and not broadly generalizable. Identity and intimacy also are concurrently measured, therein blurring any potential temporal prediction between identity and intimacy.

To overcome these two limitations of previous investigations, Fitch and Adams (1983) randomly selected 78 male and female respondents from a larger population of students in a project that focused on the study of ego development. These individuals represented students from 10 disciplines over 8 separate colleges at a western university. Identity and intimacy statuses were assessed at two points in time (approximately one year apart), and both concurrent and time-lagged associations were examined. Both types of analyses supported the proposed association between active and passive identities and intimate or isolated relationships.

For example, the concurrent association between identity and intimacy for one year revealed that (a) 100% of the diffused respondents were isolates, (b) 64% of the foreclosed subjects were isolates or pseudointimates, (c) while 43% of the moratoriums were either preintimate or intimate, with (d) 70% of the identity-achieved youths in intimate relationships.

The time-lagged association assessing the distal relationship between identity in one year and intimacy in the next was clearest for the passive-diffusion status. Approximately 88% of the diffused respondents were observed to be isolates or pseudointimates the next year. For foreclosed respondents, 58% were isolates or pseudointimates. A simple majority of the active moratorium (57%) and identity-achieved (54%) were observed to be either preintimate or intimate. Although a large minority were observed to be pseudointimate or stereotyped (moratorium = 42%, achievement = 46%), none of the active-identity youths were observed to be isolates.

Identity and intimacy appear to be conceptually linked psychosocial constructs. The clearest evidence suggests that passive forms of identity (diffusion in particular) are most strongly correlated with isolated interpersonal relationship styles, with active forms of identity (moratorium and achievement) tending to be more strongly related to intimate relationships. Again note that the associations are not perfect. However, the patterns are consistent across both concurrent and longitudinal assessments.

Comparative Models of the Identity-Intimacy Association

The major intention of previous research has been to establish, through descriptive research, the connection between identity and intimacy as coexisting psychosocial constructs. Collectively and integratively the evidence supports this connection. Further, much of the original research has drawn on Erikson's (1968) theorizing about the association between identity and intimacy. In recent years, important criticisms and proposed alternatives to Erikson's assumptions have been advanced. We shall briefly reexamine Erikson's general assumptions and contrast them with critical alternatives. Specific attention will be given to each model's distinctions regarding gender differences in the identity and intimacy connection. Then we shall summarize one attempt to test empirically the differences between the comparative models.

Erikson's Psychosocial Model

In brief, Erikson proposed that the resolution of a sense of identity versus role confusion is a necessary and compelling task of adolescence. Further, he proposed for males that this resolution must be accomplished before intimacy formation. Men without a firm and actively constructed sense of self will be unable to commit to another with either depth or ethical strength to abide by commitments made.

In contrast, Erikson stated for females that "much of a young woman's identity is already defined in her kind of attractiveness and in the selective nature of her search for the man (or men) by whom she wishes to be sought" (Erikson, 1968, p. 283). In essence, a woman's identity development is incomplete until she has attached herself to a man, therein being able to link her identity and intimacy needs and find fulfilling intimacy.

This model is depicted in Figure 12.1. The Erikson model would suggest that for males, identity precedes intimacy (bold arrow). However, for females, identity and intimacy appear to be fused psychosocial constructs

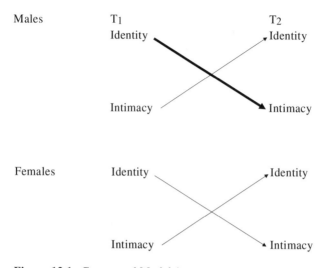

Males   T₁   T₂

Figure 12.1. Conceptual Model 1
SOURCE: From Dyk & Adams (1990). Reprinted with permission from Plenum Publishing Corp.

in which identity is based on an attachment to a significant male counterpart.

Gilligan's Different Voice

Numerous scholars have suggested that theory development has needlessly made separation and autonomy distinct from connectedness and relatedness. For example, Bakan (1966) long ago argued that a duality of existence is a natural part of social living. He argued that agency and communion are distinctly separate dimensions along which individuals differ and develop. Agency is seen in the need for separateness, mastery, and differentiation. Communion is found in belongingness, cooperation, relatedness, fusion, and emotional expression. He argued that an integrated coexistence between these two dimensions is a natural and adaptive outcome of human existence and individual development. Aspects of such thinking can be found in Josselson's (1987) writings, when she suggested that "a central aspect of identity is the commitment to a self-in-relation rather than a self that stands alone facing an abstract world" (p. 22).

Gilligan (1982) has possibly provided the most visibly recognized critique of the Eriksonian model. She noted that a contrasting pattern of male and female development should be characterized by theme, not gender. She implied that the male "voice" defines identity more in a context of individual achievement and goals (instrumental roles of agency) with a focus on the process of separation. In comparison, the female "voice" defines identity in a context of relationships that are judged by a standard of care and responsibility (expressive roles of communion) with a focus on the ongoing process of attachment and relatedness. Dyk and Adams (1990) speculated that these themes may be identified by sex-role orientations, which are indicative of masculine and feminine personality development.

Dyk and Adams's (1990) reading of Gilligan suggested the following model. For those individuals of a masculine sex-role orientation, because of their strong socialization in roles of agency, the process of individuation results in an outcome of identity functioning as a precursor to intimacy. For those individuals of a feminine sex-role orientation, because of their socialization in communion, the process of caring and responsibility results in a coexisting linkage between identity and intimacy. Thus a sense of self based on intimacy and caring results in a fusion (of sorts) between identity and intimacy. This model is depicted in Figure 12.2.

Freedman's Sex-Role Theory

Freedman (1986) noted that theoretical suppositions from social psychology suggest that the developmental progression for females may in fact be reversed from that of males. For example, she contrasted distinctions between agonic and hedonic power as modal patterns of behavior by men and women, respectively. She argued, as might many ethologists, that men tend to rely on the more aggressive and dominant forms of agonic power seen in the use of economic, status, and physical force found in men's behavioral patterns. In comparison, women's use of hedonic power to command attention is observed in their covert use of display, charm, love withdrawal, and related emotional expressions. Therefore, Freedman suggested that while male identity development is supported by assertiveness, females are encouraged to invest their time and energy in the pursuit of attractiveness resulting in intimate relationships predicting identity outcomes.

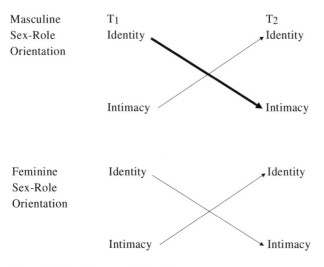

Figure 12.2. Conceptual Model 2

SOURCE: From Dyk & Adams (1990). Reprinted with permission from Plenum Publishing Corp.

Another line of reasoning can be found to support this model. It is generally assumed that women have the ability to develop a sense of caring that is manifested in empathy at a younger age than do men. As Chodorow (1974) suggested, this sex difference may be linked to early experiences where females are provided relationships with female caregivers who function as effective role models for viewing and defining the self in the context of intimate relationships. Indeed, Fischer (1981) supported the notion that adolescent females are more capable than males of developing and maintaining intimate relationships and that females develop skills in relating to others earlier than do males. Dyk and Adams (1990) speculated that these behaviors may be indicative of an earlier development of intimacy capacities by females.

This final model (see Figure 12.3) suggests a reverse relationship between identity and intimacy for males and females. For males, identity is thought to precede intimacy. For females, intimacy is thought to precede and predict identity.

An Initial Test of the Comparative Models

To assess the potential merit of the three models, Dyk and Adams (1990) conducted a short-term longitudinal study. A total of 142 college

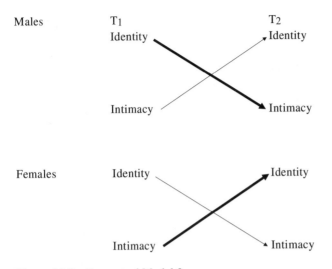

Figure 12.3. Conceptual Model 3

SOURCE: From Dyk & Adams (1990). Reprinted with permission from Plenum Publishing Corp.

respondents (71 males, 71 females; average age 19) was assessed on both identity and intimacy measures at two occasions over a five-week period. Respondents completed the Erikson Psychosocial Stage Inventory (EPSI) scale (Rosenthal et al., 1981), the Bem Sex Role Inventory (BSRI) (Bem, 1974), and the Questionnaire Measure of Emotional Empathy (Mehrabian & Epstein, 1972). The identity and intimacy subscales of the EPSI were used as continuous-scale measures for the analyses. The feminine and masculine scales of the BSRI were correlated with the empathy measure. As anticipated, empathy was positively correlated with femininity and negatively with masculinity. Therefore, the masculine and feminine scores were used as indicators of a male and female voice, respectively.

Cross-lag panel correlations were computed using a program developed by Kenny (1976). In simple terms, the cross-lag correlations are compared, assuming all other statistical assumptions are met, to determine whether one cross-lag correlation is significantly larger than the other. If so, it is assumed that the significantly larger correlation is suggestive of directional dominance.

In the first set of analyses, Models 1 and 3 were tested by conducting cross-lagged correlational assessments between identity and intimacy for males and females separately. In support of Model 1 for both sexes and Model 3 for males, a significant cross-lagged correlation revealed that identity predicts intimacy for males, whereas no statistical directional dominance was found for females.

The cross-lags then were recomputed with the intent of separating the sex of the respondent (as a basic genotype) from the identification with a given sex-role orientation. In other words, separate analyses were computed for males and females, partialing for masculinity and femininity. This analysis attempts to remove socialization factors from the basic biological or genotype difference associated with being male or female. Once these controls were included, identity predicted intimacy for both males and females. This finding contradicts both Model 1's prediction for identity-intimacy fusion for females and Model 3's prediction of a directional dominance of intimacy-to-identity association for females. Regarding Model 3, a directional dominance of intimacy-to-identity was found for neither sex.

Given that Gilligan and others have argued that the association between identity and intimacy is based on socialization and internalized psychological processes of either individuation for males or caring and responsibility for females, analyses (testing Model 2) were undertaken comparing low and high empathy, low and high masculine, and low and high feminine individuals of each sex. For males, regardless of level of empathy or sex-role orientation, all significant cross-lags revealed that identity predicted intimacy. Of interest is that the identity-to-intimacy association was strongest for the more feminine-oriented males. For masculine-oriented women, identity also predicted intimacy. Only for feminine-oriented women was directional dominance not manifested. Thus Model 2 was only partially supported.

In summary, the tests of the three models revealed significant cross-lagged correlations that demonstrated the sequential nature of the relationship between identity and intimacy, with identity occurring sequentially before intimacy. This supports the predictions of Models 1 and 3 for men. It refutes Model 3's prediction of intimacy preceding identity for women.

Sex-role orientation provided an interesting complication to this finding. So-called feminine-oriented men and masculine-oriented women demonstrated significant directional dominance patterns of identity before intimacy, while feminine-oriented women revealed no directional dominance. Thus men of the feminine or female voice countered Gilligan's theme proposal (Model 2), while women of the masculine or male voice and feminine or female voice supported her theme argument and Model 2.

Because the feminine-oriented or female-voiced men held the strongest directional dominance of identity preceding intimacy, the arguments advanced for Model 2 become problematic. The feminine orientation of connection, nurturance, and empathy does not necessitate a fusion of identity and intimacy, at least for men. Indeed, in those few instances of no directional dominance for females, with sex-role orientation not partialed out and for feminine-oriented females, one can only conclude that no sequentiality was demonstrated with regard to the relationship between identity and intimacy. The cross-lagged correlational analyses do not afford us an answer to the question of whether lack of directionality means that identity and intimacy are fused or engaged in a parallel manner without integration or interrelatedness. The findings from this short-term longitudinal study have demonstrated the need for further research focused on a specific test of the meaning of nondirectionality.

Implications for Socialization

Current debate about different patterns and processes in psychological development seem to be only partially supported by the evidence. In much of the research assessing the association between identity and intimacy, the proposed connection is observed for males and females. Both concurrent assessments and longitudinal analyses support the association between identity and intimacy. Furthermore, numerous analyses of possible gender differences (e.g., Archer, 1989; Archer & Waterman, 1988; Waterman, 1985) have found that patterns in identity formation are similar for males and females and of equal importance to the individual's psychological and social functioning regardless of gender. Boys and girls, men and women, appear to formulate identities in very similar ways.

Further, when the interconnection between agency and communion is extrapolated from the measurement of identity and intimacy, it is observed that an active, mastery-focused, self-selected identity is predictive of depth, quality, and intimacy in social relationships. This finding is found for males and females. So a sense of uniqueness, self-direction, personalized goals, autonomy, and separateness is an important factor in predicting intimate social relationships. For many, this may appear as a paradox. However, we perceive the association between these two dimensions of social functioning as mutually compatible and complementary (as does Bakan, 1966).

Elsewhere it has been suggested that human development is supported by two functions (Dyk & Adams, 1987). The social function assures that we are socialized through a process of connection, integration, union, and mutuality. It ensures that we are provided with a network of support and provides a common cultural, historical, and social niche. The personality function provides for a process of differentiation that allows one to feel unique, special, autonomous, and independent. When either the social or personality function fails to materialize, the individual feels disconnected, unaffiliated, unrecognized, vulnerable, alienated, and diffused. When the social function dominates the personality function, one is likely to be oversocialized, conformist, and foreclosed. Should the personality function overshadow the social function, one is likely to be narcissistic, egotistical, domineering, and possibly show manifestations of existential anxiety and confusion. When a balance between the personality and social function is evident, the individual appears to internalize both agency and communion and recognizes that the individual is unique within an important and broader social network. In other words, individualism is based on interdependency between an active, mastery-based self and a supporting and contributing social niche.

Partial evidence for such assumptions are found in the sex-role orientation facilitation effects in the Dyk and Adams (1990) study. Men, whom we assume are focused on individuation based on their socialization, are facilitated in their search for intimacy by the acquisition of feminine sex-role interests and characteristics. Likewise, women, whom we assume are generally focused on connection based on their socialization, are facilitated in their search for an identity by the acquisition of masculine sex-role characteristics. Such findings as these support the growing notion that the encouragement of a balance between agency and communion is predictive of greater social adaptiveness and, in our special case, capacity to establish and maintain intimacy. Thus early and continuing socialization in sex-role typing appears to set the stage for the formation of an active form of identity formation. In turn, an active form of identity development is an established precursor for greater capacity and positive resolution in intimacy.

In conclusion, the identity and intimacy connection represents the strong linkage between individuality and connectedness, agency and communion, individualism and interdependency. This connection is no less important for men than for women. In the next chapter, Raskin and Waterman propose interventions for facilitating the identity-intimacy connection.

References

Adams, G. R. (1985). Family correlates of female adolescents' ego-identity development. *Journal of Adolescence, 8,* 69-82.

Adams, G. R., & Shea, J. A. (1979). The relationship between identity status, locus of control and ego development. *Journal of Youth and Adolescence, 8,* 81-89.

Archer, S. L. (1985). Identity and the choice of social roles. In A. S. Waterman (Ed.), *Identity in adolescence: Processes and contents* (pp. 79-99). San Francisco: Jossey-Bass.

Archer, S. L. (1989). Gender differences in identity development: Issues of process, domain, and timing. *Journal of Adolescence, 12,* 117-138.

Archer, S. L., & Waterman, A. S. (1988). Psychological individualism: Gender differences or gender neutrality? *Human Development, 31,* 65-81.

Archer, S. L., Gayer, H., Campano, K., Reichman, C., Vaneerden, A., Alexander, V., Davala, A., Callahan, A., Raatzs, I., Lombardo, J., Emers, M., Eig, B., and Suabedissen, A. (1989). *Intimacy manual for romantic relationships.* Unpublished manuscript.

Bakan, D. (1966). *The duality of human existence.* Boston: Beacon.

Bem, S. L. (1974). The measurement of psychological androgyny. *Journal of Consulting and Clinical Psychology, 42,* 155-162.

Carlson, D. L. (1986). *Identity status: Its relationship to psychological adjustment and academic achievement.* Unpublished master's thesis, University of Wisconsin, River Falls, WI.

Chodorow, N. (1974). Family structure and feminine personality. In M. Z. Rosaldo & L. Lamphere (Eds.), *Woman, culture, and society* (pp. 43-66). Palo Alto: Stanford University Press.

Constantinople, A. (1969). An Eriksonian measure of personality development in college students. *Developmental Psychology, 1,* 357-372.

Cooper, C. R., Grotevant, H. D., Moore, M. S., & Condon, S. M. (1984). Predicting adolescent role taking and identity exploration from communication patterns: A comparison of one- and two-child families. In T. Falbo (Ed.), *The single-child family* (pp. 117-142). New York: Guilford.

Craig-Bray, L., & Adams, G. R. (1986). Measuring social intimacy in same-sex and opposite-sex contexts. *Journal of Adolescent Research, 1,* 95-101.

Craig-Bray, L., Adams, G. R., & Dobson, W. R. (1988). Identity formation and social relations during late adolescence. *Journal of Youth and Adolescence, 17,* 173-187.

Donovan, J. M. (1975). Identity status: Its relationship to Rorschach performance and to daily life patterns. *Adolescence, 10,* 29-44.

Dyk, P. A., & Adams, G. R. (1987). The association between identity development and intimacy during adolescence: A theoretical treatise. *Journal of Adolescent Research, 2,* 223-235.

Dyk, P. A., & Adams, G. R. (1990). Identity and intimacy: An initial investigation of three theoretical models using cross-lag panel correlations. *Journal of Youth and Adolescence, 19,* 91-110.

Erikson, E. H. (1968). *Identity: Youth and crisis.* New York: Norton.

Fischer, J. L. (1981). Transitions in relationship style from adolescent to young adulthood. *Journal of Youth and Adolescence, 10,* 11-24.

Fitch, S. A., & Adams, G. R. (1983). Ego-identity and intimacy status: Replication and extension. *Developmental Psychology, 19,* 839-845.

Freedman, B. (1986). *Beauty bound.* Lexington, MA: D. C. Heath.

Gilligan, C. (1982). *In a different voice.* Cambridge, MA: Harvard University Press.

Ginsburg, S. D., & Orlofsky, J. L. (1981). Ego identity status, ego development, and locus of control in college women. *Journal of Youth and Adolescence, 10,* 297-307.

Grotevant, H., & Cooper, C. (1981). Assessing adolescent identity in the areas of occupation, religion, politics, friendship, dating, sex roles: Manual for administration and coding of the interview. *JSAS Catalog of Selected Documents in Psychology, 11,* 52. (Manuscript No. 2295)

Hawley, G. A. (1988). *Measures of psychosocial development.* Odessa, FL: Psychological Assessment Resources.

Hodgson, J. W., & Fischer, J. L. (1979). Sex differences in identity and intimacy development in college youth. *Youth and Adolescence, 8,* 37-50.

Josselson, R. (1987). *Finding herself: Pathways to identity development in women.* San Francisco: Jossey-Bass.

Kacerguis, M. A., & Adams, G. R. (1980). Erikson stage resolution: The relationship between identity and intimacy. *Journal of Youth and Adolescence, 9,* 117-126.

Kenny, D. A. (1976). *PANAL: A computer program for panel data analysis.* Storrs: University of Connecticut, Department of Psychology.

Kroger, J. (1985). Separation-individuation and ego identity status in New Zealand university students. *Journal of Youth and Adolescence, 14,* 133-147.

Lamke, L. K., & Abraham, K. G. (1984, October). *Adolescent identity formation and sex-role development: Critical linkages.* Paper presented at meeting of National Council on Family Relations, San Francisco, CA.

Mallory, M. E. (1989). Q-sort definition of ego identity status. *Journal of Youth and Adolescence, 18,* 399-412.

Marcia, J. E. (1966). Development and validation of ego identity status. *Journal of Personality and Social Psychology, 3,* 551-558.

Marcia, J. E., Waterman, A. S., Matteson, D. R., Archer, S.L., & Orlofsky, J. L. (1993). *Ego identity: A handbook for psychosocial research.* New York: Springer Verlag.

Mehrabian, A., & Epstein, N. (1972). A measure of emotional empathy. *Journal of Personality, 40,* 525-543.

Orlofsky, J. (1993). Intimacy status: Theory and research. In J. E. Marcia, A. S. Waterman, D. R. Matteson, S. L. Archer, & J. L. Orlofsky, *Ego identity: A handbook for psychosocial research* (pp. 111-133). New York: Springer Verlag.

Orlofsky, J., & Frank, M. (1986). Personality structure as viewed through early memories and identity status in college men and women. *Journal of Personality and Social Psychology, 50,* 580-586.

Orlofsky, J., Marcia, J., & Lesser, I. (1973). Ego identity status and the intimacy vs. isolation crisis in young adulthood. *Journal of Personality and Social Psychology, 27,* 211-219.

Paul, E. L., White, K. M., Speisman, J. C., & Costos, D. (1989, April). *The self in relation to others.* Paper presented at biennial meeting of Society for Research in Child Development, Kansas City, MO.

Rasmussen, J. F. (1964). Relationship of ego identity to psychosocial effectiveness. *Psychological Reports, 15,* 815-825.

Read, D., Adams, G. R., & Dobson, W. (1984). Ego-identity status, personality, and social influence style. *Journal of Personality and Social Psychology, 46,* 169-177.

Rosenthal, D. A., Gurney, R. M., & Moore, S. M. (1981). From trust to intimacy: A new inventory for examining Erikson's stages of psychosocial development. *Journal of Youth and Adolescence, 10,* 525-537.

Tesch, S. A., & Whitbourne, S. K. (1982). Intimacy and identity status in young adults. *Journal of Personality and Social Psychology, 43,* 1041-1051.

Waterman, A. S. (1985). Identity in the context of adolescent psychology. In A. W. Waterman (Ed.), *Identity in adolescence: Processes and contents* (pp. 5-24). San Francisco: Jossey-Bass.

White, K., Speisman, J., & Costos, D. (1983). Young adults and their parents: Individuation to mutuality. In H. D. Grotevant & C. R. Cooper (Eds.), *Adolescent development in the family* (pp. 61-76). San Francisco: Jossey-Bass.

Willemsen, E. W., & Waterman, K. K. (1988). *Ego identity status and family environment: A correlational study.* Unpublished study, Department of Psychology, Santa Clara University, Santa Clara, CA.

Yufit, R. I. (1969). Variations of intimacy and isolation. *Journal of Projective Techniques and Personality Assessment, 33,* 49-58.

13

On the Bidirectional Impact
of Counseling on
Identity and Intimacy Developments

PATRICIA M. RASKIN
ALAN S. WATERMAN

As discussed in Chapter 12, the identity construct has been demonstrated to be strongly associated with a range of variables that pertain to the quality of intimate relationships. Active, self-reflective approaches to the task of identity formation, as found in the identity-achievement and moratorium statuses, are associated with greater depth and mutuality in intimate relationships. Less sophisticated, more passive approaches to identity formation, such as the foreclosure and identity-diffusion statuses, are associated with either relative isolation or traditional role-oriented approaches to relationships. One principal point of divergence for the models of the relationship of identity to intimacy involves the normative sequencing in the development of these two aspects of psychosocial functioning. Is a successful resolution of identity concerns a necessary precursor to successful intimacy development, as Erikson (1963, 1968) proposes, or can successful development proceed in the reverse sequence or simultaneously? Some theorists have proposed different answers to this question for males and females (Freedman, 1986; Gilligan, 1982).

The focus of this chapter will be on the bidirectional implications of counseling for both identity formation and intimacy development. Where the focus of counseling is on the resolution of identity concerns, the

214

outcomes may have an effect on individuals' functioning in intimate relationships. Where the focus of counseling is on relationships, the effects of counseling may involve important changes in the processes of identity formation.

In pointing to such bidirectional impacts, no stand need be taken on the normative question raised above. Whereas Erikson (1963, 1968) emphasized the sequential nature of the stages in his life-cycle scheme, he incorporated into his theory a more complex arrangement of interconnections of stage components across time. First, he proposed that each stage component is reworked at each stage after its time of special ascendancy within the context of the component that is then the focus of development. Thus an individual's standing with respect to the Stage 5 component of identity versus role confusion can be expected to change as a function of how the person copes with the focal task of Stage 6, intimacy versus isolation. Second, he maintained that the components of each later stage in the life cycle have their forerunners during any current stage. Thus as an adolescent proceeds with the task of identity formation, elements of the intimacy versus isolation component are also emerging.

Counseling Techniques

Counseling techniques with adolescents do not differ from those with adults, although it is probably true that for many normal teenagers, interpersonal or person-centered approaches generate the least resistance. Although young people are eager to learn about themselves, they are also often reluctant to discuss their innermost thoughts and feelings with others, especially adults. To some extent, counselors have an advantage over parents and teachers because authority issues are not paramount. This is especially true when the adolescent has asked for counseling and has personally chosen the counselor or therapist.

With regard to establishing rapport, the counselor's capacity to listen without making judgments is crucial, as is his or her ability to communicate that capacity. Because boundaries are so fluid in adolescence, it is not unusual for teenagers to feel that adults can "read" their minds and decide that something is really wrong with them. That projection, of course, is partly based on their own confusion about what is happening to them, as well as on the natural conflicts that occur between dependency and independence strivings. At the same time, it is important for clients to feel that they can share the things that trouble them without those concerns being minimized.

The communication approach used by the counselor is also important. Brammer and Shostrom (1982) used the term *lead* to describe "the extent to which the counselor is ahead or behind the client's thinking" (p. 197). Robinson (1950) defined it as "a teamlike working together in which the counselor's remarks seem to the client to state the next point he [or she] is ready to accept" (p. 66). All counselor responses can be placed on a continuum ranging from minimal leading—such as silence, acceptance, and restatement—to considerable leading—such as tentative analysis, interpretation, urging, and rejection. Adolescents are sometimes alienated by responses that fall into the latter categories because of emergent autonomy issues, so counselors need to be sensitive to this possibility. But clients also can be put off by responses that offer too little. Simple reflection, as in paraphrasing, occasionally results in the client feeling that the counselor is just repeating what is said. This can be experienced as condescending or frustrating. In this regard, there may be large individual differences among clients such that a technique that works effectively with one adolescent may prove to be counterproductive with another.

The importance of flexibility on the part of the therapist may also become evident when encountering the adolescent client's need to shift the focus of counseling concern from issue to issue. Of particular relevance here are the shifts that may occur between priorities placed on identity and intimacy themes. Adolescents who may have sought counseling for problems with respect to an identity search may find that it becomes more important to look at the changes taking place in their relationships. Alternatively, adolescents who initially brought relationship problems to counseling may find that changes in relationships reopen identity issues that then become more important to work through than were the original presenting problems.

Counseling With Clients in the Various Identity Statuses

If an adolescent seeks to become involved in identity counseling, it can be assumed that there is a significant degree of discomfort with which the adolescent finds her- or himself with respect to identity-related goals, values, or beliefs. It may be that the adolescent is diffuse, with the discomfort arising from the apparent inability to form desired commitments. The discomfort might also arise from pressures applied by parents or others, pressures to which the adolescent may be exerting active or passive resistance. Alternatively, the adolescent may be fore-closed or identity-achieved but in a position where the existing com-mitments are not working out as he or she may have wished. Or the adolescent may be in moratorium, experiencing increased levels of anxiety typically associated with an identity crisis (Marcia, 1967).

Status: Identity Diffusion

With respect to identity-diffuse adolescents entering a counseling process there may be quite different issues involved for clients who are not in romantic relationships and those who are. If an adolescent not in a relationship presents identity-related issues in counseling, it is possi-ble that the counseling may proceed in a relatively linear, uncluttered way on those themes. However, it is also possible for an adolescent, particularly a late adolescent, who has yet to enter into a meaningful romantic relationship to seek a romantic partner in an attempt to achieve a self-definition through the partner. Such attempts typically reflect dependency motivations. In this way identity and intimacy issues may become fused in counseling.

From a social exchange theory perspective (Thibaut & Kelley, 1959), a lack of a sense of personal identity can be considered a debit with respect to relationship formation, as can the presence of dependency motivations. In the absence of other notable assets, difficulties can be expected with respect to relationship formation. It is likely that, at a fairly early point, counseling will become focused on the question of what the client has to offer to a potential romantic partner. If the client is able to develop a realistic recognition of his or her ratio of assets to liabilities, then the focus of counseling may shift to "asset accumulation and liability reduction." This will likely include identity as well as other potential assets and liabilities.

If an identity-diffuse client is currently in a romantic relationship and seeking counseling for identity-related concerns, then it is possible that the actual impetus for change may have arisen with the partner. The partner may be making either explicit or implicit demands for more investment and greater commitment on the part of the client not just about the client's goals and values, but also about the relationship itself. Thus early in counseling it may become evident that the partner has threatened to end the relationship if the client does not change. At this point, the focus of counseling may shift to the relational themes, with a need to make some progress in this area, before it will be productive to return to identity-related themes.

Status: Foreclosure

Foreclosures are unlikely to enter identity counseling unless there is some perceived threat to their ability to effectively implement the identity commitments they have in place. Given the existing commitments and, for some foreclosures, the rigidity with which commitments are held, problem-solving, reality-based counseling techniques are likely to be the most appropriate. If the original path toward the implementation of the client's goals can be reestablished or if alternative paths toward the same end can be developed, then the client's objective for counseling will have been met. In this instance, counseling will likely proceed without the need to consider the client's relationships or broader intimacy themes. But if it becomes clear that the client will not be able to successfully implement the identity elements on which he or she has foreclosed, then efforts to help the client work through the feeling of loss and initiate the consideration of identity alternatives may have serious repercussions for an existing romantic relationship. The identity status of the partner may be an important variable in determining whether the relationship survives the identity changes taking place.

If the client's partner in a relationship is also foreclosed, and if compatibility of goals and values was an important element in the establishment of the relationship, then the prospect of the client experiencing a change in those goals and values is likely to be experienced as threatening. The partner may well have difficulty in understanding the other's ideas. Although the most likely outcome during adolescence of emerging value differences is a dissolution of the relationship, there will be instances where other factors (e.g., parental preferences or a rigid idealization of a first love experience) will be of sufficient strength to have both partners seek maintenance of the relationship. At this point, it will be clear that the focus of counseling has shifted from identity toward intimacy issues.

With a shift toward relational concerns, it may be appropriate to initiate joint sessions with a couple. It is likely with foreclosed clients that each partner will seek to have the counselor play the role of an ally in authority in the efforts to change the other. The counselor's attempts to get each person to perceive the other's point of view may be actively resisted. The goal of counseling at this point may have more to do with establishing a climate in which personal and social changes can be perceived as not unduly threatening rather than with the maintenance or dissolution of the relationship.

Status: Moratorium

The moratorium status is a state of disequilibrium with respect to goals, values, and beliefs that is experienced by some individuals with considerable psychological distress. Adolescents may seek counseling either for assistance in developing strategies for the consideration of identity alternatives or in response to the anxiety engendered by an identity crisis. In the latter instance, an adolescent may not be aware initially of the factors precipitating the anxiety.

The experience of an identity crisis poses several problems for adolescent relationships. To the extent that the premoratorium characteristics of the adolescent in counseling contributed to the attraction within the relationship, either in terms of the content of identity elements or the psychological dynamics associated with identity, those characteristics may now be in a state of flux. At some point the changes occurring may have the effect of undermining the quality and existence of the relationship.

Because the moratorium status is usually accompanied by anxiety or other dysphoric emotions, there is a natural tendency for the individual to turn inward, increasing egocentricity and self-focus as efforts are made to resolve what are perceived to be personal problems. The increased psychological energy focused on the self is likely to be accompanied by a corresponding decrease in the attention and concern directed toward the romantic relationship in which the adolescent has been involved. As a consequence, the relationship may be experienced by the partner as less rewarding or satisfying.

The emerging strains on the relationship can produce problems for both the adolescent in counseling and the partner. Either or both individuals may, with some justification, identify the source of the problems in the relationship as arising from the counseling process. This may serve to undermine the counseling.

The threat of or actual breakup of a relationship adds stress in the life of the adolescent participating in identity-related counseling. It now appears that counseling has produced greater changes in the person's life than had been initially anticipated. As a consequence, it may be necessary to temporarily refocus the counseling on relational concerns, because these may become of more focal concern to the adolescent than the identity-related concerns that initiated counseling. Depending on the priorities set by adolescents in counseling, some may drop out at this point in an effort to protect the relationship, while others will refocus again on the identity issues that brought them to counseling.

Status: Identity Achievement

Adolescents in the identity-achievement status will most likely enter identity-related counseling for reasons similar to those of someone in foreclosure status—that is, problems are anticipated with regard to the implementation of an established identity element. Alternatively, there may be an emerging feeling that the chosen goal or value will not prove as fulfilling as had been believed originally. In contrast to a foreclosed client, an identity achiever will likely feel less threatened by change and more confident of his or her exploration skills because of previous successful experience with an identity crisis. This can make the process of counseling smoother than it is with individuals in the other statuses.

The effect of identity counseling on a client's relationship will vary in part because of the quality of the relationship and the identity status of the partner. Many of the issues described above with respect to the foreclosure and moratorium statuses may emerge in counseling with identity achievers as they reenter the moratorium status (Stephen, Fraser, & Marcia, 1992).

Counseling With Clients in the Various Intimacy Statuses

Adolescents may seek counseling with respect to relationships either because they have not yet been in a meaningful relationship and are seeking to learn how to attract a partner or because they are encountering problems in an existing relationship and are seeking ways to preserve that relationship. In either instance, what starts as an intervention with respect to intimacy may become focused on identity themes.

Archer and her colleagues (1989) have expanded the intimacy-status paradigm to include broad classes and statuses, resulting in 12 possible status assignments. Individuals within the classes may present developmentally similar profiles, so that one or more examples are provided for each of the three new class categories: (a) casual, (b) traditional, and (c) intimate.

Class—Casual
Status—Isolated Adolescents

Isolated clients are not uncommon in high school and college counseling centers. They can present in two ways: They either seem highly defensive, narcissistic, distant, and unempathic or appear quite schizoid and dependent. It is unlikely that those in the first group would initiate counseling because of a relationship, but those in the second group often complain of loneliness and the inability to meet people. In both cases, the absence of self-awareness is palpable, and difficulties with peer and romantic relationships tend to be externalized. Clients in the second category can develop intense positive transference in the counseling relationship, especially if counselors are not clearly age-inappropriate. What is interesting about this transference is that it seems to occur quickly and without much stimulus. These clients seem completely inexperienced in relationships and often show a deficit in social skill. Inquiry into the past might reveal abuse or other forms of family dysfunction.

In identity terms, isolated clients are likely to appear as either identity-diffuse or foreclosed. When identity-diffuse, the transference may result in the client taking over visible aspects of the counselor's identity in a superficial, nonreflective, and inappropriate fashion. Dress, language, career plans, and so on may come to mirror the counselor's. When foreclosed, this process may have occurred with respect to some other model or transference figure in the adolescent's life. At some later point in the counseling relationship, identity issues may need to become a focus of therapeutic work.

Although isolated adolescents might be quite accomplished in technical areas and appear to be bright, one has the feeling that their complaints of isolation are lifelong and nearly intractable. Working with these clients is a challenge; they clearly need help in developing social skills. But such efforts are seen by these clients as further evidence that the counselor is the only one in the world who understands them. Both individual and group treatment is recommended. It is likely that these clients will be in some form of counseling for much of their lives.

Class—Casual
Status—Immature Casual Adolescents

Immature casuals can appear attractive and personable, but one has the feeling that dating meets general social needs rather than being a precursor for deep interpersonal fulfillment. Junior and senior high school students epitomize the immature casual status with new romantic attachments each week. Senior high school and college students who describe themselves as "playing the field" are in this status, provided there is not a developmental history of a long-term commitment to a romantic relationship,

Here again, it is unlikely that relationship issues would be the occasion for seeking counseling. Conflict between the demands of the family and a desire for greater social independence might, however, be a presenting problem. Before college, it is age-appropriate, and adolescents vary widely on this dimension in college, especially during the first three years. When this class of intimacy persists much beyond college, it is likely to be diagnostic of some deficit in the capacity to form intimate relationships.

As a status that is age-appropriate before and during the college years, there is no strong association between casual intimacy and identity functioning. Should adolescents in this category be in counseling, the focus can be placed on whatever the presenting problems may be, identity- or intimacy-related, without necessarily bringing the other into the process. For older clients, where casual intimacy may be an aspect of character, either weak or strong identity commitments may be evident. For clients who are identity-diffuse, it is likely that this represents the same casual approach taken toward commitments in relationships that has been applied to the matter of self-definition. Here the matter of commitment may be worked on in counseling with efforts made to generalize between commitments to both self and others. To the extent that the problem is characterological, however, this clinical task can be quite difficult. For clients who are foreclosed or identity-achieved, the lack of commitment to relationships may represent a conscious or unconscious priority to place identity-related achievement ahead of relationships. Here presenting problems concerning relationships can only be worked through after the client can develop a better understanding of the identity-related priorities that he or she has set.

Class—Traditional
Status—Pretraditional Adolescents

Pretraditional adolescents are looking to "settle down." They are dissatisfied with dating and often give the impression that finding a mate will help them get on with their lives. Advertising directed at preteen and teenage girls is often specifically aimed at this group, and conversation (especially with young women) sometimes reveals that they have been planning their weddings for a few years: The only thing missing is the groom. One also has the feeling that both men and women in this category can select a life partner based more on social criteria than on affect or passion, and that they are confident that if the external criteria are met, then the internal feelings will follow naturally.

In junior and senior high school students, this status is parallel to the foreclosure identity status. Unable to tolerate the ambiguity of an uncertain future, both boys and girls can articulate the wish to find someone to feel as much at home with as they do their parents or to create a home they feel they have never had. They might enter counseling to find out how to attract someone specific or to expand their options for meeting people. This status does persist into college and beyond, in the same way that foreclosure does. Counseling with these adolescents may or may not result in developmental shifts. It is important to keep in mind that clients in this status are selectively disclosing and can be quite judgmental. They are particularly resistant to having their values and beliefs called into question and will terminate prematurely if they think that change in this respect is a goal held by the counselor.

Class—Traditional
Status—Merged Adolescents

Merged adolescents are role-bound and committed; their presenting problems for counseling arise when their relationships are not going as expected. Partners' bids for greater independence or more space are perceived as threatening, and differences in opinions are not well tolerated. One has the feeling that these relationships suffer from a too rigid superstructure: Fluctuation in any domain can result in a shattering of the structure rather than a rearrangement.

Class—Intimate
Status—Conditionally Intimate Adolescents

Relatively few younger clients will fall into the intimate class, although one cannot rule out that possibility. The criteria for assignment into this status call for "a good deal of self-awareness, genuine interest in others and the absence of significant defensiveness" (Orlofsky, 1993, p. 358). Individuals who can be characterized as intimate may also be identity-achieved (Orlofsky, 1978; Orlofsky, Marcia, & Lesser, 1973). It is therefore more likely that older adolescents (e.g., college juniors and seniors) would be assigned to these statuses than would junior high school and senior high school students or college freshmen and sophomores (Orlofsky, 1976). When these students do come in for counseling about their relationships, the presenting problems are often realistic—for example, differing career goals create a dilemma of what to do and where to go for further education. These clients may seek help because they find that they are rethinking their level of commitment to the relationship or renegotiating the balance between individual goals and dyadic goals (Archer et al., 1989). These conflicts may also create separation anxiety or depression in the client. The capacity for forming intimate relationships, however, tends to remain stable, independent of the outcomes of these dilemmas.

Because the problems in the relationship may initiate a reworking of previously developed identity elements—that is, a new period of moratorium—the focus of work within counseling may shift back and forth between intimacy and identity concerns. Such shifts may occur within a single session. Given that the problems brought to counseling arise in life circumstances rather than being of intrapsychic origin, the timing of their resolution may be determined by external events—for example, the need to accept or reject a graduate school offer of admission or a new job offer.

Two Examples of Intimacy-Identity Counseling

Class—Traditional
Status—Merged Adolescents

Michael, a merged adolescent, is a 20-year-old heavy-equipment operator who has been going steady with Mary for a year and a half. Just before meeting her, he confided that if he had known how hard it would be to meet nice girls after high school, he would have made more of an effort to be in a committed relationship before graduation. Although he has vague plans for further education, he makes good money at his job, and his future seems secure to him if he continues on his current career path. Mary is 18 and has just started to attend a college an hour away from home. She lives in the dorm but thus far has been home every weekend except one. Michael visited her on that occasion.

Michael enters counseling clearly despondent. Mary has seemed distant and irritable since she started college and seems unable to include Michael in her new life. He is hurt and angry but clear that it is the situation that is causing this difficulty, not any inherent conflicts within the relationship. He says that he knows this is true because they never fought about anything until Mary left for college. Michael has given Mary an ultimatum. Either treat him better or he will break up with her. So far she has capitulated, but it is clear that the relationship is no longer "perfect."

Counseling with Michael has to begin with the acceptance of his premise—that the deterioration of the relationship is situational. Any other observation will be met with resistance or premature termination. Gentle exploration about the nature of the relationship might uncover some questioning about the similarity of their individual (identity-related) goals or about the "rightness" of Mary as a life partner. It is unlikely that Michael will be able to handle Mary's accelerated development unless (a) he can make a corresponding shift in circumstance such as going to school or taking a job in a new community (both unlikely events) or (b) she can incorporate him into her new world in a way that does not feel humiliating to him. If the commitment on both parts is strong enough, counseling can help Michael accept changes in both of them as natural and help prepare both of them for some of the developmental shifts that will undoubtedly occur over time. The key to successful counseling with this couple is in expanding their appreciation of each other as individuals rather than as role representatives. If this occurs, one might also expect identity shifts in both of them (a good example of the reciprocal relationship between identity and intimacy).

Class—Intimate
Status—Conditionally Intimate Adolescents

Irene, a prelaw student, is in her senior year of college, as is her boyfriend, Jim, a computer science major. They have been seeing each other since the middle of their junior year and recently moved in together off campus. They are planning on marrying at some point in the future, although they do not feel pressured to do so immediately. They are good students, but not in the top 10% of their class. Although they have applied to graduate programs at the same or nearby universities, there is a real possibility that if they each get admitted to their first-choice schools, they will not be able to live together. Irene and Jim are mature, and their career goals are well thought out. Abandoning those goals would be painful for both of them.

Irene seeks counseling because she and Jim are at a stalemate, and it is unusual for them to be unable to resolve conflicts. She indicates that Jim knows of and understands her concerns and that no hidden agenda is apparent. She is distressed by both the need to make such difficult decisions and her lack of knowledge about what this current inability to resolve conflicts portends. To work effectively with this client, her counselor needs to (a) respect the seriousness and reality of the dilemma, (b) create an environment in which further expansion can take place without threat, (c) enable Irene to challenge her own assumptions about her career and relationships, and (d) give her "permission" to test her assumptions. Seeing Jim would also be useful, especially if it becomes apparent that Irene is the de facto "emissary" to counseling.

Conclusions

Clearly, one cannot work with individuals without taking relationships into account and vice versa. Erikson (1963) assumed that identity precedes and influences intimacy, while others have discussed the possibility of the reverse normative sequence (particularly for women) or the simultaneous development of the two. In clinical work as well as research, it is evident that progress in either developmental stage may influence the other, and that this mutual influence can further identity or intimacy formation, retard progress, or both.

Some of the evidence for this phenomenon can be ascertained from the stories of constructive relationships and the dissolution of incompatible ones. Strong relationships can free individuals for further identity work—much as secure attachment in early childhood paves the way for eager exploration (Ainsworth, 1989; Lyddon, Bradford, & Nelson, 1993). On the other hand, clients often report surprising surges in identity formation at the end of relationships, and future relationships may benefit from such a surge. We also often see a regression in individual functioning when clients report dissolution purely as loss of partner, social standing, and so on. And these possibilities, of course, document Eriksonian theory: the recapitulation of previous stage resolution in each successive stage.

Although intimacy counseling would not be undertaken for the purpose of initiating changes with respect to identity formation, it must be recognized that counseling with respect to relationships may have the consequence of inducing movement with respect to identity themes. Correspondingly, identity interventions will in many instances have repercussions with regard to an individual's ongoing relationships. Thus counselors need to have the flexibility to shift the focus of intervention from intimacy to identity, or vice versa, as the client's priorities shift. The frequency and duration of such shifts will vary by client, based in part on his or her developmental standing with respect to identity and intimacy at the time counseling begins.

The fact of shifts within counseling between identity and intimacy issues does not in itself mean that the two stages of Erikson's theory should be viewed as merged, with successful development considered possible in either direction. From an epigenetic perspective, Erikson (1963, 1968) contended that some success in the process of identity formation is a necessary precursor for success with respect to intimacy development. Although a client may feel the need to work on intimacy issues before identity issues, and the counselor may need to act on the client's perceptions in this regard, it may still be the case that only by a subsequent return to identity questions will the client actually be able to establish the foundation to facilitate progress with respect to his or her relationships. As more is learned about the sequential or simultaneous interrelationships regarding developments of the psychosocial components of identity and intimacy, improvements in counseling practice are likely to follow.

References

Ainsworth, M. D. (1989). Attachments beyond infancy. *American Psychologist, 44,* 709-716.

Archer, S. L., Gayer, H., Campano, K., Reichman, C., Vaneerden, A., Alexander, V., Davala, A., Callahan, A., Raatzs, I., Lombardo, J., Emers, M., Eig, B., & Suabedissen, A. (1989). *Intimacy manual for romantic relationships.* Unpublished technical report. Trenton, NJ: Trenton State College.

Brammer, L. M., & Shostrom, E. L. (1982). *Therapeutic psychology: Fundamentals of counseling and psychotherapy* (4th ed.). Englewood Cliffs, NJ: Prentice-Hall.

Erikson, E. H. (1963). *Childhood and society* (2nd ed.). New York: Norton.

Erikson, E. H. (1968). *Identity: Youth and crisis.* New York: Norton.

Freedman, B. (1986). *Beauty bound.* Lexington, MA: D. C. Heath.

Gilligan, C. (1982). *In a different voice.* Cambridge, MA: Harvard University Press.

Lyddon, W. J., Bradford, E., & Nelson, J. P. (1993). Assessing adolescent and adult attachment: A review of current self-report measures. *Journal of Counseling and Development, 71,* 390-395.

Marcia, J. E. (1967). Ego identity status: Relationship to change in self-esteem, "general maladjustment," and authoritarianism. *Journal of Personality, 35,* 118-133.

Orlofsky, J. L. (1976). Intimacy status: Relationship to interpersonal perception. *Journal of Youth and Adolescence, 5,* 73-88.

Orlofsky, J. L. (1978). The relationship between intimacy status and antecedent personality components. *Adolescence, 13,* 419-441.

Orlofsky, J. L. (1993). Intimacy status rating manual. In J. E. Marcia, A. S. Waterman, D. R. Matteson, S. L. Archer, & J. L. Orlofsky, *Ego identity: A handbook for psychological research* (pp. 347-358). New York: Springer-Verlag.

Orlofsky, J. L., Marcia, J. E., & Lesser, I. M. (1973). Ego identity status and the intimacy versus isolation crisis of young adulthood. *Journal of Personality and Social Psychology, 27,* 211-219.

Robinson, F. P. (1950). *Principles and procedures in student counseling.* New York: Harper & Row.

Stephen, J., Fraser, E., & Marcia, J. E. (1992). Moratorium-achievement (Mama) cycles in lifespan identity development: Value orientations and reasoning system correlates. *Journal of Adolescence, 15,* 283-300.

Thibaut, J. W., & Kelley, H. H. (1959). *The social psychology of groups.* New York: John Wiley.

PART V

Commentary

14

Ethical Considerations in Interventions for Promoting Identity Development

ALAN S. WATERMAN

The chapters of this volume have discussed a variety of clinical, counseling, and curricula interventions for their potential value in the facilitation of identity formation. Some of these interventions involve an increased awareness of the identity implications of relatively traditional approaches to intervention: for example, individual psychodynamic therapy (Chapter 3), individual and group career counseling (Chapter 10), and cultural history curricula (Chapter 8). Others represent techniques specifically designed to change the course of identity development: for example, the reflective perspective-taking training approach (Chapter 6) and "family homework" assignments integrated into health or family-life courses (Chapter 4). These and other interventions discussed in the preceding chapters carry with them sets of ethical concerns related to intervention generally and the type of intervention specifically involved, ethical concerns that exist independently of the identity-related aspects of the intervention. In the analysis that follows, I want to evaluate how paying heed to the identity-related implications of interventions with adolescents makes salient some ethical issues that might not otherwise become the focus of our attention.

Why Interventions for Identity?

The logic for undertaking systematic clinical, counseling, and curricula interventions to effect identity change is relatively straightforward: If individuals who are advanced in identity formation possess a variety of desirable qualities that allow them to make their way in the world more effectively than those who are less advanced, then interventions to further identity formation may result in a greater number of individuals enjoying such benefits. Archer (1989) has reviewed the research literature, finding several notable strengths of individuals in the more sophisticated identity statuses (identity achievement and moratorium) in Marcia's (1966, 1980) classification scheme. These strengths appear sufficient to warrant the serious consideration of the possibility of developing intervention techniques to promote identity formation. This logic is used consistently throughout this volume, with Jones (Chapter 11) being most explicit in regard to his advocacy of identity-related interventions as a potential means to reduce the likelihood of substance abuse by adolescents as well as other forms of behavioral deviance.

Assuming potential benefits to interventions designed to affect identity formation, it must be demonstrated that there are available procedures whereby an individual's sense of identity can be induced to change in the directions thought desirable or that they can be developed if they do not now exist. Because identity has been shown to undergo characteristic patterns of development during the high school and college years (Waterman, 1982, 1985), it is plausible to look to both direct clinical services and educational practices and curricula for their potential to affect identity formation to supplement whatever is provided by the natural environment.

Assuming that there are potential benefits to be derived from intervention and that effective intervention strategies now exist or can be developed, it must still be asked whether we ought to proceed with their use. Certainly the benefits presumed to be derived from the employment of intervention programs constitute a grounds for proceeding. However, there may be attendant risks as well as benefits resulting from intervention programs that could lead to a recommendation against their use. Thus a careful benefit-cost analysis should be made for any proposed intervention strategy and its use with particular populations.

Benefit-Cost Analyses for Intervention

A partial, generalized benefit-cost analysis might take the following form:

Benefits

1. To what extent is the individual currently in need of making changes in his or her way of relating to the world to either reverse negative outcomes or increase positive outcomes? This will include an assessment of the objective difficulties encountered and the subjective experiences of the current situation. It also will include consideration of the individual's short- and long-term needs.
2. To what extent will a proposed intervention have positive consequences for individuals other than the person toward whom it is directed—for example, the person's family, classmates, or society in general?
3. What is the likelihood that the proposed intervention will actually improve the quality of life of the recipient or others?

Costs

1. What is the nature and magnitude of the risks attendant to the use of a proposed intervention, both for the client and others?
2. What is the likelihood that these risks will materialize in the form of adverse consequences?
3. What are the monetary, material, time, and other costs associated with the delivery of the proposed intervention? Who is to incur these costs? What is the subjective importance of these costs to the person(s) who will bear them?
4. Are the potential costs undertaken voluntarily or are they to be imposed on the individuals involved?

General Considerations

It should be apparent from this listing that the number of variables in any benefit-cost analysis is very high indeed. Many factors to be considered permit only probabilistic answers. In any given instance, standing with respect to many variables may not be knowable.

Further, when considering a potential intervention, it is not possible to do only a single benefit-cost analysis. A similar analysis must be conducted for whatever alternatives exist to the introduction of the proposed intervention. For the sake of simplicity, the only alternative that will be discussed here is the status quo. This makes it clear that not taking a given action (e.g., introducing an intervention) is itself an action (e.g., putting in motion the events that would occur in the absence of the intervention). The choice of a course of action will then depend on the outcome of the comparison of the two benefit-cost analyses.

To add still another aspect of complexity to the discussion of benefit-cost analyses, it should be recognized that the outcome of the comparison referred to in the previous paragraph may vary with a variety of client personal qualities. The magnitude and value of both benefits and costs may vary with age, sex, race, social class, and other personal variables. For example, as Rotheram-Borus and Wyche (Chapter 5) and Markstrom-Adams and Spencer (Chapter 6) have shown, ethnicity must be considered when deciding how to proceed with identity-related interventions.

In the sections that follow, the benefits and costs of identity-related interventions will be considered separately for clinical and counseling, and curricula interventions.

Ethical Implications of Clinical and Counseling Interventions to Promote Identity Formation

It is generally assumed that a client enters clinical therapy or counseling seeking to make changes in his or her life (albeit often with some ambivalence), and with the expectation that the therapy will facilitate the process of change. There is a presumption that the need for change is great, that a means to bring about desired change is available, and that the potential benefits outweigh the risks and costs that can be anticipated. The orientation to the therapeutic process that clients are given at the start of therapy provides a basis on which they can give a reasonably informed consent to the undertaking. Although this approach may be appropriate for most adults choosing to enter therapy, it is questionable whether the typical adolescent entering clinical therapy or counseling can be considered as either informed or consenting with respect to the process on which he or she is about to embark.

Informed Consent and the Therapeutic Contract

The matter of informed consent can be examined in the context of the therapeutic contract (Maluccio & Marlow, 1974; Seabury, 1976). Developing a therapeutic contract between a client and a clinical or counseling service provider entails the development of both explicit and implicit understandings about the nature of the outcomes sought, the processes by which such outcomes may be promoted, and the likelihood of the desired results. Clients of any age will vary widely with respect to the extent to which their expectations of clinical interventions can be considered reasonable. Given the limited range of life experiences available to most adolescents, they are poorly prepared to have reasonable expectations of either therapeutic goals or probabilities for successful change. With the exception of adolescent clients whose therapeutic histories began in childhood, they are also likely to have problems in anticipating or understanding the intervention process. Even where the therapist endeavors to be explicit with respect to what is to take place in a therapeutic intervention and the outcomes that could ensue, there can be no assurance that the adolescent client will be able to assimilate effectively the information being provided.

The problem becomes further complicated. For many adolescent clients, the motivation for the intervention arises not with them but with one or more parties in their social world—for example, parents, school personnel, or the courts. Not only may such origins for the intervention create resistance on the part of the client, but also the nature of the therapeutic contract is altered when other parties and their interests are introduced into the development of the contract. The clinician must make a decision with respect to how the legitimate interests of all parties concerned (including the therapist) can be balanced in developing goals for the intervention and selecting the therapeutic processes to be used. A thorough analysis of such "extended therapeutic contracts" is beyond the scope of this chapter.

With respect to the development of therapeutic contracts for identity-related interventions, the following points should be considered: To what extent is the client explicitly seeking to work through or rework identity-related goals, values, and beliefs? Some adolescents and college-aged youths will enter counseling with focal concerns that explicitly involve identity issues—for example, vocational indecision (Chapter 10), problems of sexual orientation or its self-acceptance (Chapter 7), or the loss of religious faith. Although the client may not make use of the language of "identity crisis," by the very nature of the presenting problem, progress in counseling will entail furthering the process of identity formation.

Where the presenting problem does not explicitly involve identity concerns, can the therapist anticipate that the consequences of the intervention process will include an undermining of existing identity elements? For example, for an adolescent or youth entering counseling for problems associated with an overcontrolling parent, the therapist can foresee that therapeutic movement toward greater independence of judgment on the client's part may entail the reworking and possible abandoning of some long-standing, foreclosed identity elements. But as Marcia (Chapter 3) has indicated, foreclosed clients may start counseling seeking interventions of a far more limited nature that do not entail the full range of possible repercussions. To raise the prospect of broad-scale identity changes in establishing the therapeutic contract may well drive the client from counseling before it has even begun. Still, the ethical dilemma of informed consent remains. Is the client being encouraged to initiate a process of change with limited objectives only to find the decision made has greater ramifications than foreseen (but which the counselor had indeed anticipated would be a possible, although not inevitable, consequence)?

Will the client be in a position to replace successfully identity-related goals, values, and beliefs lost during the intervention? This question of potential costs is essentially unanswerable at the start of a clinical intervention. It is only answerable in the affirmative if the client indeed successfully establishes new, more rewarding identity commitments than those existing at the start of therapy. The likelihood of successful identity changes will be a function of a wide array of factors, including the client's capacities, skills, and developmental foundation (e.g., in terms of her or his standing on the personality components emerging from previous stages as specified by Erikson, 1968); the presence or absence of a supportive family and social environment within which the client functions; the availability of realistic opportunities to enact alternative identity commitments; and the therapist's skills. We must recognize that the undermining of existing identity commitments in the absence of the development of suitable alternatives may leave the client more troubled than he or she was at the start of counseling. However, the difficulties involved in attempting to answer the question posed should not be used as a basis for concluding that identity-related interventions should not be undertaken. After all, any form of psychological intervention is a risk-taking enterprise with the outcomes uncertain. There is a need to compare the risks of intervention with those associated with the status quo. The process of risk assessment should become part of the process of establishing a therapeutic contract with the client's informed consent.

How are interested third parties (e.g., parents) likely to respond to the identity-related changes induced by the intervention? Among possible interested third parties in such identity-related clinical interventions are the client's parents, school officials, civil or religious authorities, representatives of the criminal justice system (e.g., judges and probation officers), and friends. Raskin and Waterman (Chapter 13) make this point explicitly with respect to dating partners. Third parties will have different legal standing depending in part on the client's age, the source of the initial referral, and the sponsorship of any agency under whose auspices the clinical intervention is to be conducted. Thus to think of the process of informed consent as only occurring between a client and counselor may well be misleading.

Some Guidelines for Minimizing
the Risks of Intervention

It is always easier to raise questions of ethical concern about an enterprise than it is to provide answers. With respect to clinical interventions, it should be recognized that appropriate answers will depend partly on the specifics of presenting problems, the qualities of the client, the qualities of significant others in the client's social world, and the goals and values of the professional agreeing to serve as intervener. Despite the breadth of the qualifiers just introduced, I would like to suggest three basic guidelines for the development and conduct of identity-related interventions with high school and college-aged clients.

First, the undermining of foreclosed identity commitments should not itself be considered a goal of clinical interventions. When identity-related problems are part of the motivation for counseling on the part of a foreclosed client, the issue is not that a commitment was formulated without the consideration of potential alternatives but rather that difficulties are being experienced with the implementation of the commitment. It is typical for the client to try to get the foreclosed commitment to "work," and that becomes part of his or her understanding of the therapeutic contract. A clinician should be prepared to explore if and how the client's goal may be attained. If in this process it becomes clear to the client that such an outcome is not attainable, then the impetus to consider other alternatives will be likely to emerge (if only after a period of mourning).

Second, identity-related clinical and counseling interventions should be directed primarily toward clients developing the skills associated with the process of making identity decisions rather than on working toward outcomes generated outside of the client's initiative, whether from the counselor, family, or social authorities. Thus when counseling with respect to erotic identity (Chapter 7) or vocational choice (Chapter 10), it is important that the client not structure the task as the discovery of the "right answers" already known by the therapist. For some clients the focus instead should be on the development of exploration techniques, while for others the emphasis may need to be placed on the process of forming and enacting commitments. Emerging capabilities in either area can be directed toward whatever outcomes the client elects to pursue.

Third, under naturally occurring conditions, identity development involving exploration and commitment can be a gradual, nonlinear process that takes years to evolve. It is not completed during the stages of adolescence or youth; individuals rework their previous identity commitments during the adult years (Stephen, Fraser, & Marcia, 1992). Termination of the clinical process thus should not depend on the "successful resolution" of an identity crisis. In many instances, termination is appropriate when the presenting problems have been ameliorated and the client has achieved a reasonable level of confidence in his or her ability to take the next steps in the identity-formation process.

Ethical Implications of Educational
Interventions to Promote Identity Formation

One basic question of educational philosophy is whether our educational system should be involved in activities that include the shaping of identity processes. The fact that educational curricula are currently in place with probable effects on identity functioning does not settle the question of whether this ought to be the case. There are several levels on which curricula interventions may be introduced that parallel the levels for prevention intervention in the field of community mental health (Caplan, 1964; Gottesfield, 1972). It will be helpful when considering benefit-cost analyses for curricula interventions to attend to the level of the intervention involved.

Primary curricula interventions are those directed or offered to the student population irrespective of the individuals' standing on particular psychological variables. (It does not appear accurate to refer to these curricula as "primary prevention interventions" because it is not clear exactly what is to be prevented.) This is the type of curricula described by Dreyer (Chapter 8). Courses here are designed to stimulate students in the exploration of identity-related alternatives and the development of commitments. Because these are for unselected populations, the need for intervention is far lower than was the case for clinical and counseling interventions, where the presence of presenting problems could be assumed. However, that there is a need for intervention is indicated by the findings (described in Chapter 1) that the majority of adolescents and youths do not explore alternatives or form commitments. Although movement toward the identity-achievement status naturally occurs, the most frequent identity statuses among adolescents and youth are foreclosure and identity diffusion. There is thus reason to maintain that educational curricula are a convenient, cost-effective, and minimally intrusive means of promoting identity formation and its attendant benefits at an appropriately targeted point in the course of personal development.

Secondary curricula interventions are those directed or offered to individuals who are considered to be at risk in some respect. The type of identity-related interventions discussed in Chapter 9 for a gender-role curriculum and in Chapter 10, group career counseling, may be thought of as falling in this category. The Choices and Challenges curricula (Chapter 9) are predicated on the assumption that sizable segments of both genders (if not everyone) can be considered at risk, although the risks are different. When a set of specified risks can be identified, the presumption of a need for intervention is higher than for primary curricula interventions. Still, the concept of "at risk" used here is probabilistic, and the case for a need for intervention is again not as strong as that for clinical and counseling interventions.

Tertiary curricula interventions are those directed or offered to individuals who are already manifesting any of a variety of problem behaviors. The curricula focused on behavior deviance discussed in Chapter 11 and the school-counselor-sponsored family education workshops described in Chapter 4 fall at this level. Here the level of need for intervention is comparable to that for clinical and counseling interventions, with the choice for the type of intervention resting perhaps on several practical and cost-effectiveness considerations.

Benefit-Cost Analyses for Curricula Interventions

The particular benefits of curricular interventions at the various levels can be addressed in terms of both students and society. Although the benefits of primary and secondary curricula intervention strategies to be considered here are not likely to involve overcoming current personal difficulties, long-run psychological health advantages are found to be associated with the reflective appraisal of a variety of identity alternatives undertaken before identity commitments are established. It is plausible that stimulating such reflection will facilitate the development of effective psychological functioning along a variety of dimensions such as self-esteem, moral reasoning, and the quality of interpersonal relationships. The potential benefits of problems avoided also should be part of the analysis. In other words, the potential psychological costs to students from not promoting the more sophisticated forms of identity functioning needs due consideration.

The reflective appraisal of identity alternatives requires the individual to perceive the world from different social perspectives and should therefore promote such social benefits as tolerance, which is an important civic virtue in a pluralistic society. The reflective consideration of identity alternatives and the ability to form dedicated and yet flexible commitments are skills that should help individuals cope with conditions in a rapidly changing society, with benefits for both the individual and society.

The justifications offered here in support of identity-related curricula interventions involve teleological moral analyses—that is, such interventions are warranted on the basis of the beneficial consequences they are expected to generate. In contrast, the reasoning offered in opposition to their use involve a more complex set of considerations.

Curricula interventions may be a highly inefficient way to influence identity formation. Because different individuals have different developmental timetables—that is, they differ in the ages at which they are most prepared to respond to particular psychology-based curricula offerings—it is extremely difficult to know when to time a given curricula intervention so as to yield the desired effect on identity formation. In most school systems, curricula are introduced on grade-level schedules with the result that exposure may be too early to benefit some students and too late to be helpful to others.

It can be acknowledged that curricula interventions may be inefficient with respect to their immediate effect on identity formation without concluding that they are not warranted in the pursuit of a meritorious objective. The variability in the developmental timetables for identity formation provides a basis for suggesting that such interventions be introduced periodically during the junior and senior high school years to increase the probability of a correspondence between personal readiness and the educational stimuli offered. Further, even when curricula interventions are presented before there is receptivity to the themes conveyed, the messages may be recalled later when identity issues have gained salience for the individual. In view of the nonreflective manner in which most identity-related decisions are made by adolescents, even an inefficient approach may yield substantial benefits.

Curricular interventions to influence identity change may face strong parental opposition. Teachers' efforts to induce the reflective considerations of identity alternatives may undermine particular values that some parents have been trying to instill in their adolescents in an unquestioning fashion. This concern is greatest with respect to primary curricular interventions because the claims for the need for intervention are the weakest. Indeed, the parents may see the educational curriculum as placing their child at risk. Under such circumstances, curricular interventions to induce identity change may serve to polarize school-parent relationships to an extent that outweighs the anticipated benefits of such programs.

The concern that curricular interventions to affect identity formation can serve to undermine goals, values, and beliefs that (some) parents are trying to instill reflects the fact that such intervention, indeed education itself, is not a value-neutral enterprise. If those involved in the formulation and implementation of educational philosophies and policies can agree that it is to be preferred that all goals, values, and beliefs (including those the educational establishment wish to have adopted) emerge from a reflective process involving the questioning of the relative merits of possible alternatives, then educational curricula should reflect that stand. Where appropriate, school officials can meet with concerned parents to assure them that the focus of the program is on the processes by which decisions are made, not on efforts to undermine particular beliefs. It is doubtful, however, that parents who equate questioning with disaffection will be reassured by such statements.

The most serious objection to the use of curricular interventions that affect the process of identity formation involves the possibility that some students will be harmed by their participation in such programs. If an intervention undermines the existing sense of identity that students bring to the program without affording a mechanism for helping them replace lost commitments with more satisfying ones, then levels of psychological distress can be expected to rise. At present, the percentage of students who might be adversely affected, and the severity of the distress that might be induced, cannot be determined. Again this concern operates most strongly with respect to primary curricula interventions. For tertiary interventions, the existence of current behavior problems creates a presumption that the status quo is not the best course of action.

Yet the potential stressful nature of identity crises can be used as evidence of the need to bring the issues of identity formation within the purview of the educational system. We should first recognize that it is not a purpose of education to protect high school students from the realities of this world, even when such recognition is unsettling. The existence of identity-disturbing questions are part of those realities, and it is likely that individuals will encounter them through such other contexts as the peer group or media, even if they could be excluded from the school. There would appear to be many potential benefits to having such questions raised within the supportive environmental context of the school in contrast to leaving the outcomes solely to the more unpredictable circumstances existing outside the schools. Still, the potential for distress on the part of students experiencing an identity crisis points to the need to identify techniques for (a) reducing the risks of adverse reactions to the interventions; (b) minimizing the debilitating aspects of a crisis, whatever its origins; and (c) facilitating a successful resolution of the task of identity formation for those actively striving to deal with identity questions.

Some Guidelines for Minimizing the Risks of Intervention

As I did for clinical and counseling interventions, I will offer a few guidelines to be used when thinking about the use of identity-related interventions in a school setting. Again, interventions designed to promote identity development should not be instituted for the purpose of undermining existing identity commitments, even those formed in a nonreflective manner. More important than the manner in which an identity commitment was formed is the extent to which it is serving adaptive functions in the life of the high school or college student. Where a commitment is functional for an individual, there is a natural, and appropriate, resistance to efforts to undermine it. It will still be valuable, however, to make the point that, if at some future time a commitment is no longer functional, then techniques can be used to find worthy alternatives that will provide a basis for commitment.

It is also important to respect the developmental timetables of different individuals. This means working against the notion of grade-level-based objectives for psychological skills or identity formation. Students may resist sound advice in a particular area, even when agreeing it is sound advice, because they intuit that they are not yet ready to take the next step. It may be that they feel the need for a stronger base in the skills that provide the foundation for further movement or that they must deal with some other, perhaps unrelated, developmental issue before proceeding. Whatever the reason, pressures to induce psychological changes before there is a readiness for such changes are likely to prove counterproductive.

Curricula to promote identity formation thus should best be viewed as stimuli to induce or entice changes in those who are developmentally ready to move. But how are we to know when someone is ready to move? The best answer may be the circular one: Apparently, the student moves in response to the stimuli provided. And for those who are not ready, we should be prepared to wait and to try again.

A Concluding Comment

Given the inherent complexity of benefit-cost analyses in the realm of applied ethics and the number of unknown elements, it must be asked whether they are worth the effort needed to carry them out. Because they represent the best available basis on which to make a decision, they have an important role to play in any decision-making process. One role of empirical research is to improve, to the extent possible, the quality of the information included in such analyses. Yet because of the existence of variables for which no information is available, from an ethical standpoint, the ultimate decision between courses of action must rest with the parties involved; hence the importance of the principle of informed consent.

From the analysis provided here, it should be evident that the interventions with identity-related implications for adolescents discussed in this volume are not ethical or unethical in themselves. Instead, a benefit-cost analysis must be done again each time a therapist works with a new client or group of clients or when a teacher begins working with a new class. What has been learned from experiences with previous clients or previous classes needs to be factored into the decision-making process the next time around. If the previous experiences have been deemed successful and the new recipients of the intervention are considered similar to the earlier participants, then this process may go

244 Ethical Considerations

swiftly. But if the next intervention represents a generalization of a technique to potential recipients notably different than those who have participated before, then some care and caution need to be taken as the benefit-cost analysis is performed. And if the previous experiences have been less than successful, then the question must be addressed in terms of how often one tries before abandoning what one believes "should" work. And each new intervener must carry out a benefit-cost analysis even for the use of techniques that have been demonstrated to be successful in the hands of others. What has been proven to be useful for one person may be ineffective or even counterproductive when attempted by someone else. Here the question becomes "Although I know this technique works, will it work when I try it?"

The level of ambiguity inherent in applied ethical analyses may be frustrating in view of the desire for clear and generalizable guidelines. An interventionist's genuine openness to the complexity of ethical analyses may be the best assurance available that identity-related interventions are being ethically pursued.

References

Archer, S. L. (1989). The status of identity: Reflections on the need for intervention. *Journal of Adolescence, 12,* 345-359.

Caplan, G. (1964). *Principles of preventive psychiatry.* New York: Basic Books.

Erikson, E. H. (1968). *Identity: Youth and crisis.* New York: Norton.

Gottesfield, J. (1972). *The critical issues of community mental health.* New York: Behavioral Publications.

Maluccio, A., & Marlow, W. (1974). The case for the contract. *Social Work, 19,* 28-36.

Marcia, J. E. (1966). Development and validation of ego identity status. *Journal of Personality and Social Psychology, 3,* 551-558.

Marcia, J. E. (1980). Identity in adolescence. In J. Adelson (Ed.), *Handbook of adolescent psychology* (pp. 159-187). New York: John Wiley.

Seabury, B. (1976). The contract: Uses, abuses and limitations. *Social Work, 21,* 16-21.

Stephen, J., Fraser, E., & Marcia, J. E. (1992). Moratorium-achievement (Mama) cycles in lifespan identity development: Value orientations and reasoning system correlates. *Journal of Adolescence, 15,* 283-300.

Waterman, A. S. (1982). Identity development from adolescence to adulthood: An extension of theory and a review of research. *Developmental Psychology, 18,* 342-358.

Waterman, A. S. (1985). Identity in the context of adolescent psychology. In A. S. Waterman (Ed.), *Identity in adolescence: Processes and contents* (pp. 5-24). San Francisco: Jossey-Bass.

15

Identity: A Construct Comes of Age and Starts to Work

JOHN PAUL McKINNEY

In the spring of 1960 at Ohio State University, George Kelly was teaching a proseminar on personality theory (also called personal construct theory) when he proposed one of his famous principles. "You're going to do your best research in areas that you care about deeply," he told the students, "in areas that relate to your core role constructs." He inquired about research interests in the class. One student was interested in research on mental retardation; another had the temerity to espouse an interest in social learning theory and the emerging construct of locus of control. One student, a fellow named Jim Marcia, said he wanted to operationalize a construct in Erik Erikson's theory, namely, identity. He wanted to find a way to measure this elusive but, according to him, vastly important variable. At that point, a fellow student across the room whispered loudly, "Right, Marcia, and I suppose after that you're going to look for the soul in the pineal gland." Few of us took psychoanalytic concepts terribly seriously at that bastion of dustbowl empiricism even as late as the 1960s, especially not in Kelly's class. "Rubber sheet theory," Kelly used to say. "Whatever it is, you've got it. If it's not manifest, it's latent. You can stretch a rubber sheet to cover anything."

That was more than 30 years ago, and since then the construct of identity and identity statuses unquestionably is one of the most well-researched areas in the whole realm of adolescent development. From

Marcia's initial interview technique to the variety of paper-and-pencil measures and projective approaches, the concept of identity statuses—along with their measurement and correlates—has taken on a life of its own in research and theory.

Despite the wealth of developmental information surrounding this concept, however, less attention has been paid to the potential practical uses of the identity construct. While the delineation of an identity disorder has been in the clinical literature for some time and recently has been included in the American Psychiatric Association's *Diagnostic and Statistical Manual,* the idea of using the concept of identity in a positive, proactive way has not been so richly explored until now.

Treating an adolescent who had been sexually abused by multiple perpetrators for several years, I was vividly impressed with his strong-willed attempt to hang on furiously to an identity that he found positive. (He had no memory of the abuse. It had been reported to me by his mother, who was in treatment with a colleague.) During one session, after having made some serious interpretations to my 15-year-old client, I waited for his reply: "You want me to change the way I've been my whole life . . . the way I've always been."

I answered, "You've got that right. Exactly right. I don't think you want to be the way you always have been. You deserve better."

"But then I won't be me. I won't be myself."

Laughing now, I said, "Look at you. You're at least a foot taller than when I first met you," and then with little more than slight exaggeration, added, "You used to look straight at my belt buckle, and now you look down to see the top of my head. And are you really a different person, somebody else?"

By now this handsome young man was smiling somewhat sheepishly. "I see what you mean," he acknowledged quietly.

We went on to talk about the power he had to keep many of the things that he liked about himself and the power he had to change and grow at the same time. Here was a boy who was afraid of identity diffusion, who used his brilliant mind to ward off any loss of ego as he moved warily toward adulthood. A straight-A student, he worked compulsively at his school assignments. "I just have higher standards than most," he would tell me to justify his obsessional attention to academic detail. Staying up until three every morning, he would type each assignment until it was letter perfect. "I want the teachers to remember me. Yes, I want to be remembered as an outstanding student. I want to make my mark."

He spoke with an articulate, adult maturity that belied his youth and betrayed his intense need to keep everything together. (He was also avoiding the terror of the night by staying up until almost dawn. His victimization had taken place at night. By staying up to do homework he could be vigilant and at the same time avoid any possibility of confronting his unconscious in a dream.)

"But you haven't done your homework on how to have fun . . . on how to have a decent social life."

"But it's irresponsible to have fun if you haven't finished your work. I feel ashamed sometimes when I want to have fun."

"Ashamed that you want to, or that you don't know how?"

"Both."

"And you make sure your work is never quite finished to your satisfaction just in case you'll be tempted to have fun. When you say you want the teachers to remember you as outstanding, I wonder if there's something you don't want them to know."

"I don't know but I think so, but I don't know what it is."

Here was a boy who did not want to remember the terrifying events of the past but was positive that he wanted to be remembered by others in the future. He wanted to be somebody, and he needed help putting the frightening past together with a more hopeful future.

In Chapter 2 in this volume, Ruthellen Josselson states, "Identity forms the foundation of adult life." She regards interventions as ways of helping this process along. In one sense, the counselor, doctor, teacher, priest, therapist, parent, or whoever helps adolescents through this process is really being asked to walk with them safely into adulthood. Someone who has taken this route before and has the map can help the adolescent on a journey that seems frightening for many of them.

Marcia comments on this adult-adolescent pact when he says, "It is primarily the relationship that cures." He goes on to make the point that the therapeutic process has the same basic components as identity formation: exploration and commitment.

He also underscores the fact that if

one is to aid in the commitment aspect of the exploration-commitment process of psychotherapy, one must be aware of the cultural context within which the individual resolved previous developmental issues as well as the extent and limitations of the culture within which [he or she] is currently trying to effect an adaptation.

Contexts for Intervention

What is the best context for this intervention? Therapy? Education? Pastoral guidance? Career counseling? Parenting? The various chapters of this book have suggested that each offers an opportunity to use the concept to promote healthy development in young people. Marcia, of course, would opt for psychotherapy, especially of the psychoanalytic sort, yet he suggests that the same intervention strategies may be "applicable to briefer interventions undertaken by counselors and educators with adolescents."

For Patricia Raskin, an appropriate arena for identity intervention is in career counseling. Of all the adolescent developmental tasks, the exploration and choice of a meaningful life's work is one that best brings into focus an exploration of previous training and education, current abilities, as well as hopes, wishes, and expectations for the future. However, like Marcia, Raskin sees the importance of attending to the constraints imposed by the cultural setting, especially the constraint of social class: "There is no doubt that the historically disenfranchised view the occupational opportunity structure with somewhat more cynicism and perhaps a healthy skepticism about the importance of 'career' to their lives."

Still, Raskin describes creative ways that students in each identity status and at various grade levels of high school can be helped to expand their views of the possible and to commit to meaningful occupational choices. Although she provides excellent examples of individual and group interventions at each level, I still wonder whether, in addition to all of the external interventions, it is also possible to help the adolescent develop the internal drive to explore—that is, to experience a sense of excitement about vocational possibilities. Perhaps simple and honest exposure to our own work lives would help.

Just last spring, one day—April 28—was designated nationally as "Take Your Daughter to Work Day," the brainstorm of the Ms Foundation for Women. In our community, various media reported on young women accompanying their mothers and fathers to factories, offices, clinics, restaurants, and so on. Some were clear afterward that they had been exposed during the day to the sort of work they themselves wanted to do when they grew up. Others were equally clear that they would not want to follow in their parents' footsteps. All of those interviewed, however, seemed to come away from the experience with not only a greater sense of possibilities, but also a greater willingness and desire to explore. Although such an experience is especially important for girls, because of their greater expectation of limited opportunities, it would appear to be almost as fruitful for boys because, in modern society, few children, male or female, have the direct experience with the work world of their parents that was available in the past.

In Chapter 9 of this book, Karen Bieri and Mindy Bingham have undertaken this issue of gender in identity interventions by developing a "gender curriculum" that can be used to help students "in determining a sense of self in the context of family and society." Their thesis is not so much about gender identity as it is about teaching freedom of choice for both boys and girls in both exploration and commitment. Addressing gender concerns of both boys and girls, the authors acknowledge that values and goals for girls are generally developed in a relational context and that choices about vocation and occupation are made with respect to family and especially children, whereas the goals and values of boys are made individually with attention to competitive achievement, and vocational choices are arrived at accordingly.

In a society that rewards individual achievement over connections and relational success, girls are at a distinct disadvantage. It has always seemed to me that one could level the playing field for the two sexes by either teaching each sex the style of identity formation of the other or valuing nurturance and communication as much as we do competition and achievement.

Bieri and Bingham would have the schools develop curricula that encourage girls to select courses of study that appeal to their interests and abilities, including mathematics and science and curricula that encourage boys to look forward as much to becoming fathers as they do to becoming entrepreneurs, to be as comfortable in relating as they are in achieving.

To some observers, this may appear to be a tall order for the schools. Yet in Chapter 8 in this volume, Philip Dreyer is able to show how the curricula in high schools can be modified to implement identity theory in a variety of ways by promoting "exploration, responsible choice, and self-determination by students," as well as "role-playing and social interaction across generations," "the student's understanding of time and how the past is related to the present," and "self-acceptance and positive feedback from teachers and counselors." These are innovations that can be implemented across the curriculum.

Finally, there seems to me to be no reason why such curricula need remain the exclusive province of schools. Families could be involved in such training and so could churches, boys' clubs, and girls' clubs. In other words, there is no reason why Dreyer's and Bieri and Bingham's "curricula" could not become a national agenda at all levels of society, much as fitness training has recently become. Such a program, which should include harmonious communication between families and schools would, it seems to me, take the entire burden of identity education off any one segment of society; it would go a long way toward reducing the potentially negative side effects raised by Alan Waterman in Chapter 14 on ethical issues. He mentions particularly the "existence of identity-disturbing questions" that, if not raised in school, may well be raised on the playground or in the streets.

One way of facilitating this sort of universal focus on the healthy identity development of youth is Dennis Papini's prescription in Chapter 4 for a school-based intervention that would involve the whole family. Few health care professionals would disagree with his observation that if "families are unable to provide an appropriate level of emotional support, many adolescents find the anxiety and guilt associated with self-exploration to be psychologically overwhelming." Most such professionals, however, are at a loss when it comes to helping adolescents and parents establish the kind of emotionally beneficial relationship that promotes healthy exploration. Surely the sort of program outlined by Papini deserves serious consideration. Several areas would need careful study if this agenda is to be attempted effectively.

First is the basic question raised by Randall Jones in Chapter 11: Who really needs the intervention? Jones reminds us not to fix what is not broken, and he suggests that we would be making a more efficient use of scant resources if we somehow targeted those most in need of identity intervention rather than developed a blanket program that covered everyone. A similar observation is made by Alan Waterman (Chapter 14) when he includes a benefit-cost analysis among the ethical issues to be considered in planning intervention strategies. One answer to that question may be that, like health education or fitness programs, some youngsters may be more in need than others, but all would benefit by some level of involvement. Nor would the sort of program that Papini proposes necessarily be more expensive to deliver to the whole community than to specific targeted families. Finally, community programs of this sort and more intense therapeutic interventions for families in greater need should not be thought of as mutually exclusive. Jones's vital call for psychosocial interventions that address earlier crises—that is, those of the earlier psychosocial stages—seems particularly suited both to the Papini model of a general educational approach and to his own proposal for therapeutic interventions for behavioral deviance.

In Chapter 14, Waterman raises a related issue concerning curricula interventions when he questions the efficiency of such strategies, because "different individuals have different developmental timetables." He wonders whether programs would have to be tailored for students who develop according to their own idiosyncratic developmental schedules.

In Chapter 1, Sally Archer also mentions this same dilemma of individual timetables in the construction of educational approaches. My only observation about that objection would be that it has rarely altered our teaching of other subjects such as mathematics, science, or languages, even though students' cognitive timetables affecting such learning also are quite different. Individualized instruction in any area may be optimal, but obviously prohibitively expensive. I remind the reader of Waterman's attention to a benefit-cost analysis as one important ethical consideration.

Motivation is another issue that arises in considering a school-based model. In depressed families or in families that struggle with getting children to do homework or be on time for dinner, the task of "family homework" may seem overwhelming.

In addition, how does one define the family? Single-parent families, gay couples with children, reconstituted families, extended families where grandparents still exercise parental authority are all examples not so much of special circumstances but of common occurrence in most school districts. Would curricula need to be devised to meet the special needs of each group? Such obstacles are not insurmountable and should not be a deterrent from embarking on the innovative sort of program that Papini suggests. Family interventions would also need to take into account the issues of social class, race, and ethnicity that are raised in Chapter 5 by Mary Jane Rotheram-Borus and Karen Fraser Wyche and in Chapter 6 by Carol Markstrom-Adams and Margaret Beale Spencer. Rotheram-Borus and Wyche stress the importance of ethnic identity among minority adolescents. Adolescence imposes a separate task for non-European-American youths, namely, the task of choosing the values and behaviors of their own ethnic group or those of the dominant group. The developmental task of identity formation is obviously more complicated for youth in the nondominant culture, and such complications may interact with family style within those cultures.

The model proposed by Markstrom-Adams and Spencer outlines the steps that can be taken to help minority youths preserve a sense of belonging to their own ethnic or racial group while also recognizing and understand:ng the dominant group's values, behaviors, and goals. The authors write of the adolescents' "aching desire to fit in" and their need to feel competent on their own terms.

As we listen to adolescents in classrooms, clinics, and counseling offices, a veritable lexicon of expressions describing this aching need pours out. Boys talk about "getting on the map" or "making a statement," while girls refer to "belonging" and "being included." This intense yearning not to be abandoned no longer refers to connections with parents, but to those with peers.

In Chapter 7, John Hazen McConnell writes of another group, namely, gay and lesbian youth, whose personal identity development is complicated by another task: coping with a society that rejects their gender orientation. We will have made an important step in identity intervention for straights and gays alike when attitudes and values are neither homophobic nor heterophobic—that is, when people do not fearfully avoid their own sex or the opposite sex and when we can talk about the identities of gay men and lesbians and mean more than their sexual orientation. Here perhaps more than anywhere else in this whole consideration of identity intervention strategies we need to remember Alan Waterman's important reminder in Chapter 14 that education "is not a value-neutral enterprise."

Adolescent Approaches to Change

Josselson says that "the prospect of growth appears terrifying rather than inviting," and I believe that for many adolescents it is, although for many different reasons that provide the bases for the different ways adolescents resolve their identities. They exhibit a variety of responses in dealing with the prospect of change—the necessity, the inevitability of becoming an adult. These responses include anticipation of the future, escape from the past, petrification that may include either clinging to the past or apprehension of the future, and finally constancy seeking.

In the first of these styles, *anticipation*, boys and girls look forward to adulthood with pleasure; they have a chance to explore a variety of adulthoods and are free to choose a pattern that makes sense for them. These appear to be the identity achievers.

A second style that is similar to anticipation but different in its orientation is *escape*, whereby adolescents, just as in anticipation, reach toward the future but primarily out of a desire to leave the past behind. They appear to be less involved in exploring options but still maintain a firm conviction that they want something different out of life than they have had in the past or than they perceive as their parents' fate. Given the opportunity, these adolescents are more likely to foreclose, excepting any option that appears better than either what they are leaving behind or what they believe to be the lot of their parents.

I call a third style *petrification*. It is the style of those who are too frightened to try anything new or different. Some of the petrified cling to the known past, whereas others are more apprehensive of the unknown future. The *clinging* behave like Lot's wife. They keep looking back, thinking about what they are leaving behind and feeling unable to let go. One boy, a senior in high school, had distinguished himself both academically and musically but had a limited social life. He went east with his father to explore the colleges he might attend. His parents were planning to sell their home of 20 years and move west with his younger brother. Finally accepted at a college of his choice, the young man began to think seriously of leaving home as his senior year drew to a close. One day he reported the following dream to me: "We were all getting in the car to go somewhere. We had all our stuff in the trunk. I knew we would never come back to the house. In fact, I think the house was on fire. Then, I wondered if I had brought everything that I would need for the trip." Although not petrified—in fact, this boy engaged in a good deal of anticipation—there was still that momentary looking back and wondering whether the past had prepared him for the future. Some of these youngsters appear to be in a state of mourning over the loss of childhood. Were they able to explore new possibilities, they might be in moratorium.

Although Lot's wife was turned to a pillar of salt for looking back, *apprehension* is characteristic of those adolescents who fear the crystallization that may take place if they move forward. To them it seems that adulthood, the final stage of development, leaves no room for further change. If physical growth is over, then so must be psychological growth. More than anything else, they fear being locked forever into one pattern of living without any avenue for escape. It is as if their life plans were etched in stone forever. As one young Dutch student told me when I asked him what his life would be like 15 years hence, "I can tell you one thing: I won't be driving the same car to the same office in Amsterdam at the same time every day and coming home to the same house and the same wife and children without anything ever being different." Although these adolescents fear foreclosure or even identity achievement, lest the change signal permanence, they remain in a perpetual state of moratorium, afraid of any commitment.

Finally, there are those adolescents who are fearful of the process of change itself. This *constancy seeking* does not seem to be a fear of adulthood so much as a fear of the process of going into adulthood. Transitions are difficult for this group. Thus such individuals may become either foreclosed or identity-diffuse, unwilling to explore. In *The Golden Cage,* Hilde Bruch describes such a girl, an anorexic who "was afraid of becoming a teenager, not of growing up. She wished she could go to sleep—like the Sleeping Beauty—and then wake up as an adult at the age of twenty."

Just as the anorexic in early adolescence may attempt to avoid adulthood physically by trying to stay with the body of a child, the schizophrenic individual in later adolescence may try to escape adulthood by retreating into a world of make-believe.

One 16-year-old boy who was referred to me for psychotherapy had a seizure disorder, was diabetic, and had been diagnosed a few years earlier as schizophrenic. In fact, like many schizophrenic patients, he seemed to have found a way out of the problem of growing up. He simply retreated into his make-believe world when the real world was too frightening. He denied any interest in sexuality, saying that any interest in girls was "stupid." I quickly learned that *stupid* was almost a code word for "sexually exciting" for him. One day George acknowledged that he was often embarrassed in school when he had to stand up because people might notice the "bulge in my pants." Suddenly, I remembered something Professor Kelly had taught us about "therapeutic stupidity": "Don't make assumptions," he used to say. "It's better to play stupid."

"What bulge?" I asked innocently.

"The box of sugar cubes that I keep in my pocket. Look," he said, pointing to the bulge made by the tin of sugar cubes. He insisted on denying his sexuality, although it was not far beneath the surface.

George was completely dependent on his parents. His physician mother had given up her practice when George was a young boy so that she could devote herself entirely to his needs. He had no pressing reason to grow up and was frightened to do so. On his way to school we would walk two blocks from his house to the bus stop, a trip that would sometimes take him an hour to an hour and a half. For every two steps forward George would take a step or two backward. He clearly was not anxious to move ahead either in going to school or in becoming an adult. Exploring occupations, sexuality, and adult social relations with someone other than his parents, on whom he had become almost completely dependent for medical and psychological help, seemed to be the sort of identity intervention that George needed. He graduated and went away to college. He began to teach the violin and to enjoy the company of young women, albeit on a very limited basis. He may continue to need therapeutic support on occasion but has begun to come to terms with being an adult.

The Identity and Intimacy Linkage

It seemed that identity and intimacy were two sides of the same coin for George and, as we can see in the work of Gerald Adams and Sally Archer (Chapter 12) and Patricia Raskin and Alan Waterman (Chapter 13), the development of intimacy is directly linked to identity. We are reminded by Adams and Archer that identity is an essential milestone on the road to adulthood. The authors particularly note that for both boys and girls an active, rather than passive, formation of identity is essential to the later establishment of intimate relationships. This is obviously a much easier route for some than for others. Social class, ethnicity, gender orientation, and a variety of other social and cultural variables serve either to encourage or impede an active approach to development.

Given the sequential linkage between identity and intimacy, one should not be surprised that an intervention aimed at identity formation may also involve relational components and vice versa. Raskin and Waterman provide a useful primer to the practice of counseling with adolescents taking into account the various identity statuses and the sort of intimacy issues that may be associated with each. They conclude by saying, "Clearly, one cannot work with individuals without taking relationships into account and vice versa." I would only add that such a consideration also must include the relationship between client and caregiver, thinking again of Marcia's comment that it "is primarily the relationship that cures."

Students often want to know about the affective nature of that relationship, about transference and countertransference, questions that are not always easy to answer. When asked by a group of psychiatric residents if I would address the issue during rounds of what it was like to work with a boy like George—"We understand the data. But what did it *feel* like to you?"—I responded at our next session with the following poem I had written for them:

> To be with a boy or girl
>   On their last night in the nursery;
> And to be there again when they awake
>   On the morn of their adulthood
> Is like watching a heron unfold
>   Its massive wings and lift itself
> Into the unknown sky—
>   Cautious at first—and then
> Swerve, almost with abandon,
>   Into the wind.
> To listen to their stories of Never-land
>   And hear their hidden fears
> Of Captain Hook—or going mad
>   And when their cries have ended
> To walk with them quietly into tomorrow
>   Is like fighting with the
> Rainbow trout, trapped in a shallow pool,
>   And waiting patiently until its strength is spent.
> Then, having reeled it in—
>   Gently set it loose
> To dart upstream
>   Free in a new and forceful way
> For the one who watches birds fly away
>   Or sets the trout free
> Yes, there is a sense of loss
>   But a larger sense of gain.

Listening to the adolescent's fears of change—of growing up—and the corresponding yearning to remain forever a child like Peter Pan arouses the desire to help adolescents recognize their own power. This often involves resistance and the paradox of trapping them with interpretations so that they can be set free to recognize their own strength and leave the therapist with a firm sense of independent adulthood.

A Closing Thought

Despite the skepticism of his classmates 30-odd years ago, it is clear today that Marcia was right. Identity has proven to be a rich and

powerful construct, one capable of providing a fertile network of linkages with other constructs in our understanding of adolescent development and behavior. In this volume we can see that identity may well be
equally powerful as a guiding concept in our interventions with youth
as we escort them toward a fuller, more satisfying adulthood. By the
way, Jim, if you ever do decide to go on a physiological safari in search
of the soul, let me know. I want to come along. If it is anything like the
last intellectual safari you went on, it is bound to be exciting.

Author Index

Subject Index

Adaptability, 20, 47, 50, 54-55, 57-58, 73, 182-184
Adjustment, 19, 73
Adoption, 75
Agency, 204-205, 209-210
AIDS, 78
Apprenticeship, 87, 100
Assimilation, 87-88
Attachment, 52-53

Behavioral deviance, 8, 174-188, 251
Biculturalism, 71-73

Cognitive processes, 87, 92, 95, 123-126, 159, 180-182
Cohesion, 50, 55, 57
Commitment, 4, 17, 37-38, 42, 50, 55-56, 58, 63, 80, 90, 107-109, 128-129, 145, 156, 163, 165, 168
Communications, 50, 54-58
Conflict, 53, 76
Conformity, 19, 66, 68
Connectedness, 49-50, 145, 204, 206, 209-210

Culture. *See* Society
Curricula. *See* Schools

Deidealization, 48
Delinquency, 66, 95, 176-177
Destructuralization, 58
Drugs, 78, 176-177, 180, 184

Educational reforms, 126-128
Egocentrism, 95, 126
Employment, 87, 98
Enculturalization, 69, 80
Erotic identity, 102-104, 114-116
Ethnic identity, 4, 7, 62, 70-76, 84-100, 251
Ethnicity, 63-80, 134-135, 157, 252
Exploration, 4, 17, 37-38, 42, 50, 53, 55-56, 58, 63, 75, 80, 90, 98, 107-109, 128-129, 145, 156, 162-163, 165, 167-168

Families, 6, 39, 47-61, 68, 74-76, 99, 142, 150-151, 250-251
Family affect, 51-52

About the Authors

Sally L. Archer (Ph.D., University of Pennsylvania) is Professor of Psychology at Trenton State College in New Jersey. Her research focuses on personality and social development, with a special interest in identity and intimacy formation across the life span and gender-role socialization. She has published numerous articles that have appeared in books and journals such as *Child Development, Human Development,* and *Youth & Society*. She also edited a special issue of the *Journal of Adolescence* on an appraisal of health and intervention for adolescent identity development in 1989. She is coauthor of the recent *Ego Identity: A Handbook for Psychosocial Research.*

Gerald R. Adams (Ph.D., Pennsylvania State University) is currently Professor of Family Studies at the University of Guelph in Ontario, Canada. His research interests are in personality and social development during adolescence and young adulthood, marriage and family relations, and social problems during adolescence. He is an associate editor of two book series—Advances in Adolescent Development and Issues in Children's and Families' Lives and is coauthor of three books—

Understanding Research Methods, Adolescent Life Experiences, and *Today's Marriages and Families.*

Karen Greenlaw Bieri (M.A., Rutgers University) is a County Extension Agent in the Home Economics Program, Cooperative Extension Service, at the University of Hawaii. Her special interests include identity development throughout the life span and its effect on relationships, decision making, education, and sense of balance and well-being. For several years she trained members of the American Association of University Women and other organizations as facilitators for integrating the Choices, Mother and Daughter, and Challenges programs into educational institutions and community groups throughout New Jersey.

Mindy Bingham is publisher of *Academic Innovations,* a part-time college professor, a seminar leader for educators, an author, and a community activist. She has written or coauthored 15 books, including *Choices: A Teen Woman's Journal for Self-Awareness and Personal Planning* and *Challenges* for young men. Among her children's picture books are the Ingram top best-selling *Minou* (1987) and the 1989 Ben Franklin Award winner, *My Way Sally.*

John C. Coleman is currently Director of the Trust for the Study of Adolescence, a research and publications organization based in Brighton, England. Since 1984 he has edited the *Journal of Adolescence.* He also edits the Routledge book series on Adolescence and Society. He has written many articles and nine books, including *The Nature of Adolescence* and *The School Years* (both in their second editions), *Working With Troubled Adolescents,* and *Youth Policy in the 1990's.* His research interests include the effects of divorce on young people, adolescent sexuality, early parenthood, and normal adolescent development.

Philip H. Dreyer is Professor of Education and Psychology and Director of the Institute for Developmental Studies at the Claremont Graduate School. His previous research focused on life-span issues of identity formation, self-esteem, sex-role orientation, and sexual behavior among adolescents and young adults. His recent research involves the study of identity status and personality measures among high school students from monolingual and bilingual home backgrounds. His publications include "Youth" in *The 74th Yearbook of the National Society for the Study of Education* and "Sexuality During Adolescence" in B. B. Wolman (Ed.), *Handbook of Developmental Psychology*. He has edited the two most recent editions of the Claremont Reading Conference Yearbooks: *Knowing: The Power of Stories* (1991) and *Reading the World: Multimedia and Multicultural Learning in Today's Classrooms* (1992).

Randall M. Jones (Ph.D., University of Arizona) is currently Assistant Professor of Family and Human Development at Utah State University. His research uses youth-related problem behaviors as a focal point for identifying at-risk children and adolescents, generating recommendations for prevention activities, and monitoring the effectiveness of interventions in school settings (the frequency of disciplinary behavior referrals, school attendance, and academic performance). He is associate editor for the *Journal of Early Adolescence* and the *Journal of Adolescent Research* and has published many articles appearing in books and such journals as the *Journal of Adolescence, Journal of Drug Education,* and *Personality and Individual Differences.*

Ruthellen Josselson (Ph.D., University of Michigan) is Professor of Psychology at Towson State University, where she directs the clinical concentration program. She recently has been a Visiting Professor of Education at Harvard University and Forchheimer Professor of Psychology at the Hebrew University of Jerusalem. She has received a Fulbright research scholarship and has published many articles on normal development in adolescence. She is also a practicing psychotherapist. Her books include *Finding Herself: Pathways to Identity Development in Women* and *The Space Between Us: Exploring the Dimensions of Human Relationships.* She is coeditor of the annual *The Narrative Study of Lives.* Her research interests are in phenomenological and psychoanalytic explorations of development in late adolescence and adulthood.

James E. Marcia (Ph.D., Ohio State University) is Professor of Psychology at Simon Fraser University, where he also has been Acting Director of Clinical Training and Director of the Clinical Psychology Center. His clinical interests are in individual psychotherapy with adolescents and adults, as well as in community mental health. His research interests are in construct validation of psychosocial developmental theory, ego identity, life-cycle stages of adulthood, and developing measures for a variety of other Eriksonian stage components. He has served on the editorial boards of the *Journal of Youth and Adolescence* and the *Journal of Applied Developmental Psychology* and is currently on the editorial board of *The Narrative Study of Lives.* He is coauthor of the recent *Ego Identity: A Handbook for Psychosocial Research.*

Carol Markstrom-Adams (Ph.D., Utah State University) is currently Assistant Professor in the Division of Family Resources at West Virginia University. Her research interests are in identity development among ethnic and religious minority adolescents, the processes underlying identity formation, the role of contextual factors in identity formation, identity intervention, the effects of perspective-taking training on identity formation, Erik Erikson's ego virtues, and contextual and developmental factors operative in adolescents' attitudes toward interfaith dating. She has published articles in such journals as the *Journal of Adolescence, Family Relations,* and *Child Development.* She is the coauthor of *Adolescent Life Experiences* (3rd ed).

John Hazen McConnell is a psychologist in private practice in San Diego, California. He specializes in working with gay men, lesbians, bisexuals, and persons with alternative erotic and gender orientations. He has taught at both the University of San Diego and National University. His clinical approach combines aspects of self psychology (Kohut) and the Mount Zion psychotherapy research group (Sampson and Weiss).

John Paul McKinney (Ph.D., Ohio State University) is Professor of Psychology at Michigan State University, where he has taught in both pediatrics and psychology since 1966. In 1969-70 he was a Fulbright scholar at the University of Utrecht in the Netherlands; in 1989 he was a visiting scholar at Cambridge University in England. With H. Fitzgerald and E. Strommen, he has coauthored the three-volume *Developmental Psychology.* His main research interests are adolescent social and moral values, engagement style (agent versus patient) in children and adolescents, and faith development.

Dennis R. Papini (Ph.D., West Virginia University) is Associate Professor of Psychology and Director of Experimental Psychology at Western Illinois University. He serves as editor of the *SRA Newsletter* (Society for Research on Adolescence). His research interests include child transition into early adolescence in the family context, the role of parent-adolescent attachment relations on adolescent emotional well-being, and the effects of attachment relations on parental emotional and marital adjustment. He has published articles in journals such as the *Journal of Early Adolescence, Journal of Adolescent Research,* and *Journal of Youth and Adolescence.*

Patricia M. Raskin is Associate Professor of Psychology and Education at Teachers College, Columbia University, in the Department of Social, Organizational, and Counseling Psychology. Her research interests include identity status, the career development of women, mentoring, and the relationship between love and work. She has recently written a chapter on asssertiveness for nurses; she previously wrote a textbook on counseling, *Vocational Counseling: A Guide for the Practitioner,* which is currently being revised. Her interests are in helping individuals and corporations adapt to the increasing presence of women in the workplace.

Mary Jane Rotheram-Borus is Professor of Psychiatry in the Division of Social Psychiatry, Department of Psychiatry, University of California at Los Angeles. She has designed and evaluated preventive interventions for adolescents at risk for multiple problem behaviors, particularly HIV and suicide. She has examined how ethnic identity influences adolescents' risk acts and mental health adjustment. She has published extensively and has received funding from the National Institute of Mental Health, National Science Foundation, National Institute of Drug Abuse, and William T. Grant Foundation.

Margaret Beale Spencer (Ph.D., University of Chicago) is Board of Overseers Professor of Education at the Graduate School of Education, University of Pennsylvania. Her developmental research interests include resilience and the identity and competence formation processes of African-American children and adolescents. Her most recent work focuses on the unique developmental experiences of African-American males during their transition from middle childhood into adolescence. She has written more than 50 chapters and articles and has coedited (with G. K. Brookins and W. R. Allen) *Beginnings: Social and Affective Development of Black Children* (1985; currently being revised); a special issue of *Child Development* (1991) on minority children and families; and a multiethnic volume (with G. K. Brookins), *Ethnicity and Diversity* (in press).

Alan S. Waterman (Ph.D., State University of New York, Buffalo) is Professor of Psychology at Trenton State College, New Jersey. His interests include the philosophical foundations of personality theories, the nature of optimal psychological functioning, and identity formation from adolescence to adulthood. He has written *The Psychology of Individualism,* edited *Identity in Adolescence: Processes and Contents,* and coauthored the recent *Ego Identity: A Handbook for Psychosocial Research.* His articles have appeared in such journals as *Developmental Psychology, Journal of Personality and Social Psychology,* and *Psychological Bulletin.*

Karen Fraser Wyche is Assistant Professor of Education and Afro-American Studies at Brown University. Her research interests include identity and gender development in minority children and mental health and educational issues in African-American women. Among her recent articles are "Minority Women in Academia," *Psychology of Women Quarterly* (1992), and "Psychology and African-American Women: Findings From Applied Research," *Applied and Preventive Psychology* (forthcoming).